# DIVIDED

# WE STAND

# DIVIDED

# WE STAND

### HOW AL GORE

### BEAT GEORGE BUSH

### AND LOST THE

### PRESIDENCY

## ROGER SIMON

 CROWN PUBLISHERS    NEW YORK

Published by Crown Publishers, New York, New York. Member of the Crown Publishing Group.

Random House, Inc. New York, Toronto, London, Sydney, Auckland www.randomhouse.com

CROWN is a trademark and the Crown colophon is a registered trademark of Random House, Inc.

Printed in the United States of America

*Design by Barbara Sturman*

Library of Congress Cataloging-in-Publication Data
Simon, Roger, 1948–
    Divided we stand : how Al Gore beat George Bush and lost the presidency / Roger Simon.—1st ed.
    1. Presidents—United States—Election—2000.  2. Gore, Albert, 1948– .  3. Bush, George W. (George Walker), 1946– .
4. Clinton, Bill, 1946– .—Influence.  5. Political campaigns—United States—History—20th century.  6. United States—Politics and government—1993–2001.  I. Title.
E889.S56  2001
324.973'0929—dc21                   2001028213

ISBN 0-8129-3204-8

10 9 8 7 6 5 4 3 2 1

First Edition

FOR MARCIA

# CONTENTS

Two friends are out camping in the woods late one night when they hear a bear clawing through their tent.

The first man jumps out of his sleeping bag and begins pulling on his running shoes.

"Don't be a fool!" his friend says. "You can't outrun a bear!"

"I don't need to outrun the bear," the first man says. "I just need to outrun you."

You don't need to be a great candidate to win a presidential election. You don't need Lincoln's wisdom or Teddy Roosevelt's energy or John F. Kennedy's wit. You just need to outrun the other guy. In 2000, it looked like neither man was capable of doing that.

The great divide that occurred—a popular vote victory for Al Gore and an electoral vote victory for George W. Bush—made the election difficult to analyze. Following Election Day, the media usually do stories about what the winner did right and the loser did wrong, neatly wrapping everything up in red ribbon and giving everyone the feeling that wisdom is rewarded and stupidity punished. But this was difficult to do with the 2000 election. Analyst after analyst listed what Gore did wrong: Didn't manage to get credit for a booming economy, didn't carry his home state, didn't connect with voters, didn't use Bill Clinton properly and did run a terrible campaign. But the analysts were then left with one problem: If Gore was so bad a candidate, how did he beat his opponent by more than a half-million votes? If he was a loser, how come the

American people made him their winner, at least when it came to the ballots they cast?

Well, yes, some grudgingly admitted, Gore did "beat" George W. Bush in that sense, but really it was a tie, because it had been the "closest race" in U.S. history. Except that it hadn't been. Gore's margin of victory was almost five times the size of John F. Kennedy's margin over Richard Nixon in 1960. Nor was the electoral vote margin even the closest in history. Bush won in the electoral college by five votes, four more than Rutherford B. Hayes's single vote margin in 1876.

Had Bush run a good campaign? Few, if any, bothered to ask. After all, he was sitting in the Oval Office. So basic questions such as why Bush did not do better in Florida—considering that his brother was the governor and the Republicans outspent the Democrats there—or why he did so poorly among African Americans nationwide, considering how assiduously he had courted their vote—were never asked or answered.

Typical of the post-election analysis was the observation by one veteran analyst on December 25 that: "The 50 million-plus votes he won this year will not excuse Gore from having to explain to party activists why he should be nominated again after losing a race widely viewed as a sure thing."

Widely viewed as a sure thing? Al Gore? The actual view of Gore and his chances were best expressed in the *New York Times* on May 13, 1999. Rick Berke managed to cram all Gore's deficiencies into a single sentence (which was no small feat): "Many Democrats point to the quick and unanticipated rise of former Senator Bill Bradley of New Jersey as a challenger; polls showing that Mr. Gore's popularity is not particularly deep, that he may be damaged by Mr. Clinton's scandals and that he would be easily defeated in a general election by Gov. George W. Bush of Texas or Elizabeth Dole;

a sense that Mr. Gore has deficient campaigning skills and has fumbled, making gaffes like taking credit for inventing the Internet; a view that he has not adequately articulated positions, and that he was trying to run his campaign singlehandedly."

That was the true state of the Gore campaign a few weeks before he announced his candidacy. Given that 18 months later Gore would win the popular vote and lose the presidency by a single vote in the Supreme Court, his achievement was actually quite impressive or at the very least worthy of a second look, just as Bush's campaign effort was.

There was a third major figure in the 2000 campaign, one who generated thousands of campaign stories even though his name was not on the ballot (though he sincerely wished it were). For nearly eight years, Bill Clinton, through a combination of charm, energy, commitment, stagecraft, seduction, and no small amount of deception, made likability—the magical ability to connect with people on a personal level—one of the essential qualities the public sought in its next president. Both candidates tried to imitate what they found worthy about the Clinton presidency, while doing a delicate dance around the scandalous.

In America, anyone can become president. That's one of the risks we take. When Adlai Stevenson expressed that sentiment decades ago, he was being sardonic. Today, that comment looks like popular wisdom.

# DIVIDED

# WE STAND

# ELECTILE DYSFUNCTION

"A WISE MAN DOES NOT TRY
TO HURRY HISTORY."

—Adlai Stevenson,
September 9, 1952

THE VICE PRESIDENT OF THE UNITED States rides in the back of the black Cadillac limousine, its tires hissing over the rain-slick streets, the only sound he hears except for the soft sobbing of his children. His campaign is now over, and the stark simplicity of losing comes to him as he looks out through the armored glass onto the empty streets of downtown Nashville: Lose and they call you unable to take advantage of your incumbency, unable to connect with the American people, unable to take credit for a booming economy. Win and they call you Mr. President. Which they will not be calling Al Gore. Not now. Maybe not ever.

He has the same trouble wrapping his mind around his popular-vote victory as everyone else this night: Getting more votes than the other guy is usually the point of campaigning. You get more votes and you not only win but there is also a bonus: Winning makes everything you did during the campaign look like an act of genius. Victory is the great answerer of questions. Win and the questions don't even get asked. Lose and they never stop. Should he have embraced Bill Clinton, championed working families, picked Joe Lieberman, kissed Tipper like that? Win and nobody cares. Nobody is asking George W. Bush where he went wrong with his

Social Security privatization plan or his giant tax cut. No Sunday papers will be analyzing his bonehead mistakes or syntactic bobbles. And that's because Bush is now clad in the Kevlar of victory: Nobody asks winners where they went wrong. But where did Al Gore go wrong? Well, he came back from a 17-point deficit in the polls to get several hundred thousand votes more than his opponent on Election Day and so he went wrong . . . where, exactly? Florida. He did not win Florida. Though Gore does not know how he lost it and by so many votes at that. Something like 50,000 last time he turned away from the TV at his hotel where the CBS anchorman was speaking in pure stream-of-Rather: "Let's give a tip of the Stetson to the loser, Vice President Al Gore, and at the same time, a big tip and a hip, hip, hurrah and a great big Texas 'howdy' to the new president of the United States. Sip it. Savor it. Cup it. Photostat it. Underline it in red. Press it in a book. Put it in an album. Hang it on the wall. George Bush is the next president of the United States."

Al Gore has not slept in nearly four days and he would be the first to admit his judgment is not at its knife-edge best. But, as he turned away from the TV set, even he knew it would inappropriate to kick the fucker in.

IN THE BACK OF THE LIMOUSINE, GORE HAS HIS concession speech in a red cardboard folder on his lap, a scarlet symbol of his failure. He had gone through it once quickly and done what he has probably not done in 24 years of giving political speeches: He has suggested no changes. The man known for managing every aspect of his campaign—down to personally designing the swoosh in the logo—now could not care less. He will go out and give it and be done.

The motorcade glides up in the inky, pre-dawn darkness to the back of the War Memorial Building, where two years earlier Gore had given his father's eulogy and where decades earlier his father had met his mother in a diner not a hundred yards away where she was making 25-cent tips to work her way through college. When his father lost his Senate race in 1970, there had been no small amount of bitterness. Tennessee had defeated him, his father said, even though he had devoted his life to Tennessee. Now, the son also loses. Tennessee would have won him the presidency, but instead it has flung him into the abyss. Perhaps it was a predictable punishment: Trying to maintain a foot in two worlds, he is comfortable in neither. In Washington he has always been criticized for not playing the game, not being part of the social circuit, not building up a network of fanatically loyal staffers and aides. In Tennessee he has always been criticized for being too much a creature of Washington. When Bill Clinton had come down to Tennessee or Arkansas during his presidential campaigns and had taken on the NRA over gun control, the hunters believed him when he said he wasn't trying to take their guns away. He was a Bubba if there ever was one, and they could see him in the early morning mists, standing behind a duck blind with a 12-gauge in his hands. When Gore said he didn't want to take their guns away, hell, they figured he was keeping a list of gun owners on that dorky Palm Pilot he kept strapped to his hip just waiting for the confiscation program to begin. Connecting with people, that is what everyone said it was about. Bill Clinton owned the franchise, George W. Bush was darned good at it, and Al Gore was a lummox, that is what people said. Except Gore had gotten more people to vote for him than Bush, hadn't he? So how were the critics going to explain that? And if he had been about to give his victory speech instead of a concession—a victory speech he had tweaked and retweaked—people would have learned the essential difference between the two candidates. Gore had looked upon the entire presidential campaign as a job interview. Bush had looked upon it as a date.

THE LEAD LIMOUSINE IN THE MOTORCADE COMES to a halt. There are always two limousines, always identical. They change places in underpasses and tunnels to throw off potential assassins. So sometimes Gore arrives first and sometimes he arrives second. Tonight he is first. A Secret Service agent pulls open his door—it is so heavily armored it takes a strong person to do so—and the vice president steps out into the cool dampness. He and the limousine are inside a gaily striped canvas tent, another security precaution meant to hide from snipers the exact instant of his exit from the car. This is one of the moments the Secret Service agents like least. They don't want him lingering. They want him to go either to the holding room or to the event site in War Memorial Plaza, about a two-minute walk down a passageway, where a lonely lectern covered with a garbage bag stands in the rain and from which he will give his concession speech.

Gore usually goes to a holding room. It gives him one last chance to go over the speech and to get last-minute instructions and information from his staff, which is stretched out behind him in the motorcade. This particular motorcade is so long that the tail end of it is still pulling up as Gore's car comes to a halt. He exits and immediately heads for the lectern. He doesn't want to read the speech again—it will be on the TelePrompTer anyway. He doesn't need any instructions on how to concede—even though in 24 years, he has never had to give a concession speech in a general election. And, his shirt still wet with the tears of his daughters, he doesn't need any more rooms filled with the people he feels he has let down. More important, the people in the War Memorial Plaza have been standing in the rain for hours waiting for him, and they deserve to have this long nightmare of an evening brought to an end.

Gore turns from the car and heads quickly down the passageway, a Secret Service agent preceding him. The back of the War Memorial Building is lower than the front, so when you enter from the back, you go through a passage, walk up a set of stairs and then are at ground level. Gore will then walk out through the tall pillars to the stage and up to the lectern, where he will put a dagger through the heart of his campaign. He is taking long, determined strides—the agents have learned to hurry in order not to be run over by him—his wife, his daughters, his son trailing him in the narrow passageway.

There is a small commotion behind him and he feels the presence of someone coming up quickly upon him before he turns and sees a slightly winded David Morehouse, his trip director. Gore does not stop walking.

"Sir," Morehouse says, trying to match him stride for stride, "we need to go to hold."

Gore gives him a look that could toast bread. "I'm not going to hold," he says. He picks up his pace.

Morehouse has been having trouble with a stiff knee and now he is hobbling after the vice president. The steps that will lead up and out to the War Memorial Plaza are only a few yards away.

"Sir, we need to go to hold!" Morehouse says, praying the vice president does not ask him why. In point of fact, Morehouse does not know why. He just knows that moments ago his cell phone rang with a frantic call saying that the vice president should not, could not, must not, go out to the plaza and concede defeat.

Over his shoulder, Gore now explains to Morehouse why there will be no delay. "I just talked to the governor," Gore says. He already conceded to Bush in a telephone call a few minutes ago back at the hotel. Bush is waiting for Gore to concede publicly so Bush can go out in Austin and declare victory. That's the way it's done. "He's waiting on me, and I'm going straight to the stage," Gore says.

With Gore now almost at the bottom of the steps and Morehouse running out of any option he can think of, he limps quickly in front of Gore and blocks his way. Just blocks it. Just like that. Morehouse is six-foot-one and solidly built, and now he is blocking the path of the vice president of the United States.

Gore is six-foot-two and a weight lifter, but if it is still possible to have something beneath your dignity after running for president for 18 months, then wrestling one of your own aides to the ground is beneath his dignity.

Gore stops short and glares at Morehouse. Both of them can now hear the crowd noise from the plaza.

The words tumble from Morehouse's lips. He isn't even sure what he is saying, but it goes, "Sir, you need to get to the hold for five minutes. Daley has to talk to you. It's going to be fine; it's going to be fine." And he sticks out his left hand like a traffic cop, motioning Gore to the holding room. Morehouse cannot quite believe what he is doing. "It is the worst day of his life, and I am standing in front of him telling him what he has to do," Morehouse says later.

Gore is annoyed, Gore is irritated, Gore is . . . and then he figures, well, it's been that kind of day, and he shrugs and walks toward the holding room. It is 3:17 A.M., and he is thinking this had better be worth it.

T HE WORST DAY OF AL GORE'S POLITICAL LIFE begins at 12:46 A.M. on Election Day. A brilliant half-moon hangs over Miami as if it had been cut from yellow construction paper and pasted on a black satin sky. A warm breeze heavy with the iodine smell of the ocean blows over the sand dunes and ruffles the hair of Al Gore. He has gone without sleep for nearly three days now, but he cannot rest. "Be not weary in well-doing," he told the parishioners of the New Jerusalem Gospel Church in Flint, Michigan, a few hours earlier, quoting the Apostle Paul. "You shall reap if you faint not." Gore is fainting not. The couch in his cabin aboard Air Force Two pulls out into a bed, the only bed on the plane—he and Tipper, who are all hugs and kissy-faces even when the cameras are not around, sometimes climb into their jammies, pop out to say good night to the staff and retire to it—and when the bed is not in use, staff members curl up on the carpeted floor around it and try to catch some sleep. But now nobody is sleeping. Gore knows Florida will make or break him. Two days ago, he gave an interview to WFLA, the NBC affiliate in Tampa, and said, "The last formal campaign stop of Campaign 2000—after my opponent has gone to bed—is in central Florida because I know that's where the future is going to be written." Gore cannot stay out of George W. Bush's face; he cannot resist comparing his own last "day" of campaigning—a murderous 30-hour visit to 15 cities in 11 states without stopping—to Bush's habit of turning in early with the pillow he always carries with him when he travels.

Gore is now totally wired. He seems to vibrate rather than speak. In Philadelphia two days ago, he went to the Morris Brown AME Church and told the parishioners, "There's an old African proverb that says, 'When you pray, move your feet.' Tuesday is the day to move your feet! You'll be able to say that we had a race so close, that I, personally, made a difference." As the crowd roars its approval, Gore's long motorcade sits idling outside the church. Unbeknownst to the vice president, Eli Attie, his chief speechwriter, has crawled aboard a van in the rear to write Gore's concession speech.

.  .  .

A T 33, ATTIE IS ALREADY A MASTER OF DISASTER. After graduating from Harvard in 1989, he went to work for New York Mayor David Dinkins. In 1993, when Dinkins lost reelection to Rudy Giuliani after a bruising and divisive campaign, it was Attie who wrote the concession speech, considered by some to be the most moving speech of Dinkins's career. "Mayors come and go," Attie wrote, "but the life of the city must endure. Never forget that this city is about dignity; it is about decency." Attie then went to work for House Speaker Richard Gephardt, and when the Democrats lost both houses of Congress in 1994, it was Attie who wrote the speech after which Gephardt turned over the speaker's gavel to Republican Newt Gingrich. "We may not all agree with today's changing of the guard," Attie wrote. "We may not all like it, but we enact the people's will with dignity and honor and pride. In that endeavor, Mr. Speaker, there can be no losers, and there can be no defeat." No doubt about it, Attie knew how to do failure, although there were some in politics who liked to say, "Show me a good loser, and I will show you a loser." When Gore's father had lost his Senate seat after a tough and bitter race—Al Jr., who was opposed to the war in Vietnam, had enlisted in the army in vain to soften the effect of his father's antiwar stance—in his concession speech he quoted the poet Edwin Markham: "Defeat may serve as well as victory to shake the soul and let the glory out." The words had always stuck in young Al's memory.

Now, Attie climbed into the empty van marked Staff One in the motorcade, sprawled out on the back seat and opened up his Dell laptop. Writing a concession speech was a ritual of his. "I wanted to have it in my pocket and not dwell on it," he said later. "It's a superstition. If you have it, you won't need it." After Gore was done speaking in the church, Attie headed for the airport and took a commercial flight to Nashville, while Gore continued flying around the country. At Gore headquarters, Attie would write a victory speech, and an array of odd variants. "Some people were discussing what our strategy would be if Gore won the electoral vote and lost the popular vote," Attie said. "And then there was one scenario for winning the electoral and losing Tennessee. In the end, I had five different speeches written. It got very weird. I even had one he could deliver if the outcome was unknown. A bunch of people thought that was possible. So I drafted something that said this was a well-fought and a great campaign, but we don't know the outcome." Attie kept all of the speeches on the hard drive of his laptop. Victory was Option A, concession was Option B, and a "hung jury," as Attie put it, was Option C1. He decided to show none of them to Gore.

PERHAPS THE FIRST PREMONITION THAT THINGS might not go exactly as planned in Florida occurs when the Gore campaign assembles a huge crowd on South Beach in Miami for a midnight rally to kick off Election Day. There is not a lot a candidate can do on Election Day because the time, energy, and money it takes to assemble crowds to hear his speeches could better be spent getting voters to the polls. At best, the candidate is irrelevant on the last day of his campaign. At worst, he can screw things up. Which is why Gore has scheduled this very early morning speech to be followed by a cancer forum at a treatment center in Tampa at 4 A.M.—Gore insists that the last event be "substantive," and his staff agrees because what else are you going to do with him at 4 A.M. anyway?—after which Gore will go back to Tennessee to vote and that will be that. But for his last speech, his advance people want to show off their stuff, and they have put together a crowd they estimate at anywhere from 30,000 to 50,000. So figure about half that. The crowd has gathered and night has fallen when some guy from the fire marshal's office appears and tells them they can't have that many people assembled in one place. And the Gore advance people are like: "What, you're kidding, right? The fucking sand is going to catch fire? The seaweed is going to burst into flame?" But in the end they move most of the people down the beach behind barriers and let only a few thousand stand in front of the stage. It is still an impressive crowd, and Gore is so glassy-eyed anyway he is already seeing double and triple. Punchy from lack of sleep and a combination of adrenaline, caffeine, and the Cepacols he keeps sucking to soothe his speech-ravaged throat, he is liable to do or say just about anything at this point. Which has Bill Daley, his campaign chairman, a little worried.

Early in the year, at a time when the media had decided that Florida was safely a Bush state—because, after all, Bush's brother, Jeb, was the governor—and that the campaign would really be decided in a battleground swath of states stretching from Pennsylvania to Missouri, Gore's strategists cooked up a plan to concede Georgia and North Carolina and instead concentrate on Florida. Gore personally approved the gamble. While some in the campaign considered it foolish, the payoff was considerable: 25 electoral votes out of the 270 needed to win. "It cost us a lot of money," Daley said later. "I mean, we went toe-to-toe and they outspent us two-to-one, but we spent a ton of money, maybe $11 million, $12 million just in Florida." Now, as the first minutes of the last day of his campaign tick by, Gore is happy with the strategy. The Bush campaign has tried to sucker him into spending a lot of time in California in the last weeks—some polls have shown the race closing dramatically there—but Gore refuses to take the bait, visiting California only to scoop up money in Hollywood and Silicon Valley. "Some people got weak and thought we had to go there to campaign, but we were comfortable with our strategy," Daley said.

Some weeks before Election Day, however, Daley hears why Bush has spent so much time in California (which Bush will lose by 12 percentage points to Gore) and so much time in New Jersey (which he will lose by 16 percentage points). "There is some reason to think Bush has gone to New Jersey and California to pump up his popular vote, knowing he may lose the electoral vote," Daley says later. "Bush has given the word that if that happens, he will try to get Gore electors to switch and go with him. We are game-planning that now." Nobody is taking this too seriously, however. This is just end-of-the-campaign, cover-all-the-bases stuff. A split between the popular and electoral vote is history-book stuff. And Bush's campaign guru, Karl Rove, is publicly predicting that Bush will win the popular vote by 6 percentage points and will get 320 electoral votes. The Gore campaign is not too terrified at this prediction, however. Rove had predicted that Bush would win the New Hampshire primary; instead John McCain shellacked him by 19 percentage points. Gore will stick to his game plan. He will end his general campaign in the same place he ended his primary campaign: Florida. Some 36 hours before he hears the word "chad" for the first time, Gore already knows he will live or die in the Sunshine State.

Now the celebrities are assembled onstage in front of a sand dune on South Beach. Everything is black except the moon high up above and the brilliantly lit stage. The celebrities are standing on risers, and the risers are crowded with Stevie Wonder, Ben Affleck, Glenn Close, Robert De Niro, and Jon Bon Jovi, among others. Gore's motorcade pulls up on Ocean Avenue, and he and his press corps wade through the sand, ignoring the boxes of multicolored flip-flops that have been provided for their convenience. They are too tired to take off their shoes and socks anyway. Affleck, wearing an unbuttoned blue shirt over a white T-shirt, is speaking to the crowd. The klieg lights make the sand in front of the stage glow an intense white. Behind the stage, you can see boats cruising slowly by on the ocean with colored lights in their rigging. "George Bush is a nice guy, but I've got friends like that and I would never lend them my car, let alone vote for them!" Affleck says, reading off a notecard. A woman in gold slacks and a black tube top with a bare midriff and a diamond navel ring dances in the rear of the crowd to music only she can hear. "I've been in a working family and now I'm in another tax bracket and I'm here to tell Governor Bush, thanks, but we don't need the money," Affleck says. "George Bush is asleep right now and Al Gore hasn't gotten started yet!" Affleck is probably correct: George Bush is just about to fall asleep in Austin. He has spent a 16-hour day visiting Iowa, Wisconsin, Arkansas and Tennessee. In Chattanooga, he tells an airport crowd, "My opponent vows to carry his home state. He may win Washington, D.C., but he's not going to win Tennessee!" (And Gore will not, with cataclysmic results. The last person to win the presidency without winning his home state was Woodrow Wilson in 1916. The last presidential contender to lose his home state was George McGovern in 1972. Losing at home just doesn't happen. Unless people at home can't remember the last time they saw you.) Bush will get four to five hours of sleep, arise at 6:30 A.M. on Election Day, feed his two cats and his dog, make coffee for Laura and then call his parents and tell them not to worry. "I trust the people," he tells a small group of reporters who have been assembled in the governor's mansion to hear his words. "I trust their will. I trust their wisdom." Aides begin to usher the reporters out. "Don't take any of the silverware and don't knock over the chandelier," Bush calls after them.

When Gore takes the stage in Miami, he is gravel-throated, intense, almost passionate. He has always been a late bloomer. In all his general election campaigns—four for the House, two for the Senate, two for vice president—he has gotten better as he goes along and has gotten good only at the end. In his very first race for Congress in 1976, he showed an energy level that was downright scary. "He was famous in the campaign for climbing telephone poles to shake hands with linemen," former Democratic U.S. Representative Jim Cooper of Tennessee said. "He covered every possible base." Now Gore tells the crowd: "It's after midnight in Miami! The moon is over Miami! I am getting a very powerful message from your cheers, from your faces, from the feeling in your hearts: We are going to carry Florida." Gore is jacketless. He is wearing a white shirt with the sleeves rolled up and a red tie. "I want to fight for you and your families and your future and your communities, not the wealthy, not the well-connected. Are you with me?" The crowd shouts its approval. "I won't always be the most exciting politician. But I will work hard for you every day, and I'll never let you down. And I'll fight for you with all my heart, and we'll win these battles together."

All of which is fine; all of which is the standard stump speech. His aides no longer even hear the speech—it is like living near the ocean and not hearing the waves—but any break in the rhythm, any slight misstep, is instantly apparent to them. Which is why, when Gore begins to veer off, the staff members standing along the fringes of the stage area beneath the palm trees stop talking among themselves and fall silent. "You know," Gore says, "Robert Kennedy always closed his speeches by quoting George Bernard Shaw: 'Some people see things as they are and ask why. I see things that never were and ask why not.'"

And Bill Daley thinks, "Whoa! Where did that come from?" When you get right down to it, Gore does not need to compare himself to Robert Kennedy in the closing hours of this campaign; not with his journalistic wolf pack still searching for a new lead for their stories. And, more important, you don't need to bring up the Kennedys in Miami, because pretty soon that leads to the Bay of Pigs, and that leads to Fidel, and that leads to Elián González and let's just not go there, OK? "Stop this! Stop it! Stop it!" Daley tells an aide near the stage, and either Gore hears him or just finally wakes up, because he brings the speech to an abrupt end. Later, back aboard Air Force Two, Gore says to Daley, "I just don't think I quite got there." And Daley replies, "No, I don't think you did. They loved you, but I don't think you quite got there." Which is just as well. Nobody is looking for spellbinding oratory this early in the morning. You just want to keep the crowds conscious enough to go and vote when the polls open.

It is nearly 4 A.M. by the time Gore gets to the cancer center and research institute in Tampa. About a half-dozen nurses are sitting around a table in the cafeteria, waiting for him. He arrives and says, "We had 25,000 people in Miami at midnight. I'm one of the millions of Americans who love nurses." Daley, hungry, turns away—how much trouble can Gore get into with six nurses at 4 A.M.? He is not Bill Clinton, after all—and wanders off to the food service area to see if he can get some fried eggs, which he can't. He then takes a piece of paper out of his pocket that has his hand-scrawled recipe for victory. A win in California and Florida and all the other states Daley can count on would bring Gore to 262 electoral votes. "We only need eight more from the little states," he says. "We deny Bush Florida and I think we win." Gore finally finishes with the nurses at 5:30 A.M. and stands up to shake their hands. One whispers to her friend, "I've had to pee since 3:30," and bolts. Gore gets back to Air Force Two, throws around a football with the staff on the tarmac for a few minutes, and then they finally manage to load him on the plane.

When Gore lands in Nashville, a helicopter is waiting to take him and Tipper to Carthage to vote. Everybody else on the staff will go to Carthage by motorcade, but everyone with enough authority and half a brain decides to skip it. They don't need to see Al Gore vote. They figure he can manage it. So they head to the Loews Hotel in Nashville, Gore's headquarters hotel, which makes them all happy because it is modern and clean and has good beds. This is a real concern on the Gore campaign. Although Gore has stayed in a few good hotels during the course of his travels, he also has holed up in some real dumps. Although his rooms are usually nice no matter what the location, the staff and press have learned to check out their rooms carefully before settling in. At one hostelry in central Illinois, a reporter enters his room to find a cat sitting on the bed and then regrets shooing it out when he realizes it was probably there to keep the mice at bay. Everyone now judges the hotels by whether they are "socks off" or "socks on" places, the latter being locations where the carpeting is so matted with crud that nobody wants to walk barefoot on it. The worst places are designated as "socks on in the shower" hotels. But the Loews is the lap of luxury, and some seek the arms of Morpheus, arms that have not embraced them in quite some time. David Morehouse, 40, a former director of strategic planning for drug policy under Clinton and a former deputy director of advance for the Clinton campaign, heads for his room and some sleep. He has slept as little as Gore and is as tired as he has ever been in his life. He gets to the ninth floor of Loews and falls into bed when he hears doors slamming up and down the corridor, and suddenly Secret Service agents are pounding on his door. He answers it, they walk in with a large dog, and Morehouse retreats beneath the covers while the dog checks for bombs under the bed.

Bill Daley showers at the Loews and looks longingly at the bed but does not get in it. He heads down to his office at campaign headquarters and immediately gets on the phone. The early news is not bad. There is a big turnout in Michigan, and John Sweeney, president of the AFL-CIO, tells Daley he feels good about Pennsylvania. Daley calls his field people in the major states. The mood is upbeat. The last poll the Gore campaign took was Friday, four days earlier, and pollster Stan Greenberg said it was dead even, which surprised nobody. Every morning it was the same story. Daley would call Greenberg at 5 o'clock and ask for the results of the previous night's tracking poll, and every morning Greenberg would say, "Even." It drove Daley nuts. "Stan, please, find a new group of people to poll," Daley would beg. But no matter what Gore did, no matter what Bush did, the numbers would not budge. "All this flying around, all this campaigning," Daley says to me. "I am not sure it really does anything."

AT CAMPAIGN HEADQUARTERS, IN THE GIANT, white chamber known as the Boiler Room, Michael Whouley, 42, a senior strategist, sits on a couch watching four television sets and going over the data. A special, magnetic keypass is required to gain entry to the Boiler Room, which has a locked door at each end. At 12:44 P.M., Whouley gets a memo from Monica Dixon, a Gore strategist, titled "General observations from the first round of exit polls." The news is about what Whouley expects it to be: Gore is losing among white Catholics and is even with independents. About 45 minutes later, Whouley starts getting some projections: Gore is up in Florida, but down in New Mexico, Wisconsin, Iowa, Missouri, Tennessee, and Oregon. The chilling news, however, is that Gore is up only half a percentage point in Pennsylvania. Whouley cannot afford to worry only about Florida. If Gore wins Florida but loses Pennsylvania or Michigan, he will be dead meat. For weeks

Whouley had been telling his people that the election is going to be very, very close—the closest since 1960, he predicts. "We are barely going to make it in the electoral college," Whouley tells them. Which is why three weeks before Election Day, Whouley assembles legal advisers and tells them to start studying the laws governing recounts in a number of key states. He also says an electoral college deadlock is possible, and plans should be drawn up to protect Gore electors from poaching by the Bush campaign. Now, Whouley is getting exit-poll results, turnout results, and reports from precincts where Gore should be doing well. He has his own number cruncher, who has his own magic software program: he can plug in the numbers and it will project the outcome. And nothing from the early numbers is changing Whouley's mind: For Gore to win, he has to carry the trifecta of Florida, Pennsylvania, and Michigan. Whouley even has buttons made up for the Boiler Room gang showing a gray map of the United States with those three states in blue and the words: "Gore/Lieberman. Winning the Trifecta. Nov. 7, 2000." The buttons are never handed out.

But Whouley is in a unique position on Election Day. Unlike others who have to sit around helplessly as they watch the numbers come in, Whouley can affect the numbers. Off to the side of the Boiler Room is an old supply closet into which eight desks have been crammed. Whouley goes there to make his phone calls and, to use his term, "move resources." Pennsylvania looks weak? Whouley can direct one of his phone banks to start telephoning voters in Pennsylvania. He can cause a million calls to go out, he figures. He can also pick up a phone, which he now does, find Jesse Jackson in Racine, Wisconsin, and ask him to get on a plane and go to Philadelphia to increase black turnout. Jackson does this without hesitation, even though he had been in Miami for the midnight rally, has been campaigning in Wisconsin, and is as seriously sleep-deprived as everyone else in the Gore campaign. ("The stakes were high, the lines were clear, the votes were essential," Jackson tells me later. "I have gone to 250 cities in the course of the campaign. I have never traveled this many miles before, frankly.")

Whouley has 70 surrogates he can call upon—including Tipper, Hadassah Lieberman, the three Gore daughters and Clinton Cabinet secretaries—to start doing live TV and radio shows at a moment's notice. Whouley has something else, too: bodies. While Republicans have more money than Democrats, the Republicans cannot match the army of people Whouley has to bang on doors. Whouley has always been a door-banger, a field-operation, street-level guy. Most young people going into political work today want to do "message" and "media strategy" and make TV commercials. Whouley does not disdain that part of modern politics, he just feels comfortable around people who also know how to get signatures on a petition or a voter to a polling place. He smokes, he drinks, and he uses bad language in a Boston Irish accent so thick you could skate on it in the wintertime. And today he is using it to be sure the bodies are out there for Al Gore: The NAACP is supplying bodies, mayors are lending bodies from their political organizations, and the AFL-CIO has maybe 100,000 people in targeted states all doing what is called "The Pull," what Jesse Jackson calls "getting souls to the polls," getting people to vote. Three weeks before Election Day, Whouley launches what he calls his "No Excuses Tour" of targeted states. "Tell us what you need to win," he says to the state operations. "You need bodies to get out the vote? You need a mailing to go out? You need Bill Clinton to tape a radio interview for a black station?" Virtually no request is denied. "If it sounded rational, we found the money for it," Whouley says. Whouley also has two other things the Republicans don't have: A candidate who will work himself past the point of exhaustion on Election Day and a president of the

United States. Like many Gore operatives, Whouley has worked for Clinton. He was a key factor in Clinton's second-place finish in New Hampshire in the 1992 primary, which was widely viewed as a great Clinton victory, considering the Gennifer Flowers scandal and draft-dodging accusations that became public there. And it is Clinton who calls Whouley in the supply closet at noon on Election Day. Whouley is not surprised. Clinton loves politics, Clinton breathes politics, and he is feeling a little left out of things. He is up in New York anticipating a victory for Hillary in her Senate race (a victory helped by the big turnout of Democrats for Gore), and now Clinton wants to feel he is still part of the action.

"What are the exits?" Clinton asks. "Is there anything I can do to help?"

Whouley is not sure if Clinton is just being polite, but he says, "Sir, I could use you." Whouley is in his "balls-to-the-walls" mode and he would ask anything of anybody. In Colorado, a Gore organizer by the name of Mike Stratton has just carried a woman in his arms through a snowstorm to a polling place. That is the kind of behavior Whouley expects from people.

So Whouley mentions to Clinton that there are some talk-radio shows that he could help with and a gospel station in Little Rock that would love to get him on the air. Clinton eagerly agrees.

About 6 P.M., Clinton calls back. "What do you think?" he asks Whouley.

Whouley doesn't know what to think. By now he is in what he calls "a well-organized but desperate frenzy." He is phoning around the country asking his people if they need more phone calls to go out, if they need a surrogate on radio or if they want Gore to call a mayor for them.

Gore calls him twice and asks the same thing as Clinton: "What do you think?"

Some states are breaking their way, Whouley tells him, but something strange is happening in Florida. It is so strange that the Gore campaign in Florida has put out a press release that says: "In Palm Beach County, a number of voters have experienced a problem with confusion over the arrows pointing at the Presidential candidates on the ballot. When ballots are placed in the slide for voting, Al Gore and Joe Lieberman are the second names on the ballot, but the third hole to punch." The release does not use the term "butterfly ballot." Hardly anyone has ever heard that term before. Many people soon will.

Later in the day, an aide pops her head into the supply closet to say, "The Big Guy is trying to get you," meaning Gore is on the phone.

"I'll have to call him back," Whouley says. "I'm looking at the Florida numbers."

But Whouley never does find the time to call Gore back. Florida is about to suffer a massive episode of electile dysfunction.

2

# GETTIN' SNIPPY

"DEMOCRACY MAY NOT ALWAYS
GIVE US THE OUTCOME WE WANT."

—Line from never-delivered
Al Gore concession speech,
November 7, 2000

ELI ATTIE HAS SET UP A SPEECH PREP room on the seventh floor of Loews. There is a TelePrompTer in case Gore wants to rehearse the speech, and a printer for Attie's laptop, in case Gore wants changes, which is inevitable. Gore always wants changes. On Gore's private schedule for Election Day, his speech prep time is listed as optional, however. "To make him walk through victory and defeat scenarios seemed abusive," Attie says. Attie has the victory speech down to eight or nine minutes, which means it takes up less than three pages, single-spaced. When Gore gets back from voting in Carthage, Attie sends a copy of the victory speech, Option A, up to Gore's suite. About 4 P.M., Gore comes down carrying it. "I am supposed to be taking a nap," he says. "But I am not."

Nobody is surprised. Gore seems to be operating on sheer force of will. He sits around talking about which states look good and which ones look close, but he makes very few comments about the speech. This is odd for him. "You could tell he was tired, because he didn't completely overhaul the victory speech," Attie says. Gore tells Attie he just wants to make sure the speech is substantive and that it talks about issues and his plans for the presidency rather than just being ceremonial. Gore tells him he especially wants it to contain his pledge to hold open town hall meetings as president. Attie brings up the possibility that Gore might lose Tennessee, and Gore thinks for a moment and talks about how, when his father had lost his Senate seat in 1970, he had said that the people of Tennessee defeated him, but that he would never stop loving Tennessee and that he would always be a Tennessean. Attie says he will write this into the speech and put it in brackets in case Gore has to deliver it. "When you have a new version, bring it to my room," Gore says. Attie does not bring up Option B, the concession.

IN AUSTIN, GEORGE W. BUSH IS HEADING FOR A workout at the University of Texas gym when his top strategist, Karl Rove, calls him on his cell phone. Rove, who is usually optimistic, breaks the bad news: the exit polls are not that good and key states look like they are slipping away. "I got the smell," Bush later told Dan Balz of the *Washington Post*. Bush works out, goes back to the governor's mansion and tells his wife, Laura, that he may have lost. Then he goes to see his twin daughters, Jenna and Barbara. "Girls, it could be a long night," he says. "Your dad may lose the presidency and the numbers don't look good now." Later, he will tell his parents the same thing. "Defeat," he said, "was settling in."

GORE GOES DOWN TO THE MEZZANINE OF THE hotel where a TV camera has been set up and does 16 live satellite TV interviews, hitting markets from east to west, targeting those identified by the Boiler Room. Brandon Thomas, 25, is handling the satellite TV, radio, and Internet webcasting operation for the Gore campaign. In addition, Thomas has had a person on the press plane with a digital video camera shooting each day's events (though few reporters know of his existence). At the end of each day, the video shooter would edit a package on his laptop computer and e-mail it to Thomas, who would put it up on the Gore 2000 website. Thomas also streams digitally compressed audio of each event over phone lines and then streams that live onto the website and feeds it to radio stations for soundbites. All this was foreshadowed in 1988, when Michael Dukakis held up his campaign in San Francisco on Election Day to stand on the tarmac at the airport and do a series of satellite interviews. Twelve years later, it is an industry. From July 1 to Election Day, Thomas has put Gore and his surrogates on 869 satellite interviews and 300 talk-radio interviews. On Election Day itself, the surrogates will do another 200 radio interviews. "We'd call a station and say, 'Hey, what is your news show talking about today? Education? I've got Secretary of Education Richard Riley.' And they'd say, 'Naw.' And I'd say, 'OK, how about Vice President Gore?'" Thomas's operation was also used in an attempt to correct some odd problems being reported from Florida. "The Boiler Room would tell us that people were being turned away from the polling places in West Palm and we should get somebody on radio down there telling people where they could get help." Afterwards, Thomas's evaluation of his tiny part of the campaign could serve as Gore's motto for the entire Election Day effort. "Our ferocity was unmatched," Thomas said.

Gore finishes with TV and goes back upstairs when he is told, hey, if he really wants to, he could do some radio, too. So Gore does 17 live radio interviews, one after another. Finally, he returns to his suite to eat dinner and greet the Liebermans.

Most of the staff groups around the TV sets on the seventh floor or in the Boiler Room at campaign headquarters. When the networks call Florida for Gore, everybody starts cheering in both locations. Tipper goes up and down the halls of Loews congratulating people and hugging them and telling them how great they are. Bill Daley is at headquarters and feels the election is now over. "My sense was that if we won Florida, we won the election," he says, and so he gets in a cab and heads for the hotel to congratulate Gore. But as he arrives he sees a big crowd in the lobby grouped around a large TV set, and Mark Fabiani, the deputy campaign manager, grabs him and says, "They just pulled back Florida from our column." Daley heads upstairs. He is disappointed but not devastated. As long as the networks don't give Florida to Bush, Gore is still alive.

Eli Attie has just arrived back at Loews after eating at a barbecue joint a few blocks away. He immediately notices the shift of mood in the lobby. Nobody is talking about defeat, but the euphoria is definitely over. He heads for the seventh floor, where most of the senior staff has now gathered. Gore keeps popping in and out, asking Daley what is going on. Daley tells him what he knows, which is not a great deal. After Gore walks away, Daley goes over to Attie. "You have a concession speech, too?" he asks quietly.

Attie nods.

DAVID LANE, BILL DALEY'S FORMER CHIEF OF staff at the Commerce Department, is trying to get the speakerphone to work in the seventh-floor meeting room so everybody at Loews can hear the people in the Boiler Room at headquarters. It is something like 1:30 A.M. They have heard from their sources in Austin that Bush is not going to go out and address his supporters until Gore goes out and addresses his. Suddenly, Gore and Lieberman appear in the doorway. Gore is in jeans and a casual shirt and Lieberman is in a suit. Gore bends over the speakerphone and starts asking some rapid-fire questions—What counties are still out in Florida? What do they look like? What are you projecting?—and people are answering the best they can.

Afterwards, people will come away from the meeting with different impressions. The vote count is rapidly coming to a close in Florida, with the unreported vote in largely Democratic counties. Some staff people get the impression that if the networks give Florida to Gore once more, which looks possible, he will go out and make an acceptance speech. Others get the impression that the most he will do is delay any decision until the morning, until every last vote in Florida is certain. In any case, the numbers start tumbling in and at first they are not good: Gore is down something like 90,000 votes in Florida. Then the Bush victory margin starts dropping rapidly. It's 80,000, then 70 then 60, 50, 40—spirits are soaring over at Gore headquarters—then the sky falls in. Fox TV reports that Bush's margin has spiked back up to 50,000 votes with very few votes left to be counted. A silence falls over the room at Loews.

Gore is standing in front of the TV set on the seventh floor when Fox calls Florida for Bush and announces he will become the next president of the United States. CBS and NBC follow a minute later and Daley immediately gets on the phone with Tom Brokaw to try to argue him out of it. "What are you calling this for?" Daley asks. "This is crazy. No one's pulled ahead!"

Then CNN calls it for Bush, and his picture appears on screen after screen with the words "winner" and "43rd President" beneath it.

At campaign headquarters, Michael Whouley, the Boiler Room chief, and his top aides fall silent in the supply closet for maybe 90 straight seconds. Outside in the Boiler Room, people start crying.

"I'm calling Nick," Whouley says. Nick Baldick is in charge of Florida for Gore. Whouley calls him just out of courtesy, just out of loyalty. The networks never get these things wrong.

"What are your numbers?" Whouley asks Baldick.

"I think the networks are wrong," Baldick says. "Broward is out. Palm Beach is out. This will be 1,000 votes either way."

Somebody comes into the closet with a printout of the Florida secretary of state's website. The Bush total is down to 6,000 votes. Whouley knows that under Florida law, a recount is automatic if the margin of victory is less than half a percentage point. With 6 million votes cast, that means a recount would be required if Bush's margin is less than 30,000 votes.

"This is fucked up," Whouley says. "Why are the networks saying we lost?"

Outside in the Boiler Room, Gore operatives begin calling network TV producers. "You're wrong!" they say. "Your numbers are wrong!"

Whouley tells somebody to call Bob Butterworth, the attorney general of Florida and one of the few Democrats to hold statewide office, to make sure they can send cameras to his house so the entire nation can hear him say that a recount is automatic.

Whouley is now in full gear. He knows that a recount will save the day and there is nothing to worry about. He has no idea that over at the Loews Hotel, a very different conclusion has been reached.

AL GORE STANDS IN FRONT OF THE TV SET, ONLY about three feet away from the screen, his arms crossed, quietly rocking back and forth on his heels as he sees the networks call the race for Bush. He turns and sees Attie. "Do you have another statement?" he asks. He seems subdued and resigned.

"I do," Attie says.

"Why don't you bring it up to my room?" Gore says. Then he turns to Daley. "Let's talk," he says.

The two of them go into a small room across the hall and close the door.

"What do you think?" Gore says.

"I think you ought to call him," Daley says, meaning Gore should call Bush and concede. Brokaw has told Daley they are pretty confident about the projection. Gore is down by 50,000 votes, he says, with only about 2 percent of the vote left to be counted. Daley has to think about the future. In America, when the networks call a race, that is it. If Gore looks like some kind of crybaby, somebody who refuses to accept the infinite wisdom of network television, he may never get to run for president again.

Gore is silent.

"I don't think we have a lot of options here," Daley says. "We have to make some decisions. We've got people waiting."

Gore is still not saying anything, which is not unusual. He is famous for long pauses.

"It's over," Gore finally says. "Let's concede." Then Gore heads for the staircase to go to his room upstairs to tell his family.

Daley places a call to Don Evans, Bush's campaign chairman. "There'll be a call coming shortly, so don't do anything, don't go out," Daley tells him. He wants Gore to do his public concession before Bush does his public acceptance; otherwise, Gore will look ungracious. Evans agrees, and Daley hangs up. He looks out the window and sees the rain falling past the street lights below. He thinks of all the people standing outside waiting for Al Gore.

. . .

JIM LOFTUS, DIRECTOR OF ADVANCE FOR GORE, HAS had a team working on the election night celebration in Nashville's War Memorial Plaza for six weeks. He loves what he calls the heroic architecture of the War Memorial Building, an enormous Greek temple with six towering, fluted columns in front. When Gore eulogized his father from inside the building, he recalled how, after his father lost his Senate seat, the two of them were floating down the Caney Fork River in a canoe and his father asked him, "What would you do if you had 32 years of service to the people, given to the highest of your ability, always doing what you thought was right, and had then been unceremoniously turned out of office? What would you do?"

"I'd take the 32 years, Dad," Al Jr. responded.

But now the choice was not that easy, not that up or down. Had the people really spoken? Gore knew he was winning the popular vote. He also knew that if he lost Florida, he would lose the electoral vote. But had he really lost Florida? The Associated Press did not think so. Its numbers did not show Florida going for Bush, and it was not about to call the race. But the Associated Press was not a television network. And the networks were going full-steam ahead with their anointment of Bush. Out in the plaza, standing in the rain, 6,000 people had gathered. Loftus had made sure there were giant 20-foot-by-20-foot TV screens for them to watch—"We didn't want anyone to leave the plaza to go watch the results in a bar," he said—and they have seen what Gore has seen. But they also look up at the building, in front of which stands a lonely microphone on a lectern covered with a plastic garbage bag to ward off the rain, and most know they are not going to leave until they hear from Al. Loftus has spent $250,000 for this evening, on everything from the blue lights that illuminate the columns, to the huge American flag painted on panels between the columns, to a monster fireworks show afterwards. He has Gore's entrance music, "Let the Day Begin," all ready to be blasted over the sound system and now, like everyone else, he just waits.

CARTER ESKEW, A SENIOR ADVISER, GOES INTO THE big room on the seventh floor and says, "He wants to talk to Tipper, and I think he may want to go down to the War Memorial."

And now everybody knows it's going to be a concession, and people start getting the motorcade organized and getting people loaded into the cars. This is not easy. The motorcade has to be expanded to include all the extra visitors and guests and family and the entire Lieberman campaign. In the hubbub nobody thinks to call Michael Whouley to tell them Gore is about to concede.

Gore and Secret Service agents take the stairs to the ninth floor. As Gore walks down the long corridor to his suite, the sound of crying is audible from many of the rooms.

Attie takes the concession speech and his laptop to the ninth floor. As he gets off the elevator and looks in the open door of Gore's suite, Gore is standing hugging his daughter Kristin, who is crying.

"It's going to be OK," Gore tells her. "It's going to be OK."

Rather than barge in, Attie hands the speech to an aide, who brings it to Gore. After a few minutes, the aide returns. "He's fine with this," the aide says.

The fact that Gore does not want to make changes is the first sign Attie has seen that defeat has really drained him. But you can't see it from Gore's exterior. He is holding his children and his wife to him, one after another, patting their backs, being the strong one.

As Attie is about to return to the seventh floor to print out the concession speech in big type for the TelePrompTer, Gore appears in the doorway and holds up a piece of paper to Daley, who has joined him in his suite.

"Is this Bush's number?" he asks.

Daley tells him it is.

Gore goes back inside the room, calls Bush and congratulates him on becoming the next president of the United States.

"You're a good man," Bush tells him.

The Gore kids are still weeping, and everyone is still upset. Daley calls Don Evans back and says, "It will be a half-hour." Daley figures the Gore kids have to get dressed and a whole bunch of people have to be stuffed into the motorcade and then they have to drive in the rain to the plaza. Nobody is feeling very good and everybody is moving as if they were underwater. He figures a half-hour is about right.

Don Evans, however, seems very nervous over the length of time. "A half-hour?" he says to Daley, concern in his voice. "That's a long time. Can you speed that up?"

"Well, you know, it's hard," Daley says. "We're trying to." And the thought flashes across Daley's mind: What is Evans so impatient about? Weeks later, Daley tells me: "I should have gotten suspicious right there. I didn't think that they may have been nervous about what was happening in Florida. I never put it together, to be frank with you, until a couple of weeks ago. But maybe they knew the numbers had already begun to slip. And, well, there were all these people waiting in the rain."

Just before Daley is about to hang up, Evans tells him to hold on a second and Bush comes on the phone.

"Congratulations," Daley says to him.

"I know it's hard, but you guys did a great job," Bush says.

.  .  .

BACK ON THE SEVENTH FLOOR, ATTIE PRINTS OUT
the large-type TelePrompTer copy and hands it to the Tele-
PrompTer operator. Then he prints out a regular-type copy for Gore,
which is placed in a red folder and taken up to Nine so Gore can
carry it with him in the limousine.

David Morehouse is on Nine with Gore and trying to figure out
how to get everybody in the elevators and still give the Gores some
modicum of privacy. He secures one elevator for Gore; Tipper;
Frank Hunger, who is Gore's brother-in-law; Karenna and her husband, Drew Schiff; Kristin, Sarah, and Albert. The other elevator
carries the Lieberman family, Daley, and Donna Brazile, the campaign manager.

"I remember the walk from the elevators in the bowels of
Loews, through the kitchen and down this long hallway to the
motorcade," Morehouse says later. "It was a very long, very quiet
walk, with nobody talking, with really deafening silence, except for
the sound of whimpering from the Gore and Lieberman children.
That was the only noise."

They get to the loading dock where the limousines are waiting
and the other vehicles of the motorcade are positioned. Tonight,
Gore gets in the first limousine with Tipper and the children. Morehouse gets in the second limousine, the identical spare limousine,
and does what he always does, which is to sit on the back seat and
then pull down the jump seat in front of him for a Secret Service
agent. The driver is also an agent and Tony Zoto, the head of the
vice president's Secret Service detail, sits in the front passenger seat.
Next to Morehouse sits a doctor, who is always present in case of
emergencies. (Often, Morehouse will get in the first limousine,
which means when he pulls up to the event and gets out, people

start snapping pictures assuming it will be the vice president.) Zoto turns around from the front seat. "It's a shame," Zoto says. "It's been a pleasure working with you." Morehouse thanks him and then stares out the window at the rain. He doesn't want to talk about it.

The motorcade is abnormally large this night: It begins with Pilot, which is a police car; Lead, another police car; the limousine; the spare limousine; Follow-Up, a Secret Service Suburban loaded with automatic weapons; Control, a sedan containing Gore's chief of staff, Gore's military aide, who always carries the top-secret nuclear attack codes in a satchel known as the Football, and a Secret Service driver; Support, which is a mini-van containing Gore's photographer and senior staff; WHCA, which contains the personnel and equipment of the White House Communications Agency that videotapes all events of the president and vice president for history; Staff One, a 15-passenger van; followed by three other 15-passenger vans designated as Staff Two, Guest and Family; followed by Lieberman's limousine; Lieberman's spare limousine; Lieberman Support; Lieberman Staff; Lieberman Family; Mrs. Gore Support; Mrs. Lieberman Support; Press One, for the pool reporters; Follow, a police car; and an ambulance. Not counting the dozens of extra police cars that are needed to block traffic for it, the motorcade stretches for something like three city blocks.

But everybody is impatient to get this thing over with, and nobody is exactly sure who is going and who is not, and so staff people just begin jumping in whatever van or car is available. This means Daley, who is usually up front in the motorcade, is now in the back in a van with Eskew, Attie, and the TelePrompTer operator. As Daley crawls into the front seat of the van, his cell phone rings and it is Howard Fineman of *Newsweek*. "Do you know it's only 10,000 votes?" Fineman says, meaning the race in Florida has tightened since the networks have called it for Bush. "No," Daley replies, "we're just leaving." The motorcade pulls away from the curb, and Daley hangs up on Fineman. He doesn't want to talk to reporters now.

"But I kind of had a bad fucking feeling," Daley says. "A bad fucking feeling."

Michael Feldman, Gore's traveling chief of staff, is supposed to be up front in the motorcade, too, but he ends up in a 15-passenger van in the back. Nobody is talking. About three blocks from the War Memorial Plaza, his Motorola Skytel beeper starts vibrating on his belt. He is being paged by White House Signal, the mysterious telecommunications arm of the White House that can put anybody in touch with anybody. It is not a secret agency, but few outsiders know about it. White House reporters, for example, can call White House Signal and leave messages or ask to be connected to anybody on the White House staff. Only White House employees can be reached through Signal, so it turns out to be unbelievable luck that Feldman is a hybrid: though working for the Gore campaign, he is still on the vice presidential payroll and so he has his beeper on his belt. He pulls it off and looks at it. It says (with the confidential coding removed): "Call Switch. Call Holding with Michael Whuley. ASAP."

B ACK AT THE BOILER ROOM, WHOULEY HAS NO idea why he can't reach anybody at Loews. He can't believe any major decision would be made without checking with him; he is in charge of the vote, after all. But now he is getting antsy. Something doesn't feel right. His phone should be ringing with questions from the people at Loews. So Whouley asks Jeff Yarbro, his assistant, to call Michael Feldman. Yarbro calls White House Signal.

Feldman looks at the message on his pager and then reaches for his cell phone and calls White House Signal—he gets through, which is amazing because the circuits are so busy most cell phones in Nashville are not working—and he asks to be connected to Whouley. Whouley gets on the line.

"Where are you guys?" Whouley asks.

Feldman looks out the rain-smeared window. "I don't know," he says. "We're very close. One more block. We're pulling up to the War Memorial now."

Whouley's heart skips a beat. "You're what? Why?" he yells.

"We're going to concede," Feldman says.

"Why?" Whouley asks. "*Why?*"

"'Cause we *lost,*" Feldman says.

"No, no, no, we haven't!" Whouley says. "We're only 6,000 votes away. That triggers a recount. And we might win!"

"Hold on! Hold on!" Feldman says. "I'll get you Daley." Feldman has a conference call feature on his cell phone; he calls Daley's cell and immediately gets thrown into voice mail. Feldman thinks for a moment and then calls Graham Street, the aide who travels with Daley. The call goes through, and Street hands the phone to Daley.

"What's up, Mike?" Daley says.

Whouley starts talking. "Billy, this thing has collapsed for Bush." Somebody hands Whouley another printout from the secretary of state's website. The victory margin for Bush is now down to 1,300 votes. "You can't go out there!" Whouley says. "It's an automatic recount."

"Oh, shit!" Daley says.

Daley, who had been slouched in the front seat next to the driver, straightens up and snaps around. "We're only 1,300 votes behind," he says to Eskew.

Their section of the motorcade begins slowing to a stop, which means Gore's limo, at the front, has already come to a complete stop, and Gore is about to get out.

"Get hold of Morehouse," Daley tells Feldman. "As soon as Gore gets out of the car, get him to the hold room and tell him, 'Don't do anything!'"

Daley turns his attention back to Whouley. "We're going inside and I'll call you back on a land line," he says.

As their van comes to a halt, Attie leaps out into the rain and darkness. He is worried that Gore might skip the holding room and deliver the speech. Attie runs down the long line of cars to catch Gore, trying not to look like a mad assassin. "But the motorcade is like a gazillion blocks long," Attie says. He starts running faster.

Feldman reaches for the secure radio phone that is always in the car where the chief of staff sits, one that will connect to the radio phone in Morehouse's limousine, but Feldman is not in the chief of staff car tonight. That's the bad news. The good news is that Morehouse's girlfriend, Vanessa Opperman, is sitting next to Feldman, and she calls Morehouse on her cell phone, praying the call goes through. One of Morehouse's many responsibilities is to signal the Secret Service agent when it is OK to open the door to Gore's limo and let him out. So if they can reach Morehouse, they can keep Gore in the car.

But this night, for the first time in anyone's memory, Gore does not wait for Morehouse's signal to the agent. He gets out of the car as Morehouse's phone begins to ring. Opperman hands it to Feldman, "David, he's got to go to the hold!" Feldman shouts. "Take him to the hold!"

"Why?" Morehouse asks. Morehouse's limousine comes to a stop directly behind Gore's. He knows he has a minute or two because Gore never exits the limousine until Morehouse says so. "Why?" he asks Feldman again.

"I can't tell you why!" Feldman says. "Just stop him from going to the event!" Feldman's van pulls up, and Feldman jumps out, running toward Gore's limousine as he talks to Morehouse. "We need to go to hold!" Feldman yells into the phone. "Absolutely, positively. Before we do anything, we need to go to the hold."

Morehouse walks into the little tent, and to his astonishment Gore is not in the limousine. He looks down the passageway and sees Gore walking swiftly to the plaza, his family trailing him. Not ever in the 15 months that Morehouse has been doing this has Gore decided to exit the limousine on his own.

And Gore, Morehouse sees, is walking faster than usual.

His bad knee sending out twinges of protest, Morehouse rushes after him.


THE HOLDING ROOM IN THE WAR MEMORIAL Building contains some metal desks, a bookcase, and a table with cookies, chocolates, and coffee. It reminds everyone of a high school principal's office. The only phones in the room are the boxy black secure phones that are always set up for the vice president. Feldman rushes inside, grabs one and calls Whouley.

"We still at 6,000?" he asks.

"We're down to 1,000," Whouley says.

By the time Tipper enters a moment later, the number is down to 600. Six hundred votes out of 6 million cast!

Gore enters behind Tipper. Attie cannot resist. He doesn't care about protocol now. He runs up to the vice president. "With 99.7 percent counted, you're only 600 votes behind, and I think we need to change some language, and Daley and Carter need to see you," he gushes.

The room is not that big, and a lot of people are now crammed into it. Everybody is hugging, and some are crying. Daley goes up to Gore.

"We have a little situation going on here," Daley says. "Bush's victory margin keeps shrinking."

Lieberman is standing next to Gore and says, "My God, what does it mean?"

Gore asks Daley to get Whouley on the phone.

"We've got an automatic recount," Whouley says. "Attorney General Butterworth is going to make a statement. It's down to 600 votes."

"Thank you," Gore tells him. "Thank you very much."

In the Boiler Room, Whouley stands up. "We're coming back!" he yells.

AT THE WAR MEMORIAL, DALEY IS NOW TRYING to figure things out from Bush's point of view. Do the Bush people have the same numbers they do? Have they known that the network call has been bullshit? And what if Bush just goes out and claims victory, based on what the networks have been broadcasting?

Everybody has the same thought at once. They've got to get this on TV. TV is God. If Brokaw, Rather, and Jennings say Florida is still in play and Bush is not president, then Gore still has a chance.

Attie goes over to a desk and opens up his laptop. A new speech is going to be needed.

Daley calls Don Evans for the third time that evening. "Hey, we've got new information here," Daley says. "Our conversation from before—we need to basically pause things so we can find out more information. Don't let your guy go out. It's a problem. I'll have to call you back."

But that just holds things.

"Everybody's running around in circles," Daley remembers. "We didn't want to look like an ass. What if Florida changed again?"

Ron Fournier of the AP calls and says, "This is nuts. You guys don't know? We stopped calling it. We're not going to call it. Nobody else is calling it."

They rush to see what TV has, but there is no TV. Just a set with a closed-circuit monitor showing the War Memorial Plaza and people getting soaked in the rain. Somebody goes running down the hall to try to find a real TV, finds one with an old rabbit ears antenna on top and lugs it to the holding room.

Daley calls Brokaw's cell phone and can't get through. "It was chaos, totally chaotic," Daley says.

"All of a sudden we were injected with a new sense of life," Attie remembers. "Like a cancer patient told there is a new treatment."

Gore decides that he and Lieberman should go out and tell the crowd to go home. Eskew thinks that is a bad idea. Candidates go out for victory or concession. They don't go out to say there is a delay.

But Gore wants to go out. "People have been waiting in the rain for hours," he says. "Joe and I need to go out and say something."

Then Drew Schiff, Gore's son-in-law, speaks up and says that if Gore goes out and speaks, he may look like he is a sore loser trying to delay the inevitable.

Gore thinks about that and nods. But who is going to go out?

Daley volunteers. "I felt real bad because I felt I had kind of encouraged the concession, and I felt real bad that it was my fault," Daley says later. "I thought it was over. I thought after all the networks called it, after a long night, it was like 2:30 in the morning with not a hell of a lot of votes left to count, 97 percent was in or something. I thought it was the right thing to do, and he did, too, he did, too. I mean, they were reporting 97 percent of the votes or whatever, and we were down 50,000, and at that point nobody was saying, 'This is bullshit.'"

So Daley will address the crowd. He turns to Gore: "You guys ought to leave here."

Then people start shouting for everybody to get back in the motorcade, and Eskew starts dictating to Attie as Daley and Karenna and others start offering ideas and Attie just pounds it into his laptop. He prints it out and hands it to Daley.

Gore remembers one little thing is left to be done. "I want to talk to Governor Bush," he says.

Daley places yet another call to Evans. "Don, I've got the vice president here calling for Governor Bush," Daley says. Then he hands the phone to Gore, who is sitting on the edge of the desk.

Gore says: "Look, Governor, the circumstances have changed in Florida, and we have to put the plans we discussed earlier on hold."

"Are you saying what I think you're saying?" an astonished Bush replies.

"The vote is close," Gore says, "and we have to put our discussion on hold. If you win, I'll be very happy to move ahead with what we discussed."

"Let me make sure that I understand," Bush says, still incredulous. "You're calling back to *retract* that concession?"

"You don't have to be snippy about it," Gore says. "Let me explain: If in fact I lose in Florida, I will immediately concede. But it's not in any way clear I have lost, and until it is clear I can't concede."

Bush starts to explain that his little brother Jeb is standing right there and has been on the phone to Tallahassee all night and has assured him that he has won Florida.

"Your little brother doesn't get to make that call," Gore says.

There are a couple more exchanges and then Bush says, "Do what you have to do."

"You're welcome!" says Gore. Then he hangs up the phone and

with one hand makes a motion as if he were a lifting a dumbbell from his waist to his shoulder, pumping iron. The room bursts into applause, and Gore smiles.

MOREHOUSE GOES OUT TO THE PLAZA AND makes sure everything is ready for Daley. Jim Loftus, the advance man, asks Morehouse what song he should play over the loudspeakers. Should it be "Let the Day Begin," which is the song they play every time Gore is about to speak, or should they play the orchestral music they played for Gore at the convention?

Morehouse looks at him as if he has gone insane.

"Jimmy," he says, "no music. It's not a real event."

"Oh," Loftus says and then pauses. "So no fireworks, either?"

"No," Morehouse says gently. "No fireworks either."

DALEY WALKS OUT THROUGH THE GIANT PILLARS and down the steps to the lectern. A huge throng is still there, some with Gore/Lieberman signs bent over their heads to keep off the rain.

"They had been standing there for hours, although they were all cheering," Daley says later. "They were standing in the rain cheering me at 3:30 in the morning or whatever time it was. I just assumed they were all drunk."

Daley steps up to the lectern. The garbage bag has been removed. "Let me say: I've been in politics for a long time. But there's never been a night like this one," he begins. "Just an hour or so ago, the TV networks called this race for Governor Bush." The crowd boos madly. "It now appears," Daley continues, "that their call was premature. As everyone in America knows, this race has come down to the state of Florida. . . . But this race is still too close to call—and until the recount is concluded and the results in Florida become official, our campaign continues. So I want to thank you all, on behalf of the vice president, for waiting out here so late tonight— and we hope to have you all back here very soon."

The crowd goes nuts.

Daley walks back up the steps and looks at the giant pillars, dripping with rain, the huge beacons of blue light, the wildly cheering crowd.

"What am I doing here?" he says.

BACK AT THE BOILER ROOM, WHOULEY STEPS outside, smokes two cigarettes and then returns to work. He convenes a meeting with the lawyers and the rest of the staff, parcels out who is going where and then arranges for Lieberman's plane to take everyone to Florida. Assignments are already being printed out. On the plane, the lawyers start briefing everyone on election law and how to conduct a recount. Nobody has slept. They arrive in Florida at 7 A.M. By 9 A.M., everyone is in place and hard at work.

In Nashville, Daley calls Warren Christopher, the dignified, former secretary of state who ran the vice presidential selection process, and asks him to supervise the legal battle in Florida. Christopher catches a 6:30 A.M. flight to Nashville.

Daley showers. In a few hours, he has to go live on the "Today" show.

At 4:18 A.M., Bill Clinton calls Al Gore. The Clintons have forgone a snazzy victory celebration for Hillary at Elaine's in Manhattan out of respect for the uncertainty of Gore's situation. Both men are in philosophical moods. Clinton assures Gore that Gore has done all he can. Gore agrees.

. . .

DALEY MANAGES TO GET TWO HOURS OF SLEEP. Then he gets up and meets with Gore and Lieberman. Whoever else they send to Florida, Lieberman says, they have got to send Michael Whouley.

"This guy is a wartime consiglieri," Lieberman says.

WHEN GORE'S FATHER LOST HIS LAST RACE AND had to concede, one of the last things he said was: "The truth shall rise again."

Years later, the elder Gore was asked if it ever had.

"Oh, yes," he said, "in my son."

The son's concession speech still sits in its red folder. It is a speech the son will not now have to give. Later, Attie reads it to me:

"Friends, fellow Tennesseans, fellow Americans: The people of our country have spoken. And I accept their judgment. Just moments ago, I called Governor George W. Bush and congratulated him on his election as the 43rd President of the United States.

"When you seek to carry the mantle of progress, it's hard to find glory in defeat. But I want you to know: Even in this hard hour, my heart is full. And that is because of you.

"Democracy may not always give us the outcome we want. But the United States of America is the best country ever created—still, as ever, the hope of humankind.

"We all share in the privilege and challenge of building a more perfect union.

"We still have a long way to go on that journey. And I can't promise it won't be a long and winding road.

"But this I know in my heart: You ain't seen nothing yet."

Now young Al would show them all. The truth would rise again and in Florida. He would fight there as he felt he had fought throughout the entire campaign: harder, longer, smarter. The numbers were good, the trend lines were clear, the votes were there. All they had to do in Florida, Gore knew, was to count the ballots.

And how difficult could that be?

# 3

# THE BOY DEBUTS

"DON'T TRY TO BE CHARMING, WITTY, OR
INTELLIGENT. JUST BE YOURSELF."

—Laura Bush's advice to
her husband, June 1999

THE CANDIDATE FOR PRESIDENT pretends to push the aluminum cart down the aisle of the TWA charter, laughingly taking orders from the reporters. He is wearing a blue, basketweave shirt, a red Ferragamo tie, dress slacks, and a big Western belt with a huge State of Texas belt buckle that has "George W. Bush" embossed on it. He is wearing ostrich-skin boots. About 100 journalists are on the plane, which has "Great Expectations" printed on its nose. This is Bush's June 1999 kickoff tour, and he shakes the hand of every one of the reporters, talking easily, laughing, and joking with them. A few seconds earlier, he got out his half-glasses, perched them on his nose, and read from a piece of paper into the intercom.

"This is your candidate speaking. Please stow your expectations securely in the overhead bin as they may shift during the trip and they could fall and hurt someone—especially me," Bush says, and the reporters laugh. "Please understand that while you are traveling with a well-trained crew, for many of us, this is our first solo flight. Thanks for coming along today—we know you have a choice of candidates when you fly, and we appreciate you choosing Great Expectations."

Everybody applauds. Most know this is part of Bush's highly calculated "charm offensive," but they are charmed nonetheless. Reporters don't get this kind of treatment on Al Gore's Air Force Two, a beautiful but austere Boeing 757, all gray and blue leather inside and packed with all sorts of electronic goodies that Gore had insisted on before the plane was delivered. Immaculately maintained and with first-class seating throughout, even in the rear press section, it is, however, utterly devoid of anything like charm. When Gore ran for vice president in 1992, things were different. He had a chartered 727 that was festooned inside with bunting, streamers, pom-poms, and goofy photographs. Back then, Gore even did what no candidate did: He went sky-surfing. He would plant his feet on a plastic meal tray, face the rear of the aircraft and then, as the plane lifted off, Gore would hurtle down the aisle at an impressive speed. The FAA would not have been amused. Even more amazing, Gore did imitations of James Brown ("Ah-feel-gooooood!"), and the beer and booze and small talk flowed all night. Then, something terrible happened to Al Gore: He won. He became vice president and went into what everybody on his staff called (though not to his face) his "crouch," second-guessing himself constantly and becoming intensely deferential to the president because that is what vice presidents do. Not only was his every speech cleared by the White House, but Gore censored himself to a ridiculous degree, adopting what he called a two-second "time-lapse" or "time-lag" in which inside his own head he would examine each word before he spoke it to make sure it utterly and completely advanced the cause of Bill Clinton. This did not exactly contribute to Gore's spontaneity.

George Bush doesn't worry about such things. Bush doesn't know from crouches and time-lags. What he knows is that reporters like stuff, and so when they came aboard each reporter's seat had resting on it a T-shirt that read "I Have Great Expectations for Governor Bush," a star-shaped yellow "tension-reliever" toy labeled "Squeeze to lower expectations," and a laminated luggage tag marked "How Did He Do?" with possible grades: "Grand Slam," "Triple," "Double," "Single," and "Back to Minors." The reporters were delighted.

Now Bush makes his way down the aisle chatting amiably about baseball and basketball and the new Austin Powers movie—"God, it was weak," Bush says. "I liked the first one, though"—and immediately he runs into a little hitch. The reporters have started acting like reporters. Some have huddled to see what they remember about the novel "Great Expectations," and somebody says that it was more about dashed hopes than optimism. And so a reporter asks Bush why he named his plane for that particular book.

Bush looks back at him quizzically. "It started out as High Expectations and I suggested Great Expectations," he says.

But the book, the reporter says.

Bush shrugs. "If I read it, I can't remember it," he says. There is a pause. "I'm going to the Knicks-Spurs game this week."

Does it matter that Bush has never read what some consider Charles Dickens's greatest work? No. Does it matter that Bush may not even know there is a book by that name? Well, probably not. The press is learning that Bush is not a reader—the bookshelves of the governor's office in Austin are filled with 250 autographed baseballs—and later, when asked by a schoolchild to name a favorite book of his while growing up, Bush cannot name a single one. He keeps short days, does not like long memos, and rarely spends more than 15 minutes on any decision, even when it is to recommend that a person be executed. He is not, he says, especially introspective. "I'm not really the type to wander off and sit down and go through a deep wrestling with my soul," he tells reporters.

There is, however, a more basic question that reporters are struggling with: Is Dubya dumb? He will admit he is no highbrow, but could a man be elected and reelected governor of Texas and run for president of the United States and be, well, stupid? OK, so he doesn't know Slovakia from Slovenia or Greeks from "Grecians," but this begs the question: How bright do you have to be to be president? True, Bush attended Andover, Yale, and Harvard—but that doesn't *prove* he's dumb. And too much intelligence can be a drawback for a presidential candidate. Voters react negatively to intellectuals such as Adlai Stevenson. And when Bill Clinton's campaign staff found out in 1992 that people associated him with Georgetown, Yale, and Oxford, it took great pains to "dumb down" Clinton and stress his roots in tiny Hope, Arkansas, and his love for Big Macs, Ray-Ban sunglasses, and the Astroturf he had in the back of his pickup truck as a youth. (Voters probably should have paid more attention to that last one.) In that respect, the Bush campaign is one step ahead: It doesn't have to dumb down its candidate for public consumption.

"Just because I happen to mispronounce the name of a country doesn't mean that I don't understand how to lead," Bush will say later. "What matters is: Do I know how to see clear goals? Do I know how to lead? Do I shoot straight? And that's all I know to do." Ronald Reagan made dozens of misstatements both as a candidate and as a president—some, such as the one in which he claimed to have been present at the liberation of Nazi concentration camps at the end of World War II, were just plain lies—but the public never seemed to mind much. "The press just never got the point, which is that people look for leadership and character and principles, and they don't expect complete mastery of every detail," says then–Bush spokesman David Beckwith. "In fact, the public knows that sometimes if you are worried about tiny details, you are not looking at the big picture." Some Republicans disagree. Dan Quayle may not know how to spell "potato," but he knows that George W. Bush is getting breaks from the media that Quayle never got. "Use your wildest imagination and multiple it by a factor of three and then you'd come close to what would be happening to me if I had made similar gaffes," says Quayle. Multiple it? It is revealing that the Bush campaign does not make any great claims as to Bush's intellect. "When you are out taking questions from reporters, the public realizes that it's stressful and somewhat risky," Beckwith says. "If someone handles it with aplomb, the voters care about that more than the precise answers."

"We're going to make mistakes," says Karl Rove, Bush's chief strategist. "But we need to avoid the biggest mistake of all, and that is to be tepid." Tepid, they are leaving to Al Gore. "Gore is very smart, but he is almost too smart," says former Texas Agriculture Commissioner and radio commentator Jim Hightower. "He's too controlled. He sits around planning on how not to make mistakes and so he will never make a bold stroke. Let's face it, Gore vs. Bush is going to be a race between Dull and Dullard." Still, Bush does seem to be separated from the American people by a common language. Bush's every gaffe is catalogued by Jacob Weisberg in *Slate* magazine's "Bushism of the Week." And they include some real howlers like, "Will the highways on the Internet become more few?" and "I know how hard it is for you to put food on your family." Then in Florence, South Carolina, on January 11, 2000, Bush speaks perhaps the ultimate Bushism: "Rarely is the question asked: Is our children learning?" It should be noted that in spite of this, Bush goes on to win the South Carolina primary, a fact that seems to have escaped the vice president. In an interview with the Associated Press, Gore is directly asked if he believes that Bush is "too dumb" to be president. His reaction: "Gore convulsed in laughter while taking a drink of Diet Coke. He grabbed a towel to hold against his mouth then, finally swallowing, insisted the tape recorder be stopped for an off-the-record observation."

Bush was not worried about the dumb thing. He liked being underestimated. Ann Richards, whom he defeated for governor in 1994, underestimated him, assumed he would be terrible in debates. Bush, however, stunned political analysts when he achieved victory by sticking to a few, well-rehearsed positions and refusing to stray "off-message" no matter what he was asked. But if Bush thought running for president would just be an enlarged governor's race, he soon learns differently. For one thing, he is now always fair game. Part of the charm offensive is to get to know reporters really well, giving them nicknames, asking about their families and engaging in the locker-room physicality that is very much a part of Bush: He rubs their cheeks, musses their hair, throws an arm around their shoulders. But Bush can't get to know everybody. Scores of reporters don't travel regularly with the campaign; they just come and go. And at first Bush doesn't realize that to reporters he is always wearing a target on his back. So when he is asked by a TV newsman to name the leaders of four world trouble spots then in the news— Chechnya, Taiwan, India, and Pakistan—Bush tries to answer instead of trying to duck. As it turns out, Bush can come up with only one partially correct answer, the family name of the leader of Taiwan, but even that didn't earn him many points. As Jay Leno put it: "He only knew one, the head of Taiwan. He said, 'A guy named Lee.' Taiwan—Lee? You've got a 50 percent chance of being right."

Then there was Poutine-gate. During the Michigan primary, a man who turned out to be a Canadian comic told Bush that "Canadian Prime Minister Jean Poutine" had endorsed him "as the man to lead the free world into the twenty-first century." Bush did not question why a Canadian prime minister would be making an endorsement in a U.S. election. Instead, he sought to show off his knowledge of foreign (or, at least, continental) affairs, by replying: "I appreciate his strong statement; he understands I believe in free trade. He understands I want to make sure our relations with our most important neighbor to the north of us, the Canadians, is strong, and we'll work closely together." Ouch. The prime minister of Canada is not "Jean Poutine." A "poutine" is a Canadian fast-food concoction of French fries, gravy, and cheese curds. The real prime minister, Jean Chrétien, is highly amused, however, and his office issues a statement: "Clearly, Canada is not in the Bush leagues."

The other problem with the charm offensive was that it got Bush close to the media and often revealed more about Bush than the campaign intended. Making his way down the plane aisle on the morning of his announcement tour, Bush looked a little tired. A reporter asked how much sleep he had gotten the night before. "I only got six hours' sleep last night," Bush replied with a weary shake of his head. "I need more than that." He was lucky to get six. Typical of the infighting that occurs in new campaigns, his fundraising people had taken control of the day before his announcement speech and scheduled two closed fundraisers for Bush, one in St. Louis and one in Chicago. The events would end up raising $1.5 million, but the Bush press staff was not pleased. "We didn't think it was a good way to start the campaign to have him going to two fat-cat fundraisers that excluded the press on the day before he announced," one aide told me. A compromise was worked out: Bush would go to the fundraisers, but he would also go to a reading center and a baseball game. Then somebody told Bush about it. He exploded. "What you're telling me is that because you guys fucked up, I got to break my ass all day and won't get home until midnight?" he said. "We're going back to Plan A." The reading center and baseball game were canceled. Bush went only to the fundraisers, but he still didn't get back to Austin until 11 P.M., about 90 minutes past his usual bedtime, resulting in a tired candidate and a nervous staff. It was a small insight into Bush: Gore would never have canceled the reading center—and child literacy was supposed to be one of Bush's signature programs—and Bill Clinton would have gone to all the events including the baseball game. Clinton loved campaigning and would do it until the wee hours of the morning. Bush pretended to like campaigning, but actually he tolerated it. And he wasn't about to go read to a bunch of kids if it meant losing sleep.

But when Bush did campaign—and he was better in the mornings—he did it with what looked like relish and ease, and crowds appreciated it. When, in Iowa, Yvonne Peasley reached out to shake his hand, Bush noticed a camera dangling from her wrist. "Let me have that," Bush said, taking the camera from her and handing it to an aide. "Let's get us a picture." (The moment had the desired effect when a reporter interviewed Peasley later. "What a sweet, nice man," she said.) Turning to another woman on the rope line, Bush said to Dorothy Thompson, "I like those shades." Then he put his hands on her shoulders, peered behind her sunglasses and said, "I like those eyes!" Bush knew that campaigning was a courtship. Why did everybody make such a fuss about it? Media experts knew that the last part of the twentieth century had become an age of visual images and that what played well on TV was important. Candidates had to speak not only with words but also with pictures. Thus to a large extent campaigns had become theatrical productions, just as political journalism began to be indistinguishable from theatrical reviews. "Artifice" was the key, said historian Gil Troy. "It is more important to act rather than to be. The role of the candidate is to fulfill the role not of commander in chief, but celebrity in chief. Clinton was excellent at it, but he learned it from studying Ronald Reagan." So whether by design or through simple affability, when

Bush put his hands on people in the rope line (or on the press plane), it had a real effect. "He's very good connecting with people both in person and on TV," Don Sipple, a Republican media consultant who worked for Bush in his campaign against Ann Richards in 1994, told me in 1996, way before Bush was planning on running for president. "He has good eyes." One thing Bush could do was to slow down his blink rate and laser his eyes into whatever he was looking at—a single voter or a crowd or a TV camera. "Eye contact is everything in this business, and he knows how to connect, in person or through a TV screen," Sipple said.

But the Bush campaign knew the candidate's announcement speech was much too important to leave to mere affability and eye contact. So in May, in South Carolina, Michigan, and California— three critical states in the election of a president—the campaign assembled groups of average citizens to watch films of Bush. Each person was given a meter with a knob on it. If they liked what they were seeing and hearing, they turned the knob one way, and if they did not like it, they turned the knob the other way. The farther they turned the knob, the greater degree of like or dislike. A computer assembled the responses and created a graph line that was superimposed over the films of Bush speaking. That way Bush and his aides could watch the films and learn exactly which spoken lines, which gestures, which facial expressions made people like or dislike him. This testing method is called people-metering, and it was made famous—or some would say infamous—by Bush's father. In his 1988 campaign, his aides put together fake news broadcasts for people-meter groups, telling them that Michael Dukakis had let convicted murderer Willie Horton out of jail and that Dukakis opposed the Pledge of Allegiance. Both scored big people-meter negatives and helped persuade Bush to launch his attacks against Dukakis. His son's campaign assured me that only real footage was used in its people-metering and that it was used to select speaking styles, not issues. "Most of what Bush said in the films, people liked, but it depended on how Bush said it," an aide told me. "The more passion he showed, the more involved he looked, the better he did on the people meters. When he struggled through a speech or was unprepared, the people didn't like it." Campaigns are about more than style and stagecraft, of course. They are also about issues and substance. But both Bush and Gore were firmly convinced that you couldn't get people to concentrate on the substance without perfecting the style.

Most of the early profiles of Bush contained the same observations: that he was relaxed, easygoing and, unlike Al Gore, "comfortable in his own skin." The latter was considered a great asset. Gore seemed constantly trying to reinvent himself, and the press portrayed him as a political chameleon: Put him on a plaid rock and he would turn plaid. The media spent little time considering whether the ability to change could be a plus and whether political rigidity could be a minus, especially if events changed rapidly, as they often did in presidential politics. Bush's father had, in fact, been an example of one of the great reinventions in modern political history. In 1988, "Poppy" Bush got clobbered in the Iowa caucuses, coming in third in a state he had won eight years earlier. Dan Rather called it a "nightmare." Tom Brokaw said it was "an embarrassing defeat." Bernard Shaw called it "a stunning upset." The *Des Moines Register* said it represented "a worst-case situation." With the New Hampshire primary just eight days away, Bush could have stuck with his game plan—his son probably would have—but instead he took off his coat and tie and put on a parka and a green and white baseball cap from East Coast Lumber and went to the Cuzzin Ritchie's Truck Stop in Hampstead, New Hampshire. There he drove an 18-wheel Mack truck—slowly and with two Secret Service agents clinging to the sides and looking somewhat ill. (After all, it was Barbara Bush who later said: "George Bush said if he loses on January 20, he is going to get in a car and drive away from the White House, and I said you'll be by yourself. Because I'm not leaving the White House in a car with a man who's never driven in eight years.") He had a friendly snowball fight with reporters, he invited them to his suite for drinks, and he transformed himself from the "wimp" to the "regular guy." He stood around with reporters in an open-necked shirt with a margarita in his hand. (This was his "casual" drink. His real drink was a martini with olives and he usually had at least one a night. In the South, in public, he would drink Tecate beer.) He suddenly developed a fondness for pork rinds and horseshoes. It wasn't that Bush tried to hide anything by these maneuvers. Everyone knew that by manner, speech, and upbringing, he was an old-money, Northeastern WASP, a member of America's most privileged class. But his reinvention was enjoyable, and people went along. "Contrary to popular belief," historian Daniel J. Boorstin once wrote, "Barnum's great discovery was not how easy it was to deceive the public, but rather how much the public enjoyed being deceived. Especially if they could see how it was being done. They were flattered that anyone would use such ingenuity to entertain them." Only after getting into office did Poppy revert to form, dropping all the horseshoes and pork rinds and other downscale crap, and even going so far as to refuse to sign autographs on rope lines in his 1992 reelection campaign. (Instead, he had an aide hand out "pre-autographed" cards with the presidential seal. People hated them.) For his son, however, no reinvention would be necessary. Dubya was a natural. His ease, his insouciance—well, smirk, actually—seemed to make him at home anywhere. You could see him downing beers and eating nachos at any ballpark in America. Geography didn't matter. And if Poppy had been dismissed by his

Republican foes in the 1988 primaries as the "Résumé Candidate" because he had been a congressman, U.N. ambassador, CIA director, envoy to China, and vice president, Dubya wouldn't have that problem either. His only record of public service was being the governor of Texas for about five years, which meant that if he were elected, he would have one of the thinnest résumés in presidential history.

A L GORE HAD THE ENTIRE WHITE HOUSE STAFF TO call upon for his campaign effort, plus all their machinery and the expertise learned over the previous seven years. Everybody expected Gore's campaign to work like clockwork, which it often did and sometimes did not. So the Bush campaign decided it had to look like a big-league operation from the first day; it could not be a typical, seat-of-the-pants campaign. Along with raising more money than any candidate in presidential history—around $100 million—the campaign sweated the small stuff like precisely duplicating the official little White House schedules for reporters, which were covered in yellow or orange or blue stiff paper and were small enough to stick in a pocket or purse. It also took baggage handling extremely seriously. Lose a reporter's luggage and you were likely to see a story about how the campaign was in "disarray" and "not ready for prime time." Here, however, the two campaigns diverged. At the end of each campaign day, Gore's baggage handlers delivered the individual bags, which were carried in the hold of the campaign plane, to each reporter's hotel room. That way you could get undressed and collapse into bed. When you heard the knock on the door about an hour later (*if* you heard the knock on the door), you could dash out into the hallway in your underwear and drag the suitcase inside. On the Bush campaign, luggage was taken to a hotel meeting room and each reporter had to go there to find it. As a result, reporters would usually just gather in the hotel bar and drink for an hour until their bags arrived. There were pros and cons to both approaches, but it was about the only real difference between the two campaigns' logistics, except for the fact that Bush was almost always on time to events—he would apologize to crowds if he was even a few minutes late—while Gore was almost always late, largely because he would stay and shake hands much longer than Bush. Gore had learned this from Bill Clinton: Never stiff the crowd you are with to get to the next crowd. Treat each crowd, each person, as if they were the only crowd and only person in the universe.

Bush has on board for his announcement flight aides from his father's White House, Ronald Reagan's White House, and from the campaigns of Bob Dole and Jack Kemp. They want to give the appearance that this campaign is a juggernaut and, except for some bad sound systems, they pull it off. McCain campaign aides, watching the evening news that night, are extremely depressed with the coverage about how Bush lands in Iowa, goes to a large shed for a speech, and the doors are pulled back to reveal a gorgeous Iowa field with ankle-high corn and large red farm machines behind him for a picture-perfect backdrop. They knew that visual on TV would get Bush good reviews in the print press. "The press coverage that day was almost like heraldic," a McCain aide told me afterwards. "It was just, 'Oh, my God, did you see how they got that door to swing open like that? What a campaign! These guys are organized—you know, a red tractor behind him!'"

(Al Gore's announcement, which followed Bush's by a few days, was a disaster. It was written in stone at the Clinton White House that at outdoor events the stage could never be less than four feet high so sign-waving crowds would not block the TV cameras. But the stage in Carthage, Tennessee, where Gore announced, was only about three feet high, and during much of his speech, Gore's face was obscured on TV by signs being waved by the crowd. "We wanted the stage three feet high so the backs of people's heads would be in the TV shot," a Gore aide moaned to me. "But signs were supposed to be banned!" They never got banned, however, and the network cameras, which were on the lower portion of the camera riser, could not get a clear picture of Gore. If you were watching live on cable television, you mostly saw waving signs. For the nightly news, the networks managed to get the pictures from their local affiliates, which were higher on the riser. It was an ominous sign for a campaign that was supposed to be overflowing with expertise.)

Bush lands in Iowa—his campaign plays Stevie Wonder singing "Here I am, baby! Signed, sealed, delivered, I'm yours!" over the loudspeakers at the Cedar Rapids airport—and he draws a good crowd at his first event at Amana. "There's no turning back—and I intend to be the next president of the United States," Bush says. It is not a job he has always wanted. In 1992, as "owner" (he had a 1.8 percent stake) of the Texas Rangers, he lobbied hard to become commissioner of baseball, even though state Republican leaders had already asked him to run for governor against the incumbent Ann Richards. Only when his attempt for the baseball job failed did Bush decide to run for governor as a fallback. And he made clear why he was running. "I'm not running against her," he told a friend. "I am running against the guy in the White House." He was running against the guy who had defeated his father.

Now in Iowa, Bush tries out the speech that he had been practicing in front of the fundraisers that were closed to the press. Bush was not a natural speaker—he would deliver this speech head down, reading off the paper—and it took him a long time to be able to deliver his stump speech from memory. But he draws real cheers when he delivers the core message of his campaign—"I am proud to be a compassionate conservative. I am running so that our party can match a conservative mind with a compassionate heart"—which was his attempt to move to the middle of the political spectrum early on in 1999 as Bill Clinton had done in 1991. Clinton and other Democratic centrists realized after the defeat of Walter Mondale and Michael Dukakis that Democratic leftists were just not going to get elected in a nation where people increasingly identified themselves as being near the center. Now, after eight years of Clinton's centrism, Bush was gambling that victory still lay in the center and that Republicans would retake the White House only when they shed their image—an image hardened throughout the Clinton impeachment struggle—as a party that was too mean. "This approach has been criticized, but why?" Bush asks. "Is compassion beneath us? Is mercy below us? Should our party be led by someone who boasts of a hard heart?" Most of Bush's Republican primary opponents are arrayed to the right of him, and Lamar Alexander immediately recognizes compassionate conservatism for what it is. "You don't beat Al Gore by trying to sound like Bill Clinton," Alexander thunders the next day. "People are tired of Bill Clinton's weasel words." Both Bush and Gore were constantly compared to Clinton throughout the campaign. Less than a month after he announced for the presidency, Bush flew to Los Angeles and talked to a group of school teachers. Dee Dee Myers, the former White House press secretary to Clinton, showed up at the event and said afterwards: "He's utterly Clintonian in his style. It's a totally Democratic audience and he connected with them." When in October Bush sharply criticized Republicans in Congress for "trying to balance the budget on the backs of the poor," the front-page story in the *Washington Post* began: "Texas Gov. George W. Bush has stolen a page from President Clinton's political playbook, distancing himself from the unpopular congressional wing of the Republican Party in the same way Clinton played off congressional Democrats as he mounted his recovery after the GOP landslide of 1994." To both Bush and Gore, Clinton became like the man in the Hughes Mearns poem: "As I was going up the stair/I met a man who wasn't there/He wasn't there again today./I wish, I wish he'd stay away." Bush, who said he wanted to restore "honor and dignity to the Oval Office," tried to be careful never to criticize Clinton by name. He would never forgive Clinton for defeating his father, but he knew that his father in 1992 and Bob Dole in 1996 had used the character issue against Clinton and had failed. Americans were clearly conflicted about Clinton, and Bush was determined not to get sucked into the same mistake. "I'm not running against Bill Clinton," Bush told Brian Williams of MSNBC. "And I was never running against Bill Clinton."

THE GORE CAMPAIGN, HOWEVER, WAS GOING TO use Clintonian tactics to try to defeat Bush. In Iowa, Democratic National Committee Chairman Joe Andrew shows up at Bush's speech. This is very much from the Clinton tactics of 1996, which said that you always had to try to rattle the enemy, get in his face, stand on his neck, suck up his oxygen. "Compassionate conservatism is a contrived cop-out," Andrew tells the reporters covering the Bush campaign. "Is Bush really any different from Newt Gingrich, Pat Robertson, or any other old-fashioned right-wing conservatives?" Andrew then hands out a leaflet that quotes a line from Bush's speech—the speech that has just been delivered. Reporters had received an advance text about an hour earlier, but how did Andrew get a copy? "I think from a reporter," a DNC staffer tells me. This, too, is very Clintonian. As the campaign goes on, Gore will assign an aide full time to keeping in contact with the Bush press corps, spreading and gathering information.

BUSH DOES VERSIONS OF HIS ANNOUNCEMENT speech throughout the day. It will soon grow very familiar. One line from it will later be dropped, however. "This dream's for you," Bush tells the crowds. It sounds a little too much like "This Bud's for you," and the Bush staff decides there is no need to remind people of when Bush's life was dominated by what he called the "the four B's—beer, bourbon, and B&B."

Bush is charged up on his debut day and, waiting for reporters to file their stories, he is everywhere. Most candidates go to a holding room and stay there, making fundraising calls (a process that never stops) or returning messages. Bush prefers to wander and talk to reporters, slapping them on their backs, kneading their shoulders and at one point coming up to a TV reporter and snapping his suspenders. Campaigning for president is still very new to Bush—running for governor is nothing like running for president—and Joe Andrew's presence has upset him. "Can you believe that?" Bush says. "I come out and they're right on me. Well, I like it: I'm talking about me and they're talking about me!"

The next day, the Bush campaign demonstrates that it can copy not only Clinton's politics, but also his visuals. Bush and the press corps fly to Walker's Point just outside Kennebunkport, Maine, to visit Bush's mother and father. The "W" in Dubya's name stands for Walker, and Walker's Point could be a picture postcard for old-money America. The house stands on a promontory that juts out into the Atlantic Ocean. Waves topped by sea foam crash up against the rocks around it. The house has a gabled roof of weathered green shingles, a stone chimney, and two flagpoles, one flying the American flag and the other flying the Lone Star flag of Texas. There is a swimming pool, a tennis court, and a salt pond. The wind whips off the ocean and blows the tall grass that leads up to a stand of pine trees. Twenty-eight camera crews have been positioned on the front lawn of the house as inflatable boats carrying Secret Service agents nervously prowl back and forth in the bay. Barbara and George Bush slowly descend the front steps— Barbara hates the moniker Dubya: "His name is George. And that one over there," she tells Gail Sheehy, pointing to her husband, "is Poppy"—and walk over to where the journalists wait in a pack. Typically, Poppy, dressed in a jacket with the presidential seal on it, is friendly—"Are all of you looking for the perfect angle?" Poppy says to the huge pack of still photographers arrayed around him— and Barbara has a sharper edge. "Where were all of you in '92?" she says, speaking of the year her husband was defeated.

Just as the Gore campaign is wrestling with how to use Bill Clinton, the Bush campaign is wrestling with how to use Bar and Poppy. They are popular figures, and the Bush campaign is depending on the guilty feelings of people who did not vote for Poppy's reelection and want to make up for it by voting for his son. Only once before—in 1824, when John Quincy Adams was elected—has a son followed his father into the White House. But the Bushes have this old-school habit of calling Dubya "the boy," and the campaign is worried that next to his father, Dubya looks callow and unready. So, of course, the first thing Barbara says to the cameras is, "I'm crazy about him and I loved watching him on TV yesterday, and he's talking about all the things I think America is concerned about. I feel like we done good with this boy."

But Poppy is perfect: smiling, friendly, modest. And when he is asked about a Bush dynasty, he says: "I don't like dynasties. We never felt we were entitled to something. To me, dynasty [carries] a connotation of expectations of something to come your way, and I've never felt that way." Then he goes on to say, "I think George is mentally prepared for this because he was there for me in the good times and the bad." But the father is also wistful, noting that "the business [of politics] is rough" and "He doesn't need advice from me. I'll be there to support him if he just needs help and needs someone to love him." (In reality, Poppy calls Joe Allbaugh, his son's campaign manager, at least once a day for updates and to give advice. Allbaugh is careful to keep Poppy in the picture.)

"I was unpopular, but what goes around comes around," the elder Bush says. When reporters insist that he wasn't really that unpopular, Bush grins and says, "I guess I was elected president once."

Now it is the son's turn. He begins with a memorized quip that he uses a lot but doesn't seem quite right for this sun-washed and nostalgic moment. "I inherited half his friends and all of his enemies," Dubya says.

He is asked what he has learned from his father. "I've learned that life doesn't end if you lose a campaign," he says. "That's why I feel comfortable about what I'm getting into. I come into this race liberated in a sense that if things work out, I believe I know what to do. And if they don't work out, I'll still have a great life. Me and the old boy, we'll spend some time fishing together."

Later, Bush is asked to evaluate his debut.

"I felt I connected with the people and they appreciated it," Bush says. "And I'm glad it's over!"

When some on his staff read this, they wonder if Bush quite gets it. This was just the debut. This was the easy part.

# 4

# KICK THE TIRES AND

# LIGHT THE FIRES!

"WE ARE HAVING FUN."

—John McCain,
explaining the difference between
his campaign and the others',
September 1, 1999

JOHN McCAIN WIGGLES AROUND IN THE seat, leans the back of his head against the window of the bus, whips out a pair of dark, happenin' sunglasses that make him look like Senator Blues Brother, and begins to talk about his old friend Barry Goldwater. "Goldwater said to me, 'If I had been elected president, if I had defeated Lyndon Johnson in 1964, you never would have been in a Vietnamese prison camp,'" McCain says and waits a moment as the reporters scratch this furiously into their notebooks. "And I said, 'You're right, Barry. It would have been a *Chinese* prison camp!'" Everyone roars. The bus rocks. And John McCain plunges into another story, this one about how when his plane was shot down and he was imprisoned by the North Vietnamese from 1967 to 1973, he was his cell's "movie teller" and had to tell the plots of movies every day to help everyone survive the crushing boredom. "I must have told a hundred movies," McCain says. "Of course, I didn't know a hundred movies. So I just made them up." But McCain's master work, his Christmas present to his fellow prisoners of war, was going to be the staging of Dickens's *A Christmas Carol.* Using a sliver of bamboo for a pen and ink made from cigarette ash, McCain laboriously wrote out every part on toilet paper. "And then the goddam gooks came into the cell and took three of my stars out!" McCain roars.

Strictly speaking, one does not say "gooks" anymore. It is simply not done. But John McCain says "gooks" and who is going to tell him not to? And when he starts another story, talking about how he fell in love with one of the prison camp cooks and is asked what *his* name was, McCain says, "Please! It was a female! I never got *that* bad." Strictly speaking, McCain might want to avoid that joke, considering that Barney Frank once called him "a thousand percent anti-gay." And when McCain enters VFW Post 1670 in Laconia, New Hampshire, one evening and spies a couple of Marines in the crowd, he begins his speech by saying, "After the Naval Academy, I tried to get into the Marine Corps. But my parents were married." Strictly speaking. . . .

"It seems to me," says his campaign manager Rick Davis, showing a certain flair for understatement, "the rest of the field is not conducting their campaigns the way John McCain is." The rest of the field is not even coming close. Nobody campaigns like this. The last time a presidential candidate came back to the press bus with any regularity was Ronald Reagan in 1976 and that was the year he lost the nomination. Now, in an age when "controlling the message" has become a mania and candidates are viewed by their staffs as errant children who must be kept from the media lest they commit news, McCain is unique: Every day, he sits down with reporters, talks on the record with reporters, jokes with reporters, and just plain schmoozes with reporters. For hours and hours and hours. Is he eventually going to get burned? Sure. Does he care? Not much. "Other campaigns I've seen, you see this kind of almost a class thing, you know what I mean?" McCain tells me. "They're back there and you're up here. One out of a hundred [reporters] may be trying to sandbag you, but that's a risk you take." So far in his attempt to win his first contest, the Republican primary in New Hampshire, McCain has gotten terrific press. The coverage has been so lavish, in fact, that some media critics have dubbed it the "McCain Swoon" and there is something to that criticism. McCain is so open, so giving of exactly what reporters say they want—unfettered access and constant conversation virtually every waking hour of the day—that it is easy for reporters to forget there is supposed to be some distance between them and the people they cover. The reporters covering McCain almost instantly start feeling protective of him. On a five-day tour of New Hampshire in late August 1999, already his 15th Granite State trip since he began running for president, McCain unexpectedly began the day by volunteering some of the terrible things he has said in the past. First there was the time he referred to the "Leisure World" senior citizens home as "Seizure World," and then there was the time he said "the nice thing about Alzheimer's is you get to hide your own Easter eggs" and then there was the national eruption he caused with an egregious joke that went something like, "Why is Chelsea Clinton so ugly? Janet Reno is her father and Hillary is her mother." (McCain will later apologize to the Clintons, but never to Reno. He doesn't like Reno.) And as he goes on and on, a reporter pipes up and just begs McCain to shut up and protect himself. Later, at dinner, I ask why she interrupted McCain. "But he was hurting himself," she says, as if to say why should we hurt him when he is the one candidate who gives us everything we want? Why would we print negative stuff about McCain, even if it comes out of his own mouth, considering how nice he is to us? Clearly she is not of the old school of journalism, which taught that the only way for a reporter to look upon a politician is down. She was not even of that school of journalism that says a reporter should report "without fear or favor." It is difficult, spending so much time with McCain every day, basking in his glow, being a recipient of the largesse of time and words he bestows upon us, not to get caught up in his mystique and charm. John McCain is funny, irreverent, a great storyteller. He easily wins the Presidential-Candidate-I-Would-Most-Want-to-Be-Trapped-in-an-Elevator-With contest. And some reporters resolve the problem of how much distance to keep from him by deciding to keep none whatsoever. One reporter admits in a profile of McCain she does for *Vogue* magazine that she actually wet and combed his hair for him one morning because his wartime injuries keep him from doing it himself. A more common example is the many reporters who protect McCain from his own words, something McCain never asked them to do.

I was not the first journalist to hear McCain use the word "gooks," but I was the first to print it in a piece that appeared in *U.S. News & World Report* on September 27, 1999. My rule was fairly simple: If the candidate says it, I report it. There is no journalistic justification for protecting a presidential candidate from himself. (And even though McCain's use of the word would go on to create a huge stink for him, he never refused me any access or any request for an interview, during or after the campaign. Nor did he ever mention it. McCain's attitude was fairly simple: Whatever he said, he was responsible for. This attitude is not universal among politicians, many of whom believe that the media should report "what I mean" rather than "what I say." McCain's staff, whose power and authority are vastly diminished by McCain dealing directly with the media, often warns him that he is following a dangerous path. "I get a notification from the staff, and they are usually correct," McCain says. "But life is too short, and you got to enjoy it. And I enjoy the exchanges, I enjoy the company, and it's a lot of fun.")

In any case, McCain often couldn't help what he said. He was what he was, and he was not a guarded man. He was a Navy jet jockey, and while regulations (to say nothing of good sense) required him during his flying days to follow a careful checklist before each takeoff, McCain would dispense with it. "Kick the tires and light the fires!" McCain says, recalling his motto back then. "To hell with the checklist. Anybody can be slow." Which is exactly the way he runs his campaign. And which is the charming and disarming side of McCain. But the campaign is also one of conflicts: Though McCain has said he is "embarrassed" by and "bored" with the constant repetition of his Vietnam experience—"I mean, Jesus, it can make your skin crawl," he once said—his campaign exploits it at every opportunity. The Picture, a boyish, smiling, handsome McCain standing in front of his A-4 Skyhawk, is dispensed by his campaign in small, medium, and large sizes. In New Hampshire, the Picture (one of which hangs in his Senate office) is the symbol of the man, the mission, the campaign. There are also clear conflicts within the man, as those who show up at his speeches find out. McCain is always introduced with a brief recitation of his war record, and he usually begins each speech modestly by smiling and saying: "It doesn't take a lot of talent to get shot down. I was able to intercept an enemy missile with my own airplane." He rarely speaks for more than 10 minutes (he is not very good at delivering set speeches, but he has excellent stage presence and comedic timing) and then takes questions for another 30 to 40 minutes. After 16 years in public office as a congressman and senator from Arizona, he has a considerable range of knowledge and likes to demonstrate it. But New Hampshire being New Hampshire, he often gets questioners who disagree with him. And they often end up getting an earful. In Littleton, New Hampshire, Jerome Danin, a textile worker, disagrees with McCain's vehement championing of free trade, saying it was driving his employer out of business. McCain instantly turns on him. "Sir, I did not know your ambitions were for your children to work in a textile mill," McCain replies scathingly. "I would rather see them work in computers or a high-tech industry." In Lancaster, when one resident complains about the lack of availability of health care, McCain points out that people who make the "lifestyle choice" of living in a rural community are going to have to make some sacrifices, including adequate health care. McCain's positions are not outrageous, but candidates almost never take on audience members this way. Candidates kiss the mistletoe of the people who attend their speeches— they are, after all, likely voters. And not a few audience members find McCain somewhat intimidating. He is not only, as a senator, accustomed to debating, but he is also the only guy in the room holding a microphone (which he always takes off the mike stand and wanders back and forth with in what his aides call his "Phil Donahue mode"). When I ask him later why he sometimes beats up on his audience questioners, McCain replies: "Well, you know, you have to be clear on what you believe in. And I think that there are some fundamental issues, particularly trade and protectionism and many of the other issues, that there's just—you've just got to—I try to be respectful. At least I hope they have that impression." McCain sometimes loses patience with reporters, but this is very rare. Asked once to name a difference between himself and George W. Bush, McCain replies snappishly, "We do Q & A. It takes a long time to establish a reputation for candor." But more often, McCain will lapse into his Jimmy Cagney imitation. "You rat," he will say to the reporter as everyone laughs. "You stoolie, we're going to get you in the prison locker!"

McCain is nothing if not unpredictable. Mispronounce his name—as a caller to New Hampshire's National Public Radio station did one afternoon—and McCain will peevishly correct you. But ask him about being a member of the Keating Five and McCain will beat himself up. On the radio show, a caller asks him about his relationship with Charles Keating, the savings and loan crook who gave hundreds of thousands of dollars in campaign contributions to McCain and four other powerful senators in return for their intervention with federal regulators. McCain got off with a wrist slap when the Senate Select Ethics Committee found that all he did was exercise "poor judgment." But McCain says on the air, "Thank you, Charlie, for that question. I was judged to have used poor judgment, but I did worse than that. I was wrong." Reporters who covered him during the Keating Five investigation found him devastated by it. "I was in his office with him one evening talking about it when he began crying," one reporter told me. "Of course, I later found out he cried about a lot of things." Now McCain likes to admit improprieties before they happen: His wife and three children took a vote as to whether he should run for president and it came out 3–1. The opposing vote was cast by his 11-year-old son, who agreed to change it if his father, as president, could get him to the head of the line at Disney World. "So I promised him," McCain says with a deadpan expression and a shrug. "It's an abuse of office, but I promised him."

McCain's mood can also quickly turn from sunny to stormy without warning. He is capable of telling hilarious jokes about his experiences in prison, even his worst moment when, after constant torture, he signed a confession saying he was a war criminal. He still agonizes over that act and feels that it disqualifies him from the title of "hero"—which everyone bestows on him anyway. But given how he views the gravity of the act, it is almost bizarre, though very McCain-like, that he once uproariously told an aide whose child was in trouble at school: "Tell him to confess. Say, 'I am a black air pirate and have committed crimes against the peace-loving people at my school.' It always worked for me." Which is the happy, joking John McCain. But with his shades on and looking out through the bus window at water-skiers crashing through silver waves under a golden sun over Lake Winnipesaukee near Laconia, New Hampshire, one day, McCain begins talking about his Vietnamese captors. Yes, they are still alive, he says, and living in Hanoi, except for the Cuban, the man he called "Fidel," who would beat the American prisoners with an automobile fan belt. "He was particularly cruel," McCain says, his mood darkening almost imperceptibly. "It didn't leave marks." McCain says he has the CIA looking for "Fidel." A reporter asks why. "He was from a foreign country!" McCain says, his voice rising. "He had no business coming to Hanoi and killing my friends! And I'd love to bring him to justice!" And just as quickly, the storm passes. McCain adjusts his glasses a little and says, "It was a long time ago. I almost never talk about it." He looks from one reporter to another. "Really. There was a lot of humor in prison. A lot of funny stories." And soon he is off telling another one.

He doesn't much care what people make of his style. At 63, one of the oldest candidates in the race, he is relentlessly energetic, powering through as many as eight appearances a day, and in between appearances he talks to reporters. Except when he sleeps, he is virtually never silent, and when a candidate says a lot of things, some strike gold—"There is no reason a good teacher should be paid less than a bad senator"—and some strike out, as when he seemed to be changing his position on repealing *Roe v. Wade* and got weeks of angry questions and angry commentary from some conservatives. "I've had foot in mouth disease all my life," McCain says. And he has no intention of changing. It may be a high-risk way to run, but his whole campaign is high risk. "I decided that the planets were aligned and I had a shot at it," he says. "Not a very good shot, but a shot. I'm not going to be driven by a fear of losing. I'm going to have fun and enjoy it because I'll never do this again." The key tactical decision for McCain was to skip the Iowa caucuses in order to concentrate on New Hampshire, where there are 140,000 veterans.

With only 165,000 people voting in the 1996 Republican primary, that veteran army could lead him to victory. Besides, it was an easy plane trip from Washington to New Hampshire and a much longer one to Iowa. This strategy flew in the face of political orthodoxy. Ever since 1976, when Jimmy Carter decided he had to run everywhere, it was understood that a candidate could not pick and choose primaries. The press also believes in the Iowa "bounce"— that the Iowa winner gets a boost going into New Hampshire, which follows eight days later—even though there is evidence that the bounce may be imaginary. Every week McCain's campaign aides discuss getting into Iowa—the media, they fear, will not take a candidate seriously if he does not stand in an Iowa farm field fondling soybeans for the cameras at least once—but McCain holds firm. Besides, he has opposed government subsidies for ethanol, a gasoline additive made from corn. The subsidies mainly benefit huge agri-business concerns in Iowa, and McCain believes that going to Iowa would be like painting a target on his chest. Knowing what it feels like to get shot down, McCain decides not to repeat the experience. So even though he is criticized, he decides to skip the Iowa Straw Poll in Ames in mid-August, an event so deliciously vulgar you had to keep pinching yourself when you were there to make sure you were not dreaming.

IT WAS THE FIRST TIME NINE OF THE TEN Republican candidates for president met and spoke on one stage. Except for Bush, Steve Forbes and his personal fortune, and Elizabeth Dole and her name recognition, the Republican field was absurdly weak. Most of them were incapable of making news unless they stuck up a 7-Eleven. But the media bought into the notion that the straw poll—a name derived from the practice of tossing a straw into the air to see which way the wind was blowing—was a legitimate test of organizational muscle. Which meant the candidates spent millions of dollars bribing people to attend. While there were no rules against giving people actual currency to go to Ames and vote, instead the candidates gave them free $25 tickets, free barbecue, free rides, free entertainment, free T-shirts, and free body-painting. (The thought of body-painted Republicans was difficult enough to grapple with in the abstract, but was profoundly disconcerting to see in actual practice.) The vote was held at the Hilton Coliseum, which is where the Iowa State University Cyclones play basketball. Outside the coliseum, the candidates had tents for food and entertainment. There were also tables where you could buy pins and postcards. One postcard depicted Hillary Clinton in a black leather bra spanking a nude President Clinton who was sprawled across her lap and smiling. "This is our bestselling postcard," the guy behind the table told me proudly. Debbie Boone sang "Crazy" and "Someday My Prince Will Come" at the Forbes tent; Orrin Hatch had convinced Vic Damone to come croon for him. Nobody could figure out why Hatch, a senator from Utah best known for his pubic-hair-on-the-Coke-can questioning of Anita Hill and his vigorous defense of the single-bullet theory in the assassination of President Kennedy, had entered the presidential race. (And he seemed to be as baffled by this question as anyone.) As it turned out, he would come in ninth at Ames, garnering only 558 votes out of more than 24,000 cast, and it occurred to some that if Vic Damone had announced for president and Orrin Hatch had come to Iowa to sing for him, the numbers would have been about the same.

Inside the coliseum, a large stage had been constructed on the basketball floor. At the appointed hour, the lights went down and the music that they play before the Chicago Bulls take the basketball floor came pounding through the speakers at maximum volume.

You could feel the bass notes as well as hear them. It was like some-body punching you in the chest. "Lay-dees and gen-um-men!" the announcer said. "It all starts in Iowa and on this stage is the next president of the United States!" Then fireworks went off behind the stage with a huge bang. Indoor fireworks are a lot louder than the outdoor variety. And the smoke tends to linger a lot longer. Through the smoke came the candidates. They were announced in alphabetical order so Lamar Alexander came onstage first, followed by Gary Bauer, followed by George W. Bush. Alexander had been saying very nasty things about Bush to reporters. "I admire Bush for raising the most money, but I never met a Texas politician who couldn't," Alexander said. "What's he going to do in a tough debate with Gore? If Bush gets a tough question, is he going say, 'Bring me my pile of money'?" It was clear from Bush's body language that he wanted nothing to do with Alexander, but Alexander stuck out his hand and Bush shook it with a curt nod of his head. (Alexander did poorly in the straw poll, coming in sixth. He would drop out a few days later.)

Eventually, all the candidates came out onstage. They posed for a photograph and then just stood around, not knowing what to do. They didn't speak to each other, they just stood there. Finally some-body came up and led them away and they all looked more com-fortable. Eventually, the candidates came out one at a time to speak, and the tone instantly got gloomy. "This is not the bread and cir-cuses of the Roman Empire," Alan Keyes told the crowd, which had just been enjoying both. "This is the dignity of the American elec-toral process." Elizabeth Dole said, "Drugs are not cool; they kill," demonstrating that she was the last person in America to actually use the word "cool." Forbes set off a sound-and-light show when he appeared onstage. He is worth half a billion dollars and seemed determined to spend a good chunk of it in Iowa. Heaps of balloons fell from the arena ceiling, confetti was blown into the air, and more indoor fireworks went off. There was only one problem: So many balloons covered the floor of the coliseum that people stepped on them throughout Forbes's speech, making it very difficult to hear him. No matter, he still came in second. Money talks louder than balloons. Bush, who came in first, gave a flat speech that didn't say much, and it drew a tepid response from the crowd. But that didn't matter, either. Bush had a bundle of dough and star power, and his campaign found it relatively easy to find people, stick them on buses to Ames, and tell them to vote for Bush regardless of what he sounded like. The most important result of the Iowa Straw Poll, however, was that it narrowed the field. Even though the Ames event should have been relatively meaningless, the media gave it a lot of publicity and it was clear that few reporters would cover the candidates who did not do well. No coverage meant few dollars and few dollars meant political death. When Alexander dropped out, he dispensed some words of wisdom: "It's always said that half the money in any campaign is wasted. You just don't know which half until it's over." Dan Quayle dropped out before many realized he was even in it. Then Elizabeth Dole packed it in. Though she enjoyed good publicity for a while, audiences never warmed to her plastic, Miss America style of speaking. Finally, Pat Buchanan, who did not like his fourth-place finish in Ames with 7 percent of the vote, decided to bolt the party. In withdrawing, Buchanan might have said, "I have failed as a candidate this year. Unlike 1996, when I actually won the New Hampshire primary, my message has fallen on deaf ears. Or, perhaps, it is the messenger. Perhaps people are misunderstanding my book saying that we would have been better off not fighting Hitler in World War II. In any event, I am withdrawing from the race." But that is not what Buchanan said. Instead, he blamed the party. Standing in a hotel ballroom in the Washington suburb of Falls

Church, Virginia, in late October, Buchanan said: "As John F. Kennedy said, sometimes party loyalty asks too much, and today it asks too much of us. Today, candor compels us to admit that our vaunted two-party system is a snare and a delusion, a fraud upon the nation. Our two parties have become nothing but two wings on the same bird of prey." (Just imagine what he would have said had he come in fifth at Ames.) Most Republicans did not care if Buchanan left the party. After Buchanan's views on Hitler and World War II became known, McCain, among others, denounced him. Bush, however, refused. "I don't want Pat Buchanan to leave the party," Bush said. "I think it's important, should I be the nominee, to unite the Republican Party. I'm going to need every vote I can get among Republicans to win the election." That seemed like such a snivel, however, that when Buchanan did bolt the party, a much stronger statement was drafted for Bush by his handlers. "Pat sees an America that should have stayed home while Hitler overran Europe and perpetrated the Holocaust," Bush said. "Pat's message was rejected by Republicans across America, so he is choosing to leave the party of Lincoln and Reagan. I am confident that the vast majority of conservatives will stay with the party that represents conservative ideals: the Republican Party."

MCCAIN, HAVING SAT OUT IOWA, WATCHED THE pre- and post-Ames maneuvering closely. He knew Bush was going to be formidable, but McCain also knew that if he could make four dominoes fall in a row—New Hampshire, South Carolina, Michigan, and New York—he could finish Bush off in California. It was always going to be a tall order, but McCain was learning as he went along. "I have learned two things, one mechanical," he said. "People really don't want you to talk for a long time, they really don't." ("If we give him long speeches, he either won't deliver them, he will stop halfway through, or give it and then regret it the next day," an aide said.) "And the other thing that I found that surprised me is that no one has wanted to talk about impeachment or the president's problems with Monica Lewinsky. I've talked to thousands and thousands of people and have gotten not one question." McCain decided to take that lesson to heart. The Republicans ran against Clinton twice using character as an issue and lost twice. If they try to use the Clinton scandals against Gore, he figures they will lose again. "I'm reminded of Wile E. Coyote in the Road Runner," McCain says. "The Republicans are Wile E. Coyote, who is always after Clinton, the Road Runner. And we're just about to get him with the latest device from Acme, and then the dynamite goes off, we run off the cliff, the train runs over us, whatever it is. But, by God, we're up and we're after him again." So McCain does not raise the character issue, per se, and instead attacks Clinton and Gore through his favorite vehicle, campaign finance reform. "I don't think it's right when the president of the United States treats the Lincoln Bedroom like Motel 6 and he's the bellhop," McCain says. "I don't think it's right when the vice president asks monks and nuns to violate their vows of poverty so they can pay thousands of dollars and spiritually commune with him. I don't think it's right when the head of Loral Corporation gives $800,000 or a million or whatever it was and then a transfer of technology takes places which helps the Chinese improve the accuracy of their missiles. This is serious stuff. This is serious corruption, and we've got to stop it, and I will never quit until we do stop it, my dear friends." McCain not only has the true politician's ability to call complete strangers "my dear friends" and sound like he means it, but he also has the ability to avoid candor when he chooses, such as when he rails in nearly every speech against a Republican tax bill passed by Congress—"It's a disgrace;

it's obscene"—without also mentioning that he voted for it. He also knows how to leave some situations ripe for later exploitation. Asked if he believes George W. Bush should have to tell whether he ever used cocaine, McCain (who says he himself has never used any illegal drug, not even marijuana) says somewhat opaquely that Bush deserves "privacy" but that the media and public will determine what privacy is. Asked by an audience member how he would feel if it turned out that Bush had used drugs while a pilot in the National Guard, McCain answers instantly: "The same way I would feel if he had committed murder or set a forest fire." Polling indicates that in 2000 voters want optimism. Both Bush and Steve Forbes have been careful to position themselves that way, but McCain spends little of his speeches on the upbeat. Though he says he wants to "inspire a generation or more of Americans to be committed to more than their self-interest," he says that because of the "feckless" foreign policy of the Clinton administration, "We may have to pay a very heavy price in blood and treasure in the future." He is not downbeat about America's future, he says in an interview, "but there may be some downbeat aspects of my message because I am worried, I am worried about the future of the political system in America. And I think those concerns are legitimate."

McCain cannot possibly raise as much money as Bush has raised, but McCain has one of the few things in politics that trumps money: a story. Candidates spend millions on media massagers and TV commercials trying to craft and sell a compelling story to the public. McCain likes to diminish this by saying, "If a story was all you needed, then John Glenn would have been president." But Glenn, the astronaut, did not have a story with the same dimension as McCain's. McCain's story—an American pilot who is shot down, captured, tortured, and imprisoned—allowed people to resolve to a certain extent what is still an open wound in American life: the

Vietnam War. McCain was so clearly the innocent victim/hero and his North Vietnamese captors were so clearly the villains that it is possible for people to unite in admiration for McCain's survival regardless of whether they opposed the war or supported it. POWs have always had a special place in Americans' feelings. They resolve the ambiguities of the war: It doesn't matter whether the war was wrong or right, the POWs are sacred.

"When we started out, McCain had Kosovo [he made an early call for decisive U.S. action in the Serbian province], campaign finance reform, and five and a half years in the Hanoi Hilton," Dan Schnur, his spokesman, said. "But the open access accelerated interest in McCain. That led to improving poll numbers, which led to increasing fundraising." And since the media concentration was on McCain the person and McCain the reformer, many people supported him without ever knowing where he really stood on issues. McCain was so well known for his reform positions on tobacco (screw the tobacco companies; keep cigarettes away from kids) and campaign finance reform (screw the Democratic and Republican parties; ban soft money) that some who attend his speeches incorrectly assume he is some kind of liberal. He is not and will sometimes mention his high ratings from conservative groups, including a 90 percent rating in 1997–98 from the National Right to Life Committee. "I have two theories, and sometimes they may even appear to conflict," McCain says after one speech. "One is a conservative view of the role of government—less government, less regulation, lower taxes—but at the same time sometimes there is a role for government. Theodore Roosevelt thought there was a need for national parks; I believe there's a need for campaign finance reform. There's a need for us to try to do something about kids smoking. So I'm glad to be a conservative, but that doesn't mean that I'm completely passive in my views and in my perspectives about the role of government." But not all that many people can attend his speeches to hear this. His real image is shaped by the extraordinary amount of news coverage he is getting and that news coverage emphasizes his heroism in Vietnam and his reformer image in America. This emphasis benefits him greatly. At a dinner with the editors and political reporters of *U.S. News,* I asked McCain: "Anecdotal evidence— what we call reporting—suggests to me that many of the independents and even Democrats who are supporting you in New Hampshire have no idea how really conservative you are." He answered immediately. "Done a hell of a job fooling them, haven't we?" he said and then laughed.

Party regulars were far less amused with McCain and saw him as the skunk at the garden party, the man who could screw up the chances of their anointed one, George W. Bush. McCain's best—in fact, only—hope was to "expand the universe" of voters and draw Democrats and independents to vote in Republican primaries. This was easier to pull off in some states than in others. Fortunately for McCain, in the first three states, New Hampshire, South Carolina, and Michigan, it was very easy. To his staff, this made McCain the irresistible force and Bush the immovable object. "The Bush campaign believes that organization stops momentum," Schnur, McCain's spokesman, said. "We believe that momentum eats away at the organization fire wall. We win the early races and McCain rides a tidal wave into California." Schnur, who shared McCain's penchant for finding wisdom in movies, liked to talk about *The Man Who Would Be King* in which the natives think Sean Connery is a god—until his reluctant bride bites him and the trickle of blood reveals him to be just a man. "If people see that trickle of blood on Bush, it will be hard for him to go on," Schnur says.

But even if McCain wins the early primaries, can he remain new and refreshing and unconventional week after week? "The one thing that keeps us from being conventional is John McCain," Schnur says. "He makes one statement a day that makes us cringe."

JOHN McCAIN WALKS ONTO HIS BUS AND SITS heavily in a red leather swivel chair. His mouth is a small, grim hyphen on what is normally a sunny face.

He is remembering the good old days. Those days that came a few months ago. "We started out in a van," he says. "We started out with one reporter. And now. . . ." He pauses and looks out the window of his bus to where his second bus, the overflow bus, the bus for the reporters who cannot squeeze onto this bus, sits idling in the parking lot of the Bedford Wayfarer hotel, sending clouds of exhaust into the chill air. He shrugs. It is January in New Hampshire and McCain is now a full-fledged phenomenon. Bill Bennett, former drug czar, former secretary of education, and currently America's chief scold, maneuvers his bulk down the narrow aisle of the bus and sits in the swiveling captain's chair next to McCain's. Bennett has not given his endorsement to John McCain—he has offered to help all the Republican contenders—but he has clearly given his heart to him. They are an odd couple: Bennett is always preaching about "values" and the benefit of clean, straitlaced living, and McCain is definitely a lady's man who is not shy about talking about his past conquests. To Bill Bennett, however, it is more important who McCain is not. "He is the anti-Clinton. He's an honorable man. The American people want a president they can look up to again," Bennett says. "That idea has captured the American imagination. *He* has captured the American imagination. You need to bring people back, you need to have them believe in the possibility of politics."

On this day, however, John McCain is worrying about the possibility of John McCain. Insurgents are usually reformers, and the Achilles' heel of the reformer is hypocrisy: A large part of McCain's campaign is based on throwing the money lenders out of the twin temples of politics and government, but recent newspaper articles have been revealing that McCain has a fondness for riding on the corporate jets of his campaign contributors and that he has also been writing letters on their behalf to governmental agencies, letters that have led to some lucrative business deals. "You've got to expect this sort of stuff," McCain tells the reporters packed together in a tight semicircle around him. "With increased traction, you get increased visibility." By which he means the kind of visibility that puts you in its crosshairs.

Soon, however, he will brighten. His bus will pull up to a church in New Bedford, New Hampshire, and he will bound off to address a standing-room-only crowd. They will give him a rock-star welcome and when he is finished answering their questions, they will mob him, people clutching his bestselling memoir to their bosoms, waiting for an autograph, waiting for a word, waiting for enough proximity to reach out and touch him. Support for an underdog is a passionate support. It is what longshots need, it is what they depend on to make up the vast gulf in resources or organization or name recognition that the frontrunners enjoy. If you are an underdog, you are not the default choice, you are not the automatic answer, you must give people a reason to vote for you. During McCain's presentation, a fifth-grader stands up and asks him how he decided to run for president. "My wife claims it was because I received several sharp blows to the head while in prison," McCain says. As always, the audience laughs and as always the phrase hangs in the air: While in prison. While in Vietnam. While being tortured. He

91

does not need to say more. Just as when he climbs back onto his bus and now, in a better mood, he shows off his new black topcoat and tells the reporters without any prompting that (a) it comes from Nordstrom, (b) he bought it because he had to give a speech on the Mall as part of the nation's millennium celebration, and (c) "It only took them one day to tailor it for my shortened arms." Shortened when they were broken. Shortened when he ejected from his plane. Shortened when they were twisted and beaten by his captors. "There is no depth I won't sink to in seeking your support," McCain tells people. Most people who hear this think he is joking. Most people should think again.

# THE ROAD TO

# PALOOKAVILLE

"THERE ARE PEOPLE WHO OBSERVE
THE RULES OF HONOR AS WE DO THE STARS,
FROM A GREAT DISTANCE."

—Victor Hugo

GEORGE W. BUSH WALKS ONTO THE
stage in the cavernous auditorium at Bob Jones University in Greenville, South Carolina, and 6,000 students are
up on their feet and applauding. A broad smile lights Bush's face.
This is the largest crowd he has ever drawn as a presidential candidate, and the sight of all these neatly dressed, fresh-faced kids beating their hands together for him has him pumped. Six thousand
people! You'd have to give away free chainsaws to get that many
people in New Hampshire to come out to a political event! Nobody,
it seems, has told Bush that Bob Jones University has made attendance at his speech mandatory for the entire student body, though
Bush's briefers did tell him something or other about the university's history: How it lost its tax-exempt status in 1975 for refusing
to admit black students and, though it now does admit them, how
it still bans interracial dating. Had Bush thought about it—and he
hasn't—that would mean that his brother Jeb, who is married to a
Hispanic woman, would not have been allowed to date her at Bob
Jones. Not that the university doesn't have a perfectly logical explanation for its ban, which university official Jonathan Pait explained
in a 1998 letter to a prospective student: "God has made people
different from one another and intends those differences to remain.

Bob Jones University is opposed to intermarriage of the races be-cause it breaks down the barriers God has established. When Jesus Christ returns to the earth, He will establish world unity, but until then, a divided earth seems to be His plan."

Not much of which has registered with Bush. All he knows is that Ronald Reagan spoke here once and so did Jack Kemp and so did Bob Dole and so did Missouri Senator John Ashcroft, an old family friend, and there wasn't any fuss about it on any of those occasions. Heck, Ashcroft accepted an honorary degree and $750 in traveling expenses from Bob Jones on May 8, 1999, and told the graduating seniors, "I thank God for this institution and for you." True, there is the Bob Jones anti-Catholic thing. In 1982, the uni-versity's president, Bob Jones III, had said, "The pope is the great-est danger we face today. He's doing more to spread anti-Christ communism than anyone around. The papacy is the religion of the antichrist and is a satanic system." That same year he also said, "I believe that Mr. Reagan came into office with good intentions, but he broke his promise to us when he took on Mr. Bush, a devil, for his vice president. Mr. Reagan has become a traitor to God's people." So maybe under ordinary circumstances, George W. might have skipped Bob Jones, if only out of consideration for Poppy. But these are not ordinary circumstances.

Yesterday, before the New Hampshire primary, Bush was run-ning for president. Today, he is running for his life. This was never part of the deal, never what they promised him when they told him to run. They never said victory was guaranteed, but they never said he was going to lose the first primary, be humiliated in front of everybody he ever knew and be one defeat away from Palookaville. But John McCain clobbers him in New Hampshire—absolutely hammers him by 19 points—and Bush never sees it coming. "Karl Rove told him he was going to win," Karen Hughes, Bush's communications director, says. "Rove had the charts to prove it and every-thing." So now Bush has been creamed in the nation's first primary. And that is not the worst of it. The worst of it is that he had to call up his father that night and tell him the news.

"I actually thought I was going to win," Bush tells me a few days later. "I did. If you had asked me Monday morning how things were going, I would have said things were in pretty good shape. The crowds were big and enthusiastic. I didn't know I was going to lose until the exit polls came in. Then it was pretty clear."

How did you feel about it? I ask.

Bush laughs a hard, short laugh. "I didn't like it. Listen, I've got a feisty personality. But I understand political realities. And when people make up their minds, they make up their minds."

Then he recalls the moment he had to pick up the phone and call his dad. "We're going to get whipped," the younger Bush tells the elder. It was not a good moment. It was not a moment George W. is going to treasure. "Yeah," he says, remembering it now. "Yeah. It's much harder to be a mother or dad than it is to be the candidate. It was really hard for me to be the son when he was the candi-date. And I had to assure them I would be fine. And I will be. I don't rationalize defeat."

Now, more than anything, more than even becoming president of the United States, George W. does not want to have to make any more phone calls like that one to his dad. "I've retooled the format to show that I know what I'm talking about," he says, which means he will copy McCain's town meeting format to show that he is not afraid to take questions. "I will show I know how to lead and share my passions with the voters."

Share your passions with the voters?

He nods. "Your eyes are the window to your soul," he says very seriously, as if this is not the kind of observation you might find in a fortune cookie. "People have got to look at me and decide whether I will bring honor and dignity to the office. That's what the campaign is about at this point. And it's amazing to watch people watch. Because people are watching real carefully."

At least Bush has a game plan now: Show knowledge, show passion, show leadership, and be likable, and let the campaign staff do the rest—the campaign staff that has incredibly, breathtakingly, already spent $50 million of the $70 million collected so far.

"I have always been underestimated," Bush goes on. "You can understand why. People say, well, he's Daddy's boy and has never done anything of accomplishment. But that's good. I'd rather be underestimated than overestimated." As he speaks, he lounges on a long couch in the front of his bus as it travels through a piney swamp in the South Carolina low country. His feet are propped up across and blocking the aisle; he holds a Diet Coke in his right hand, and when I come into his cabin to interview him, Bush languidly extends his left hand as he stays slumped to one side. But when I ask if he wants to be president badly enough to really go after it, he straightens up, drains the Coke, and begins crumpling the can in one hand.

"That's ridiculous!" he says. "What do you think I'm doing? I'm up at 6:30 every morning and go to bed at 10:30 at night and I'm shakin' thousands of hands and I'm speakin' from my heart and I'm puttin' out policy initiatives that are on the edge of reform! It's an absurd statement." He stops crunching the can for a moment. "But I understand how it works," he says. "They have to say something after I got whipped."

The pine trees flash by. The Coke can emits one last muffled crunch before it can be crunched no more. "It's important for me to show you I can not only take a punch," Bush says, "but win."

The Bush campaign has decided that the best way to take a

punch is to throw a punch, and so Bush begins his South Carolina campaign by appearing with J. Thomas Burch Jr., chairman of the National Vietnam and Gulf War Coalition, a group hardly anybody has ever heard of. Burch accuses John McCain of not doing enough for veterans. "He came home and he forgot us," Burch says. McCain's main strategy in South Carolina is to win the large veterans vote, and he can't believe Bush would stoop so low as to attack his commitment to veterans. Especially after McCain has refrained from attacking Bush for ducking service in Vietnam. "I gave him a pass on the National Guard and now he comes after me on this," McCain fumes. Bush has also started running a TV ad that says McCain "solicits money from lobbyists with interests before his committee and pressures agencies on behalf of contributors." So McCain responds with two ads, one saying the Bush commercial "twists the truth like Clinton" and the other saying, "Do we really want another politician in the White House we can't trust?"

Bush adopts a tone of wounded outrage. "I don't like to be called Clinton and neither would you!" he tells me. "In a Republican primary, that's over the line . . . and I think McCain will suffer a backlash because of those ads. But I don't feel sorry for myself. It's steeling me for the job. I'm rising to the challenge—and it is a challenge."

Bush is also rankled by the McCain Swoon, believing that the media have turned McCain into the fashionable choice for president among the nation's elites. "I don't think there is any plot; I hope there isn't," Bush says, "but it's an amazing phenomenon, I'll tell you that. It's like the flap over the foreign leader deal. A guy gets up and quizzes me—it's my fault for trying to answer—but John McCain says something about the 'ambassador to Czechoslovakia.' Well, I know there is no Czechoslovakia [it's the Czech Republic], but yet it didn't make the nightly national news. I'm not going to gripe about it, but the media question is starting to pop up." They have especially started to pop up on talk-radio shows in South Carolina, but all this is kid stuff compared to what is about to follow. Bush is pouring $6 million into the state, including $4 million in TV ads (McCain will spend $2.8 million on ads), plus radio and TV ads paid for by anti-abortion and pro-tobacco groups attacking McCain, none of which costs Bush a dime. There is also a well-organized smear campaign and nobody knows how much that is costing or where the money for it is coming from. But Bush has convinced himself that he is taking the high road. "He's using his position as chairman of an important committee to raise money!" Bush says. "But I'm not going to attack him personally as he has done to me." People at Bush rallies carry signs that say: "This Is <u>Not</u> New Hampshire! This is South Carolina." And John McCain is about to discover what that really means.

"I like my chances here," Bush says.

ABOUT 15 MILES NORTH OF BOB JONES UNIVERSITY sits North Greenville College, a small Baptist school in the town of Tigerville, which is down a long country road from the main highway. Even though Bush is continuing with his unbelievably light work schedule—no matter how indignant he is at the suggestion that he is coasting, two-event days are not uncommon— he makes time to come to North Greenville College. There is a huge sign at the college this day announcing "A Reformer with Results: One on One with Governor Bush," which means, in others words, that the Bush campaign is already morphing into the McCain campaign. "He's got a good message," Ralph Reed, the former executive director of the Christian Coalition and now a private consultant working for Bush, says of McCain. "That's why we've decided to adopt some of it." If the results in New Hampshire showed that voters want a reformer, then Bush will become a reformer. If they showed people want one-on-one meetings with their candidate, then Bush will do one-on-one meetings. If they showed people want a heroic war veteran for president, Bush will . . . well, he'll do one-on-one meetings.

In a small room packed with students and reporters, the college's president, Jimmy Epting, welcomes the press "to the place where Christ makes a difference." Up in New Hampshire, candidates could get away with talking about taxes and health care and national defense. But in South Carolina, some people have their priorities straight. "We want someone to lead this nation who loves Jesus Christ and we want to meet all the candidates and see who God wants," Epting says. How God will convey this message, Epting does not say, but Bush will have his chance to make his case as God's chosen one. Epting does not want the discussion to get bogged down in issues, however. "I hope he will share his heart with us and, most importantly, I hope he shows how he stands with Jesus Christ," Epting says. "You hold him to the fire and make sure he stands strong." The students applaud lustily at this and a few minutes later Bush enters the room to recorded country music. He is dressed in a blue suit, light blue tie, and blue shirt. He has wisely refrained from dressing "country." To these people, this political meeting is like going to church. Bush is accompanied by his brother Marvin, one of the Bushes who is not a governor. (Marvin has amused the Bush press corps to no end by saying one morning: "The next sound you hear will be the media removing their lips from John McCain's blank, blank, blank." He actually says "blank, blank, blank." He cannot bring himself to say "ass.") Bush removes the mike from the mike stand and begins pacing with it. "My priorities in life are family and faith!" Bush shouts, nervously tapping his foot. Bush has been told by his handlers to be more enthusiastic and involved and to show his "passion." The staff is tired of reading about his smirk, his light workload, and his general disinterest in the nitty-gritty process of becoming president. "I think you're going to see the fire in the governor's belly," Bush spokesman Ari Fleischer promises reporters after New Hampshire. And although Bush will later learn to do it well, right now he associates fire in the belly with volume, and just about every line is delivered in a bellow. "I've got an honest disagreement with my friend, the Chairman!" he barks. In New Hampshire, Bush had called McCain his "buddy," but now he calls him "the Chairman"—as in chairman of the Senate Commerce Committee—to emphasize that McCain is a Washington insider and also because it sounds a little like Chairman Mao. "I've been a reformer in Texas when it comes to helping people's lives . . . bringing people of faith to people in need. It requires a leader who inspires, it requires a leader who elevates the spirit!" Bush roars this and soon ends his speech. This is really as far as he wants to go with the whole religious thing. As the *New York Times* pointed out a few days earlier, Bush has an almost "perfect pitch resonance" with South Carolina Republicans in part because of his "unabashed Christian conservatism that does not edge over into pietistic evangelism." But the students are staring at Bush open-mouthed. He has not mentioned Jesus Christ once, not once! What kind of presidential candidate is he? So one student stands up and asks, "Are you a Christian? And tell us a little about your faith."

Bush has been prepped for this. "I appreciate that," he says, "and 'yes' is the answer. I am a lowly sinner"—there are nods and pleased smiles around the room—"and I've sought redemption." There, that ought to hold the little bastards.

Another student rises and asks the second most important question when it comes to choosing the leader of the free world: "What about the Confederate flag?" The Confederate battle flag has been flying over the South Carolina state capitol since 1962 and there have been various attempts to have it removed. Both Gore and Bill Bradley, his Democratic primary challenger, advocate removing it, while both Bush and McCain want no part of the issue. McCain has not exactly been a profile in courage. In January he said the flag was "offensive" and a "symbol of racism and slavery." Then his staff told him he simply could not stick to that position and hope to win South Carolina. McCain tells them he is not going to change his statement, and they yell and argue and tell him he is doomed until finally he just shakes his head and says, "Fine, fine, just write down what you want me to say." Mark Salter, his administrative assistant and the co-author of his bestselling autobiography, knows him better than anyone and knows McCain is going to deliver his recantation in such a way as to make clear he doesn't believe it. Sure enough, the next day in South Carolina, McCain is peppered with questions on the flag, and he reaches into his pocket and slowly unfolds the statement his staff has prepared and reads that the flag is "a symbol of heritage."

"That was his way of saying 'I'm lying, and fuck you guys for making me do it,'" a campaign official tells me. But the next day in New Hampshire, McCain also says, "My forefathers fought under the Confederate flag [and] I believe they believed their service was honorable." There the issue sits until the Thursday before the Saturday South Carolina primary, when the wheels are really coming off the campaign, and McCain says to his staff one morning, "I sincerely believe this flag should come down and that's what I want to say today." They are sitting around a Holiday Inn and they are going back and forth and arguing and finally they convince McCain it will look too tactical, too cynical, too nakedly political, and so McCain abandons the idea. Only after the primary is over does McCain apologize for opposing the removal of the flag, and months later, after the election, he tells me: "That's the only thing that I regret, that I didn't stand up and just say, 'Look, it ought to come down.' That was the greatest display of lack of political courage, I think, in the campaign. I'm sure I took other positions that were not particularly courageous, but that sort of was the least courageous."

Bush at least has the advantage of consistency, having ducked the issue from the beginning. "It's up to you," Bush tells the students at North Greenville College. "The State of South Carolina can make up its own mind." That's the kind of states' rights talk that plays well here—the same words were once used to keep segregation in place—and the audience applauds. So much for secular issues.

Another student rises and asks, "Is it important to have a president who has Jesus Christ in his heart?" and, not waiting for an answer, he asks if Bush believes it is "God's will" that he be the next president. Pleased with himself, the student gives a high-five to a friend, which pisses Bush off. Even though McCain is supposed to be the one with the bad temper, Bush often gets angry. "You and I, brother, are humble servants," Bush says to the student in a venomous tone, and his aides look up sharply. "Far be it for me to say this is God's will. I don't get to put words in God's mouth. We're all lowly sinners. I'm doing the best I can do and I don't know whether it's God's will or not. That was not a bad question, but it doesn't deserve a high-five." There are ooohs of shock from the students. What's going on here? Isn't Bush supposed to be the blessed one?

Bush wraps up, "Takin' Care of Business" comes over the loudspeakers and he starts shaking a few hands as the students file out. I seek out President Epting to see if Bush has pandered sufficiently. "He did say he has accepted Jesus Christ into his heart," Epting says. "If he stands up in front of the press and says that, well, that means something." Yes, it does. It means he really, really wants to win South Carolina. "I don't know what's in his heart; that's the Lord's business," Epting goes on. "But it was encouraging to hear him say it. I hope he is telling it like it is. Like all of them, you have to take what they say and hope they are telling the truth."

When Bush finishes shaking hands, he wanders over to the media. "Coming in second in New Hampshire causes you to reassess, and I have reassessed," he says. "Chairman McCain has convinced people he is from outside Washington, D.C. That's a game of switch and bait." Reporters glance at each other. Isn't the expression "bait and switch"?

A reporter asks Bush about the kid and the high-five and all the Jesus questions. And the candidate who made his first stop in South Carolina at Bob Jones University and now has come to North Greenville College—"the place where Christ makes a difference"—says, "I don't like to spend a lot of time on personal religion." And he says it with a straight face.

THE NEWSPAPERS ARE FULL OF STORIES ABOUT how this is the "new" South Carolina, but the Bush forces are betting it isn't. "Republican primaries in South Carolina have always been a contest to see who is the most Republican—a mad dash to the right," Trey Walker, a former state party executive director now running the McCain effort, tells the *Los Angeles Times*. "That was conventional wisdom. But the problem is in 2000 that's changed. South Carolina is a very different South Carolina." And in some ways it is. While its median income and school spending per student are below the national average, the state has attracted $42 billion in new business investment in the last ten years, much of it from overseas. Presidential candidates line up to visit the ultramodern BMW plant in Spartanburg, which is so clean and glistening inside it looks more like a hospital than a factory. But Christian conservatives cast one out of every three votes in South Carolina in

1996. And when you get away from the seacoast resorts like Kiawah and Hilton Head and into the Piedmont region of western South Carolina, you get to towns that are centers of religious conservatism such as Greenville, where it is easier to buy a gun than a drink. So Bush's going to Bob Jones makes sense, as does ducking the flag issue. Until, that is, he has to go to Michigan and face Catholic voters or until he tries to get black votes in the general election. Mass media, 24-hour news stations, and databases available to anyone with a computer have made it almost impossible to run regional campaigns. You can try tailoring your message to one state, but it is going to be heard all over the country. The Bush campaign knows all that and also knows that it doesn't matter. Tomorrow doesn't matter because unless Bush wins South Carolina, there will be no tomorrow. Which made anything he did in South Carolina justifiable. And so he did anything.

DURING THE CLINTON IMPEACHMENT HEARINGS in the House in late 1998, McCain was so impressed with the feistiness of South Carolina's Lindsey Graham, who will later become one of the House managers of the impeachment trial in the Senate, that McCain calls and asks for his support. The two have never met, but Graham, 44, is worth his weight in gold to McCain, or so McCain believes. Graham used to work in his father's saloon, where blacks were refused service until the early '70s, and Graham does not pussyfoot around when it comes to the Confederate battle flag. "There is a guy out there named Bubba," he likes to say. "He grew up when public schools got integrated. He goes to work every day. There are women and African Americans in the workplace, and he's fine with that, but he thinks the whole world is against him and has rights he doesn't have. He thinks the flag is the last thing he has going for him, and he's not going to take it down. There are no groups sticking up for the Bubbas of the world." McCain would like to have the Bubbas of the world—though how many he can reasonably expect to pry loose from Bush is questionable—and so he is absolutely delighted when Graham agrees to support him. But McCain also needs independents and Democrats—the expanded voting universe that will make it possible for him to win the Republican nomination—and that makes Graham a risky ally, even though McCain never sees it. By campaigning with Graham, McCain has put another name on the ballot: Bill Clinton. And while there are plenty of people in South Carolina who hate Bill Clinton with a visceral passion, most of them are going with Bush. And how much good is Graham doing him with independents and Democrats when he says, "I'd like to thank Bill Clinton for doing more for my career than anyone. Anybody got Clinton fatigue? Ladies and gentlemen, I've got the antidote. John McCain is very candid and very blunt, while Bill Clinton is the ultimate master of deception." And it seems to make sense, when McCain wants to hit back at Bush for calling him a liar, to invoke the name of the "ultimate" liar and liken Bush to Clinton, but, again, who is that ad really reaching? And, of course, since all local campaigns are now national campaigns, people all over the country—including California, where McCain must do well—see Graham and remember the impeachment trial and his holier-than-thou attitude and his South Carolina drawl, and they remember why they wanted to put their fists through the TV screen. But McCain, who agrees to duck the flag controversy, cannot bring himself to duck the Clinton controversy, even though he knows that nobody is bringing it up at all the hundreds of town meetings he has gone to.

And the McCain campaign is not quite the seat-of-the-pants campaign it first appears to be. Though McCain is superstitious—he always carries a lucky penny, a compass, a feather, and a pouch of sacred stones and makes sure he is wearing his lucky shoes, eating his lucky food, and getting out of the same lucky side of the motel bed each morning—his campaign is depending on more than luck. Before it began, it engaged in scientific testing of its message and its messenger, conducting "bio tests" and "negative bio tests" to see how people reacted to good and bad things about McCain. The negative stuff included McCain's stands on tobacco and campaign finance reform and how he had allied himself with Clinton on certain votes. But he did fine in all the testing. "And so we thought we had a real shot at this," a senior aide said. "We knew that there is nobody in politics that works harder than McCain, and we knew that Bush was sort of the opposite of that—there's nobody in politics who works less hard than him. And so we figured we'd just out-hustle him."

And in New Hampshire they did. Bush had to split his time between New Hampshire and Iowa and other states like Delaware, which McCain was not contesting, and that helped enormously. Basically McCain just lived in New Hampshire and people there began to see him as a neighbor. One day there was a snowstorm and Bush canceled his events in New Hampshire, but McCain rubbed his face in it by having three town hall meetings that day. By the last one, everybody was so giddy and goofy and happy that McCain began inviting the array of publicity-seekers and head cases who follow campaigns in New Hampshire up onto the stage. So at one event he invites a guy in a shark suit up onto the stage and at another he invites a guy with a boot on his head to come up and address the crowd and when Tom Brokaw shows up for one event, McCain introduces him to the crowd as a "Trotskyite" and everybody roars with laughter. "We were punch-drunk," the aide said. "But New Hampshire made us proud. We felt this was the way a campaign should be run—an honest campaigner that gave the press access and answered the questions of the people—and we knew we were doing something that gave us more of a sense of honor in what we do for a living than we've felt in a long time."

"Honor" is a very important word to John McCain. In many ways, he judges his worth as a human being by whether or not he has acted with honor. It is, according to those who know him well, the "animating ideal of his life." Which is why he refused an early release from a North Vietnamese prison, because he knew his captors were offering it only because he was the son of an admiral (and it is why his father refused to meet McCain's plane when he was released six years later because McCain's father had not met the other planes carrying POWs). And even though honor and politics are rarely spoken of in the same breath and even though McCain admits he has done several dishonorable things in his life, he feels good after the New Hampshire primary. And when Bush calls him and makes a graceful concession, McCain says to him, "I think we both ran campaigns that we and everybody we care about should be proud of up here." And McCain believes it as he heads for South Carolina. "And we felt," Mark Salter said, "we might lose it, we might win it, but we were going down there to have a fairly honorable contest with a likeable enough opponent."

And then the roof fell in.

"FIRST-TIME CALLER, LONG-TIME LISTENER, JIM, AND I love your show. I was wonderin' if you had heard about how McCain had turned traitor in Vietnam? That he is one of them Manchurian candidates working for the Red Chinese? That's what I heard. And you know that little girl of his, the black one? They adopted her because he infected his wife with a venereal disease that he got in Nam and it destroyed her uterus and turned her into a drug addict to boot."

The calls went out all day and all night for nearly three weeks. They went out to talk-radio shows and to the homes of registered voters. They were accompanied by leaflets, faxes, and a barrage of e-mails.

"Hey, you heard about McCain, right? He had this affair with Connie Stevens, the singer, and he had this guy killed because he was going to spill the beans? Yeah, it's on the Internet. No, I am not kidding you."

Over at McCain headquarters, they kept a list of the calls. It grew longer and sicker. "'McCain beats his wife; McCain's adopted daughter is the progeny of his relationship with a black prostitute; McCain ruined his wife's uterus with venereal disease; McCain was a traitor; McCain had a Vietnamese family'; oh, it goes on and on," an aide said. "And that was from Day One. There was this guy who had his kids passing out leaflets about 'Senator McCain, the junkie.' His kids!"

"When I got some idea of the depth of this, particularly the phone campaign, the really scurrilous stuff, I mean, I was astounded," McCain said, sitting in his Senate office, a few days after George Bush was certified by the electoral college as the next president. "At first, I said, 'Come on. It's not true!' And then some people started taping these messages, and I thought, 'Good God!'

"And at that same time, I could feel it start to slip. We saw a dropoff in the crowd size, particularly in interior South Carolina, and a definite reduction in the enthusiasm of the audiences. I mean, I could just sense it. I remember the last couple of days when we were in, I think, Columbia, Greensboro, those places, and people were just sort of"—he very slowly applauds—"and I said, 'Gee, there's something happening here. There is something happening.'" And McCain turns on the TV one day to see an interview with a professor at Bob Jones University who was sending out e-mails saying that McCain had fathered illegitimate children. "And the CNN guy finds him and asks, 'Why are you doing this?'" McCain said. "And he says, 'Because it's true.' And the reporter asks, 'Do you have any proof of it?' And he says, 'No, McCain has to provide the proof that he didn't.' And I thought, 'Well, *that's* a curious standard.'"

That was the way-below-the-belt stuff. There was also just-plain-below-the-belt attacks in the form of push polls, which is when somebody calls you at home pretending to be a pollster but instead plants negative information about someone. So people got calls asking them: "Do you support McCain's effort to pass the largest tax increase in history? Do you agree with McCain's plan to give more power to the media and the unions to pick the president?"

The Bush campaign denied any involvement. Such terrible stuff must be coming from "local" people. How could they imagine that Bush knew anything about it? But the McCain people did imagine it, and, in fact, they were convinced of it. "There's no doubt in any of our minds that the Bush campaign organized all this; not a one of us doubts that," a senior McCain aide said. Did Bush himself know? On that, there was a split between those who believed Bush maintained an "upper-crust" hands-off attitude of remaining above the fray, letting others do his dirty work, and those who believed he was up to his elbows in it. McCain chose to believe that Bush did not personally know of the most vicious phone calls and that Karl Rove, Bush's chief strategist, was behind it all. He believes that, aides say, to this day. "In any case, we kind of got the idea that the gentlemanly campaign was over and we had to hit back. Hard," the aide said.

"We're going to hit back; this is not the Bradley campaign," McCain told reporters in South Carolina.

"I am going to vigorously defend myself, because I know what happens when you don't," Bush told reporters in South Carolina.

Both statements were the direct legacy of the 1988 presidential campaign, the direct legacy of Willie Horton. The campaign of 1988 was a sleazy, sordid, sad affair (the press loved it), so awful, in fact, that the winner, George Bush, Dubya's father, apologized for it afterwards by promising to be "kinder and gentler" as president. The elder Bush's main point of attack during the race was how his opponent, Massachusetts governor Michael Dukakis, had given convicted murderer Willie Horton a furlough. Horton had returned to prison from nine previous furloughs, but the tenth time he took off for Maryland, where he broke into a home, tied a man to a joist in the basement, slashed his chest and stomach with a knife, then beat and repeatedly raped his fiancée. Horton was caught and tried in Maryland, where he was sentenced to two consecutive life terms plus 85 years. The judge refused to allow Horton to return to prison in Massachusetts until he was done serving his time in Maryland. "I'm not going to take the chance you'll be on the streets again, because you're dangerous," the judge told Horton. "You should never breathe a breath of fresh air again. You should be locked up until you die."

On June 9, 1988, Bush first raised the Willie Horton issue in a speech in Houston. Dukakis's communications director Leslie Dach made the official response to Bush's speech: "The American people aren't interested in mudslinging and tearing down."

Ho. Ho. Ho.

On June 22, Bush upped the ante by using Horton's name, thereby guaranteeing that TV and print would use Horton's picture, a particularly threatening picture that stared out at people from a thousand TV sets and a thousand front pages. Speaking in Louisville to the National Sheriffs Association, Bush said: "Horton applied for a furlough. He was given the furlough. He was released. And he fled—only to terrorize a family and repeatedly rape a woman!" Bush kept up the attack, but Dukakis was not worried. He was way ahead in the polls and came out of that summer's Democratic convention some 17 points ahead of Bush.

But by August, after two solid months of the Horton attack and others, Bush was narrowing the gap. Dukakis finally struck back on August 30 by attacking Bush on foreign policy. Dukakis explained why he was now giving as good as he had gotten. "I came to a reluctant conclusion that if it continues, you have to respond," he said. "I think that's unfortunate, but I think it's very clear what kind of campaign the Republicans are running, and I think we're going to have to deal with it."

By Labor Day, the polls showed Dukakis and Bush running even. "I knew the election was over," Mark Gearan, a Dukakis press aide, said, "when I returned a phone call to a newspaper and I was told the reporter couldn't take my call because she was talking to Willie Horton." Both sides began running negative ads, but the polling showed the Horton attack had devastated Dukakis and *Time* magazine declared in a headline that Horton was "Bush's Most Valuable Player." Dukakis was sure that the voters would see through the Bush attack. "The American people can smell the garbage," he said.

Because they always do, don't they? Without knowing it, McCain made one of the most hilarious statements of the campaign in South Carolina, when he said he was surprised by Bush's attack. "He comes from a better family, he knows better than this," McCain said. McCain just could not believe the gentry would act this way, forgetting that Bush learned at his father's knee.

"Everybody says negative ads are terrible and trashing somebody is terrible—but it works!" a long-time political adviser working for another campaign said. "People want a candidate with an edge. You've got to have heat. Heat wins elections."

At a debate in Columbia, McCain and Bush met backstage. According to McCain, Bush came up to him and said, "It's just politics, John. It doesn't mean anything."

"That's just baloney!" McCain replied. "When you have a veteran say that I abandoned the veterans, that's bad, that's wrong. And I resent that. And I resent the other stuff your people are doing."

Bush was taken aback. Didn't McCain understand that it wasn't personal? That it was just about winning?

"Well, I'm sure we'll be able to work together," Bush mumbled and walked away.

"AFTER OUR VICTORY IN NEW HAMPSHIRE, THIS campaign took a turn early," McCain said after the election. "They attacked; we made a tough response. That's what you're supposed to do. And then you spiral down." McCain thought some kind of rules of engagement existed. You could bomb this part of Hanoi, but not that. You could fly north of this parallel, but not that one. This target was fair game; that one was not. And there would be a bombing halt for Christmas. But those were the rules of war. This was politics. There were no rules. Mark Salter, new to presidential politics, was astonished. "I thought, good God, you can't just slander a man, can you?" Salter said. "I kept waiting for the referee to blow the whistle, but there is no referee." One day a distraught mother called McCain and said her son had gotten one of the anti-McCain hate calls at home. The son considered McCain a hero and tearfully asked his mother why people were saying terrible things about him. At that moment, McCain decided to stop all his negative ads directed against Bush. "I wanted to be president not in the worst way, but in the best way," he said. "The cause is greater than our self-interest."

After the campaign, McCain said, "I decided not go negative for two reasons. One, I didn't want to look back and say we ran a dishonorable campaign. And clearly it was a mistake to have run these, you know, 'twist the truth like Clinton' ads. But the second reason is that we didn't have the resources to do it. We just couldn't afford to compete."

At the beginning of the South Carolina campaign, still riding the crest of his New Hampshire victory, McCain was cocky. "I'd like to have the Democratic nomination (too)," he said one day on his bus. "I think I'm better than anything they got going." But by the end of the South Carolina campaign, McCain was visibly weary, often tightly shutting his eyes and rubbing his face with his hands, and he knew victory was slipping away. He would lose by 11 points, but the worst thing was that the veterans split nearly equally between him and Bush. I asked him why.

"Because, I guess, because those negatives were reinforced almost ceaselessly for three weeks," McCain said. "That's really all they got to hear about. 'He really isn't a war hero, he really is a liberal, he's really like—he helps Clinton, he doesn't really care about you.' And there was hardly any medium in which that message wasn't just jackhammered into any South Carolinian with a radio or a computer, a television set or eyes. So it affected veterans, too. I think even the media were surprised when they began finding out how low that road was."

South Carolina would be the low point. In Michigan, McCain would win in part because of his own telephone campaign reminding Catholic voters of Bush's appearance at Bob Jones. "I'm not going to lie," a McCain aide said. "I was deeply satisfied by the Michigan win because it was our way of saying to Bush, 'Well, fuck you right back.' New Hampshire had been lofty and Michigan was low. You need both in your life. We're all sinners." To others in the McCain campaign, the success of Michigan was proof they should have stayed negative in South Carolina. "If we had stayed negative, we would have won," Rick Davis, the campaign manager, told me after the primaries. "Going positive was the worst thing we could have done."

The general election, perhaps in reaction to South Carolina, was not notable for below-the-belt attacks. And, in a *New York Times* interview that appeared on Christmas Eve, Bill Clinton astonishingly took credit. "I just think that one of the things I hope—and I saw it in this election—I noticed that there was much less appetite for the politics of personal destruction in this election than there had been in many others, and I hope that maybe that's one of the consequences of all that I did, and maybe—I mean, what we all went through, and maybe that will be something that's really good for the country over the long run. Maybe nobody else will ever have to go through this."

THE BUSH CAMPAIGN WOULD NEVER FORGIVE John McCain. Maybe it was because McCain had made their god bleed or maybe it was because he made campaigning look so easy and fun or maybe because he continued to push campaign finance reform even when it was an embarrassment to Bush. In any case, they would try to wreak their vengeance on him long after the primaries and even the general election were over. McCain would never quite understand it. "The reason why I think a few of those people are still angry at me is because we interfered with the coronation," he said. "Look, Bush and his people will have to live with the legacy of South Carolina; I don't. None of my people are particularly sore losers. But it's funny how people can be sore *winners*."

# 6

# SHOW ME THE MONEY

"I MADE A MISTAKE GOING TO THE BUDDHIST
TEMPLE. I MADE A MISTAKE IN MAKING
TELEPHONE CALLS FROM MY OFFICE. AND I
HAVE LEARNED FROM MY MISTAKES."

—Al Gore, March 12, 2000

"WE NEED TO FIX THE SYSTEM. AND WE
NEED TO FIX IT BEFORE PEOPLE START
GOING TO JAIL."

—U.S. Representative David Bonior
to author at fundraiser where Al Gore
helps raise $4 million, June 5, 2000

I N POLITICS, MONEY IS MORE THAN MONEY. Money is the first test of credibility. The media place enormous importance on a candidate's ability to raise money, lavishing stories and attention on those who do, and usually ignoring those who do not. Bill Bradley's campaign became credible not because Bradley was a sports legend or because he had been a U.S. senator but because he was able to raise tons of money early—exactly what Gore had feared. Gore knew about the power of early money. Bill Clinton raised so much of it so early in 1996 that he managed to freeze out any primary opponents. In 2000, Gore wanted to do the same thing. A primary would most likely move him to the left and he would have to spend time beating back to the center for the general election. And Gore's ability to lock up many big contributors worked: Senator John Kerry of Massachusetts, Senator Bob Kerrey of Nebraska, and House Minority Leader Richard Gephardt of Missouri all decided that challenging Gore for the nomination would have been too tough a fight. But Bradley could not be moved.

For years, Bradley had been working below the radar screen of the media to prepare for 2000. He had been giving speeches for other candidates even down to the level of country sheriff and district attorney. "He would come in and give a terrible speech," an aide for one candidate said, "but he would draw people to the fund-raiser because he was a basketball star. We loved it." Bradley, who gave the impression he lumbered along just responding to his inner voice, in fact had assembled a campaign machine: He went to Madison Avenue to learn how he could be packaged, and he went to experienced fundraisers to learn what he could reasonably squeeze from people. Rick Wright, Bradley's Princeton basketball teammate and later his national finance chairman, was an experienced fund-raiser who got his start with Bobby Kennedy. On Bradley's behalf, Wright did a demographic study of the United States and found that an astonishing 30 million Americans could afford to give $1,000 to a political campaign "without denting their lifestyle." Consider-ing that only 400,000 people gave any amount of money in 1996 and that only 31,000 gave $1,000, the Bradley campaign had a huge pool of potential donors, of which it had to tap only a relative few. "We figured if we got 2 percent, you could raise money from 600,000 individuals," Wright said. "We figured even if we could reach a half percent, we would be competitive."

The Bradley campaign raised money the best way campaigns can: The candidate got on the phone and called people. This was not new to Bradley—he had raised $11 million for a Senate race—but now he was searching out people Gore had not already locked up: sports figures, business people, people in arts and education. Bradley was not just asking them for contributions: The key was not getting people to give him money; the key was getting them to raise money for him. The Gore campaign, still looking to a general election race and not yet taking Bradley seriously, started to take notice when Abe Pollin, majority owner of the Washington Wizards and the arena they play in, raised $300,000 for Bradley. "Abe Pollin never raises money for traditional candidates," a professional fund-raiser not working for Bradley said. "He gives money, but he doesn't raise money. I am not a Bradley supporter, but his fundraising has been amazing. There is no other word for it. He is raising money from the free-throw line." Worse for Gore, money was giving Bradley credibility with reporters. "We knew we had to raise money to make Bill legitimate," Wright told me. "We had done that by June of 1999. We raised $7.4 million in the second quarter and suddenly people realized the vice president wasn't inevitable. But we still had to get our message out."

Which is where the limits of money come in. Which is why the person who has the most money early on doesn't always win. If they did, we would have had President John Connolly and President Phil Gramm and President Steve Forbes. But, in the end, money gives you only the ability to make your candidate seen and heard. And that is where Bradley hit a wall. The trouble with Bradley is that he was Al Gore, only more so. Was Gore opaque? Bradley was inscrutable. Did Gore have trouble connecting with audiences? Bradley didn't care about connecting with audiences, or at least he wasn't willing to make the changes necessary to do so. Gore was roundly attacked during the early primaries for being a chameleon, for not being comfortable in his own skin, for changing too much. Bradley refused to change at all, which was the problem. His campaign did, however, what all campaigns do when it has a candidate who has rough edges that cannot be smoothed: it calls the rough edges "authenticity" and hopes for the best.

IT IS LATE ON A COLD AFTERNOON IN JANUARY with the light beginning to fade and a few snowflakes beginning to fall when Don Benedict and David Buteau sit down to eat at Mary Ann's diner in Derry, New Hampshire. It is an ordinary day, which means the door bursts open and a roiling mass of cameras, lights, boom mikes, and journalists spills into the place. Don and Dave barely look up from their eggs and pancakes. Every presidential election season the New Hampshire state motto becomes: "Come Trample Us." In the center of the swirl, above it all both physically and figuratively, is Bill Bradley. He works his way up and down the aisles until he comes to Don and Dave. Both are wearing dark workshirts with bright patches that state in large letters: Heritage Plumbing and Heating.

"So what do you guys do?" Bradley asks.

Duh. Read much, Senator? Which is exactly what Don and Dave do not say. Instead, Don replies: "We're in plumbing and heating."

Bradley reacts as if Don has just revealed the secret of the Rosetta Stone to him. He ignores the minicam snouts peeking over his shoulder, the TV lights searing everything with a blue-white glare, the constant *whirrrclicks* of the still camera motor drives. He concentrates utterly and completely on Don and Dave. To Bill Bradley, now, here, at this moment, there are only three people on Earth and he is pleased—no, honored—to listen to two of them.

"How's business?" Bradley asks.

"Good, very good," Don says.

"You own the business?" Bradley goes on. "How many guys work there? Do you have health insurance?" He goes on and on, and Don and Dave make their replies, and eventually Bradley sticks out a hand and says, "Good to meet you. Hope you can help me out with a vote." Which Bradley often forgets to do, as if running for president was secondary to his 30-year effort to collect people's "stories," which, he says, teaches him about America and which, he believes, will make him a better, more connected president.

But how do Don and Dave feel about Bradley? Has he used them as props for the media? Has he listened with the phony half-an-ear that politicians usually use when Election Day looms? *Au contraire.*

"I like the fact he is down to earth and low-key," Don Benedict says. "To me, that's trustworthy. I know he's not real exciting, but that's not what we need. Bush, I don't trust the guy. He plays for the cameras. Bradley, he wouldn't be different if the cameras were not around." Score that a 10 on Bradley's "Voters-I-Would-Like-to-Hug-if-I-Did-That-Kind-of-Thing" chart. It is exactly the reaction Bradley hopes for and exactly what his advisers, pollsters, focus group managers, and Madison Avenue consultants hope to sell about Bradley: His authenticity.

"The homeliness of the Bradley campaign, though packaged by campaign professionals earning a lot of money, is the anti-campaign that many people desire," says David Birdsell, a professor of public affairs at Baruch College. Everything about Bradley reeks of authenticity, which is an especially useful attribute because it turns minuses into pluses: Is Bradley's speaking style somewhere between that of a dentist's drill and the hum of a refrigerator? That's authenticity. Are his clothes more easily deplored than described? That's genuineness. Is he sometimes so low key that you wonder if he has painted eyeballs on his eyelids and is really sleeping? That's the real deal.

Essential to authenticity, however, is the belief we can actually discern how "real" the candidate is and the question in Bradley's case is how well anyone actually knows him. "He's a mystery to me," a senior Bradley aide says. "I've known him for years, and he's still mysterious." At a triumphant Madison Square Garden fundraiser, Bradley's ex-teammate Willis Reed said, "When you walk away [from Bradley], he'll know more about you than you'll know about him." And Bradley wants to keep it that way. He is a collector of other people's stories, not a revealer of his own. Not his private story, anyway. When I asked him what he was willing to give up to become president, Bradley replied: "Essentially you have to be willing to give up your life." Bradley was not speaking of assassination, but something almost the same to him: the death of his privacy. "If you succeed [in becoming president] you've got six guys around you the rest of your life," Bradley said. It's not that Bradley refuses to speak about his public life or tell certain childhood anecdotes. But stray into his private life or beliefs and you meet a No Trespassing sign. "Does a person's private life reflect on the ability to serve?" Bradley asks in his bestselling memoir, *Time Present, Time Past*. Only when it is "truly pathological," Bradley replies. "Individual quirks such as preferring Bach to blues, suffering from fear of heights, choosing certain kinds of sexual pleasures, having difficulty relaxing after a period of intense work, waging a vendetta, working at a messy desk, having nightmares about death, being unable to sleep for more than a few hours at a time, cannot be correlated to one's ability to perform public service," he writes. When I asked him if he was describing himself with that list, he replied: "They're not all me."

"And we're left to guess which are yours and which aren't?" I asked.

"Yes, right," he replied.

"There has always been a search for the true, the authentic in American politics," says Gil Troy. "In the eighteenth and nineteenth centuries, people talked about finding 'virtue' in their leaders, but it was public virtue. Now, we have an inversion: we want to look behind the screen to get to the essence of a person's soul rather than judging a person by his track record." Bradley would rather we stick to his track record. Famous for his endless practice before every basketball game, Bradley knows all about performance. He has studied his own stage fright and speaking style, and while he attracts a load of l-words from the press (laconic, low-key, laid-back), this very much depends on how much Bradley decides to invest of himself in any given event. At St. Anselm College in Goffstown, New Hampshire, in front of a virtually all-white student crowd, Bradley was so low key it was impossible to tell if he was being authentic or merely drowsy. But the next day, in front of a largely African American student crowd at Morehouse School of Medicine in Atlanta, Bradley was animated and involved. What had been a series of disconnected one-liners at St. Anselm took on a flow, a context, and a texture at Morehouse. The trouble is that presidential candidates are to a great extent performers, and, like performers on a stage, they have to be ready to give the same performance, with the same energy, over and over again. Repetition is eventually what gets through to voters and as mind-numbing as it may be for the candidate (and the reporters who have to listen to it), delivering the same high-energy performance again and again is what is often required.

Only once in the months that I covered Bradley did I see him really break free. It was January 10, in Carroll, Iowa, at the community college, when Bradley decided to stop playing from the playbook and talk: "The other day, you know, it wasn't the other day, I'll be honest, it was a couple of months ago, I was in a motel and, you know, I've been spending a lot of nights in motels and this is one of those motels where the sheet comes off, you know, when you roll over, the bottom sheet comes off because the sheets aren't long enough to tuck in, you know, so it's the middle of the night and you're sleeping on an open mattress as opposed to the sheets and you ask yourself, 'Who slept here last night?' you know, and I was there and I had my head on the pillow and it was one of those rubberized pillows and you put your head down and your head bounces back up like this, you know, it was one of those places where you turn the heat on and it's too hot and I think it's 100 degrees in the room and, you know, if you turn it off, ten minutes later you're freezing. Life along the road. And I thought that night, you know: I've been on the road in America for 30 years. Thirty years. That's why I know so much about this."

The Gore campaign was openly contemptuous of Bradley trying to sell his rigidity as authenticity and his defense of his privacy. They knew the American public had been taught by Bill Clinton— who was not only willing but happy to talk about his wife-abusing father, his devil-may-care mother, and his drug-abusing brother— that a candidate had to sell his story, his personality, his humanness to the voters. That is what people could connect to. And if you couldn't connect, all the money in the world could not save you.

The other truth about money is that eventually it flows to winners. John McCain started with barely enough money to launch his campaign against George W. Bush, while Bill Bradley had more money at one point than Al Gore. But what happened? John McCain won the Republican primary in New Hampshire and raised $11.1 million the following month. Bill Bradley lost Iowa and New Hampshire and raised $710,294 the following month. One campaign caught fire and the other campaign caught it in the neck.

O N THE CROWDED NIGHTCLUB FLOOR IN MID-town Manhattan, the lawyers jostle the stockbrokers, the stockbrokers jostle the CEOs, the CEOs jostle the union bosses, and the union bosses jostle whomever they wish. It is a Democratic fundraiser and Dick Gephardt stands in front of the buffet table, hugging and kissing people, seemingly at random. Faces are flushed, spirits are high, and the night is pregnant with possibilities. If the Democrats raise enough money, they figure they can take back the House of Representatives, make Gephardt the speaker, and make Charlie Rangel, whose 70th birthday is being celebrated this night, chairman of the Ways and Means Committee. But money does not come through magic. It comes through guys like David Jones.

Jones, 34, a professional fundraiser who began his political life as a college organizer for Amnesty International, stands at Gephardt's elbow, smoothly funneling people to him. Jones sees a face in the crowd, summons up a name from his prodigious memory—"You have to be good at remembering their faces, their names, their spouses, their kids, their dogs. And when they last gave money," Jones says—and then gives them a hug and a tug and says, "Go and talk to Dick." For many, merely meeting Gephardt, the House minority leader, is enough. "They want a picture taken with Gephardt or Al Gore or Rangel or the president," Jones says. "They want to be part of the effort, be part of the scene. They want to go to a fundraising event and rub elbows with CEOs, the managing partners of law firms, business people. Maybe they'll do some business." And some business will be done tonight.

Dennis Rivera, the president of Local 1199 of the Service Employees International Union, walks up to Jones and Gephardt. They are all old friends. Rivera reaches into his suit jacket and extracts a slender white envelope. He hands it to Jones—giving it to Gephardt would be unseemly—and says huskily in Jones's ear, "This is from the union."

Jones takes the envelope without looking inside, places it in his own jacket pocket, and embraces Rivera. A moment later, Rivera tells me, "We hope to generate the resources needed to compete with the Republicans, who always outspend us." Rivera then asks if I know how much money will be raised this night. I check my notes and tell him $2.7 million total. Rivera smiles. "I think you're going to be off," he says. "By a million dollars." And Rivera ought to know. Inside the envelope he just handed Jones are three checks totaling a million dollars. Just a little surprise "from the union."

All in all, the evening will bring in $4 million, the largest amount of money the Democratic Congressional Campaign Committee has ever raised at a single event outside Washington, D.C. Though the publicity for the event lists Al Gore and Hillary Clinton merely as special guests, the Reuters headline the next day will read: "Gore, Mrs. Clinton Raise $4 Mln at New York Fund-Raiser." The event also comes more than three months after Gore has announced he wants to do away with the kind of money-grubbing he is now engaging in. As the front-page *New York Times* story said at the time: "In an audacious attempt to turn one of his greatest vulnerabilities into an asset, Vice President Al Gore said today he would make overhauling the campaign finance system a central theme of his presidential bid. He brushed aside fresh questions about his own conduct in raising money, insisting that he had learned from his mistakes and was seizing the issue with the passion of a convert."

THOUGH IT HAS BEEN ILLEGAL FOR MORE THAN half a century for labor unions to contribute to federal campaigns, the checks Dennis Rivera slips to David Jones are perfectly legal because they are "soft money," whose very name has become a dirty word in American politics, but a dirty word that politicians love to mumble to themselves as they rub their hands together in glee. Even those politicians who raise soft money decry it. Gephardt, who rakes in oodles, would like to end it, and Rangel is downright passionate when it comes to denouncing what he flies around the country to shovel in. "There is not a fundraiser that I attend or speak at that I don't express my fear that unless we have an effective campaign reform law we may destroy the legislative system as we know it," Rangel tells me. "We need people like me to say: 'Stop us before we destroy ourselves!'" Rangel's cry for self-discipline has, however, fallen on deaf ears (including his own). Soft-money totals from 2000 almost doubled what was raised four years earlier, and the fundraising is still going strong. Most of the money, however, is raised not in single, huge checks but in thousands of much smaller checks, which is why professional fundraisers like Jones are in such demand. "A national or statewide candidate needs a solid fundraiser two years in advance of the election," Jones says. "Many people planning on running for the Senate are hiring us four years out."

The largest single check from an individual for the Rangel birthday fundraiser is $150,000 from Richard Medley, president of a risk-analysis firm. Medley, a former Yale professor and Democratic Hill staffer, does not expect to have a highway named for him or to influence laws, even though he has given hundreds of thousands in soft money to the Democratic Party over the years. Sitting in his lovingly restored TriBeCa office and wearing a golf shirt, slacks, and deck shoes without socks, he says, "We don't run a business where we care about what laws are passed. I don't think I've ever made a phone call to a politician." (Politicians call him, however, 10 to 20 times a week asking for money; he ducks almost all of them.) "The reward is feeling involved, in having conversations at the highest level about policy, and, yes, about getting your ego stroked," Medley says.

Like a lot of big fundgivers, Medley is also a fundraiser, assembling groups of businesspeople to sit down and talk to big-name pols in return for hefty contributions to the Democratic Party. Why would people pay good money to talk to politicians? Some might have a hidden agenda, such as trying to influence a particular piece of legislation, Medley admits, and some may have purely altruistic motives, but most, he says, give for one simple reason: They won't miss the money. When Medley assembled a group of businessmen at his home to meet Gore, the price of admission was $50,000 each.

"A big George Bush guy wanted to confront Gore and he didn't mind giving $50,000 to do it," Medley says. "He gave Gore a hard time within the limits of civility. But he came away impressed with Gore." Who would pay $50,000 just to tell Al Gore to his face that he is full of beans? The kind of people that Richard Medley knows. In Medley's world, a non-tax-deductible $50,000 is chump change—and it's a bigger world than many might think. There are 5 million millionaires in America, with 40,000 new ones being created each month. In 1982 there were 13 billionaires in America. Today, there are 298, a 2,200 percent increase in 18 years. But few people go around looking for ways to give away money. Most usually have to be separated from it, and that's where the fundraiser comes in, a fundraiser who will do what is called the Big Ask. The Big Ask is not difficult—you just ask the person to write you a check—and Nancy L. Bockskor, a Republican fundraiser, recommends that candidates spend 35 to 50 percent of their time raising money. "Some form of fundraising should be going on every single day," she says. Some lawmakers do not like to do it. "Rangel does not like to do the Big Ask," Jones says. "I'll set up the meeting [with prospective donors] and Rangel will give a broad brush stroke on what it will mean to the country for Gephardt to be speaker and him to be chairman of Ways and Means, and then the person who does the Big Ask is me."

Later, in his pink-walled Washington office—"It used to be a dentist's office," Jones says, "but now we extract money instead of teeth"—Jones checks his 40,000-name database and grabs the phone. "I'm smilin' and I'm dialin'," he says, punching the number of Patrick Mitchell, whom he describes as a longtime Democratic activist. "Patrick! David Jones! How you doin'? You were? Good. OK. You got that letter from me, right? OK. What we need you to do is raise $20,000 in hard, federal dollars, if you can, for Gephardt. That's the priority. If you can commit to 20 and give it your best shot, that would be good. I hear you, I hear you. That would be great." Jones erupts into laughter.

Mitchell, he explains later, had just said to him, "What do I get for that? A glass of wine and ten calls from you?"

One of the reasons the public at large periodically tunes out of the campaign finance reform controversy is that the rules are so complicated that you need to be a specialist to follow them and, indeed, the parties spend a bundle on legal bills just to keep everything straight and to try to keep as many people as possible out of jail. Basically, while soft money is unregulated, hard money is not. A candidate can accept only $1,000 per election in hard money from an individual and $5,000 from a political action committee. However, a candidate can set up a "leadership PAC" and take another $5,000 from individuals, though it can't be spent on the candidate's own campaign. Political parties can accept $20,000 in hard money from individuals and $5,000 from PACs, but can raise unlimited amounts of soft money from corporations, labor unions, and individuals. Soft money is supposed to be used for "party building" activities and "issue advertising," but the Clinton/Gore campaign of 1996 pioneered in using soft money to finance sharply focused ads designed to directly benefit the top of the ticket. Parties must raise a certain amount of hard money before they can use soft money, however. This makes the $1,000 hard-money donor extremely valuable, especially considering how many of them are out there in an America experiencing unprecedented wealth.

Because politics never stops, fundraising never stops. Which is not, some argue, really as bad as we have all been led to believe. Presidential historian Gil Troy argues that the impact of money on politics is often exaggerated and that it was the growth of democracy and reforms to the system that really caused the increase in the need for money. And "currying the people's favor," which is what democracy is all about, he argues, has always been costly. The amount of money George Washington spent on his two elections to the Virginia House of Burgesses was several times the going price for a house or plot of land. Washington bought rum punch, cookies, and ginger cakes for the voters, he threw an election-eve ball complete with a fiddler and he provided money for the poll watchers who recorded the tally. (Stick enough rum punch in a poll watcher, Washington seemed to know instinctively, and things like hanging chads are no longer an issue.) As more and more people could vote, the cost of reaching them increased. Andrew Jackson's 1828 victory "may have cost as much as $1 million, much of it absorbed by the federal government, thanks to his legislative allies' convenient franking privileges," Troy writes. In 1864, every ward in Manhattan was "abundantly supplied with material aid" to assure the reelection of Abraham Lincoln. There was reform, of course, but reform increased the need for other sources of money. When the Pendleton Civil Service Act of 1883 made it illegal to assess federal officeholders for campaign contributions, the parties turned even more to private corporations to make up the loss. In 1896, Republican political operative Mark Hanna raised $6 million to $7 million from corporations to put William McKinley in office, the equivalent of nearly $100 million today. In modern times, reformers wanted candidates picked by primaries and not party bosses, which was fair enough, but it meant the candidates now had to reach the primary voters directly and that required money for television. Are the amounts spent on political campaigning really out of line with other forms of campaigning? In 1996, Bill Clinton spent $169 million to be reelected president. In that same year, the Wm. Wrigley Jr. Co. spent $247 million advertising chewing gum.

The huge amounts spent by campaigns are actually "modest,"

Troy argues, "considering how much it costs to attract attention in a nation of 265 million couch potatoes...."

So David Jones dials for dollars every day. "Vince! David Jones! Let me ask you about your check. You writing 20? Beautiful! Wonderful! That's great! Great!" Only about 10 to 12 percent of the people who tell Jones they will send a check end up not doing it. "You know what I call those people?" Jones says. "Frauds." He must make roughly 100 phone calls to get one yes and that is from a list of proven Democratic donors. "You want the *Glengarry Glen Ross* leads," he says, a reference to the David Mamet play. "Most people don't even bother to call you back." Jones admits that sometimes the right person must do the asking. "Maybe it's a partner in their law firm, the CEO of their company, or the mayor of their city," he says, citing three circumstances in which an individual might find it hard to say no to a caller. "Or the person who gets the call might want to rub elbows with other givers at the event. Maybe it's their chance to see the CEO or meet the managing partner of the law firm. Maybe they'll do some business with them. You can meet a high-end group of people this way."

But, aside from meeting high-end people who can do you some personal good, why do people give money to political campaigns? Two reasons, Jones says. "People outside Washington give because they want to be part of the action, and people in Washington give because they want their phone calls returned." This, Jones says, is how it works in our nation's capital: "If you represent the National Widget Association and Representative X sits on the Ways and Widgets subcommittee, a good way to meet him might be to give $1,000 to an event where he is the host. Give the DCCC $50,000 from Widget PAC and he'll know you even better. And then when the president of U.S. Widget Inc. comes to town, you can take him by Representative X's office and arrange a meeting. That's all. You've done your job. Most lobbyists don't care which way you vote, they just want to prove they can get in to see a member and that justifies their existence. So if they are a lobbyist for a corporation and the CEO is coming to town, they call me and I'll call the chief of staff for the member to ask for a meeting. That's the inside-the-beltway game."

All this is legal, but Jones's scenario presents a somewhat benign interpretation of why corporations and interest groups give money. In late December 2000, the *Wall Street Journal,* under the headline "Big GOP Contributors Look for Return on Their Money," listed the vast sums of money contributed by industry groups to George W. Bush, the Republican Party, and the Florida recount effort. And—surprise, surprise—groups like securities and investment companies that contributed $22.2 million to Bush, the RNC, and the recount wanted more than an appointment with some member of Congress. They wanted, the *Journal* said, the Bush administration "to get Congress to expand IRAs and 401(k) accounts, and reduce taxes." High-tech companies, which gave $7.7 million, wanted Bush to stop any taxation of the Internet.

The election of 2000 was the most expensive in U.S. history with an estimated $3 billion spent on presidential and congressional races and an additional $1 billion spent on state races. That was an increase of 50 percent over 1996. And both parties liked to brag that nobody who failed to win election did so because of a lack of funds. As Gore's representative at the Democratic National Committee—where he had the simple title "strategist"—Michael Whouley, who would prove so critical to the Gore vote effort, handled millions of dollars in soft money. He estimates he spent $30 million on TV, $30 million on "ground" costs, and an additional $25 million on administrative costs—such things as satellite time.

"I'm sure I spent more than the Gore campaign spent," Whouley says. And he did. The two presidential campaigns were restricted by law to spending $67.6 million each for the general election. Whouley exceeded that at the DNC, and the RNC exceeded Whouley's expenditures. At the time of their last report before Election Day, the RNC had raised about $211 million, 74 percent more than 1996, and the Democrats had raised about $199 million, an increase of 85 percent over four years earlier. Which is another phenomenon of 2000: What was considered audacious fundraising by Clinton/ Gore in 1996 is now standard procedure, at least in terms of the kind of money raised. As the *Washington Post* concluded, "The result, according to election lawyers and political scientists and practitioners, is that the basic pillars of the campaign finance system—a ban on corporate contributions, strict limits on individual donations, public financing for the presidential general election campaign—have been effectively eroded."

So while it has been illegal since 1907 for corporations to make political contributions and illegal since 1943 for unions to contribute to federal campaigns, in reality under the non-rules of soft money they can give virtually whatever they want. It is not just the big shots in that Manhattan nightclub who know Dennis Rivera and the Service Employees International Union. Virtually every Democrat running for office does. The SEIU was the No. 3 political donor in America in 2000, giving about $3.6 million. Microsoft was fourth, AT&T was second, and the American Federation of State, County, and Municipal Employees was first.

It is safe to say all these entities want some big things for their contributions, but one little thing they want is the right person thanking them for their dough. A call from Bill, a thank-you note from Al, or a handshake from Patrick can work wonders. Patrick is Patrick Kennedy, who became the DCCC chairman in 1998, supervising a staff of 126 even though he was only 31 and had been representing the 1st District of Rhode Island in Congress for only a handful of years. But though he looks like none of the Kennedys, he is Ted Kennedy's youngest son, which means he was a nephew of John F. Kennedy and Robert Kennedy, which means he is something in America. "If his last name wasn't Kennedy, he would be at Thom McAn helping you try on these shoes," one critic says. But Patrick's name *is* Kennedy and, as it turns out, he excels at fundraising. "Patrick Kennedy means $20 million on top of what the DCCC would raise, that's how good he is," David Jones says. "He has got access to people the rest of us can't get a call returned from. Some of them have known him since he was five years old or they know his father. The Kennedy magic exists. Big time."

PATRICK KENNEDY IS TELLING A JOKE THAT MAKES fun of Patrick Kennedy, self-deprecating humor being the only kind of humor that is safe for politicians to indulge in these days. Kennedy is standing on the lawn of the estate of Norman and Mary Patiz, high up on a hillside in Beverly Hills, the city of Los Angeles spread out like a twinkling map-of-the-stars'-homes beneath him.

Patiz is a radio mogul, and in Los Angeles, where realty is destiny, everybody knows that the Patiz estate used to be the David Geffen estate, which used to be the Marlo Thomas estate. (Few memories at this cocktail party go back beyond Marlo Thomas.) As chairman of the DCCC (which is always referred to as the D-Triple-C), Kennedy is in charge of raising millions and millions of dollars. And now he is telling this story about how he has to call George Clinton, the ultimate funk singer, and get him to appear at a Democratic fundraiser.

"They've written it all out for me on a notecard," Kennedy is saying, "and the notecard says I must say to him: 'We gotta have the funk!'"

The people standing around Kennedy begin to laugh.

"It's underlined three times on the notecard," Kennedy is saying. "'We gotta have the funk.' I have to say this to him. So I get him on the phone and say, 'This is Congressman Kennedy-Kennedy-Kennedy...'"

Everybody laughs again at how Kennedy is making fun of the power of the Kennedy name.

"And then I say to him: 'We gotta have the funk!'" Kennedy says. "And he comes right back with, 'And you're gonna get the groove, too!' He doesn't miss a beat. 'And you're gonna get the groove, too!'"

Everybody roars, pretending that they get Kennedy's joke.

In the end, Kennedy will raise $97 million for the DCCC in 2000, three times what was raised in the previous election cycle. Why is so much more money needed every time America heads for an even-numbered year? Television. The ever increasing cost of buying TV time is the greatest single reason campaign costs keep going up. Today, one out of every five dollars raised goes to TV advertising. Two kinds of people benefit from this: the media consultants, who get a percentage of all the TV time purchased—just one or two big campaigns can set a consultant up for life—and the TV station owners, who got an estimated $600 million in revenue from political advertising in 2000, a 40 percent increase over 1996. No wonder broadcasters have pre-tax profit margins that range from 25 to 50 percent.

Unfortunately for the candidates, they are getting less bang for their TV buck. "Local TV stations charge five to ten times what they did 20 years ago to deliver the same audience," said Neal Oxman of Campaign Group Inc., a Philadelphia media consulting firm.

"They're getting away with flat-out stealing compared to what they're delivering."

And TV is virtually the whole ballgame. Of political advertising dollars, 83.5 percent goes to TV, 10.2 percent to radio, 4.6 percent to newspapers, 1.5 percent to billboards, and 0.2 percent to magazines. Who, if anybody, actually pays attention to political commercials is anybody's guess. The real appeal of commercials is that they are completely controlled by the campaign. A news conference, a speech, or a debate can all go wrong. But carefully made TV commercials, ones with pleasing images and nice music, are candidate-proof. And anything that the candidate cannot screw up is considered gold to a political campaign.

THOUGH ORIGINALLY NOT A GORE SUPPORTER— he would have supported Gephardt had he run in 2000— Kennedy does have one startling thing in common with the vice president: They both raised money at the Hsi Lai Buddhist temple outside Los Angeles in 1996. Kennedy said his visit had been "a gesture of deference and respect" and that Asian Americans gave him $5,000 afterwards because they liked his positions on immigration. When it was revealed that the individuals making the contributions had been illegally reimbursed, Kennedy gave the money back. The incident was especially painful because the Kennedys, like many ultra-wealthy politicians, promote their financial status as a plus by saying it is a sign that they cannot be bought. In any case, the temple incident did nothing to discourage Kennedy from aggressive fundraising, and it must have caused more than a few smiles at the White House when Kennedy promised that anyone who contributed at least $100,000 to the DCCC would be invited to a weekend retreat at the Kennedy compound in Hyannis Port. The Lincoln Bedroom might be very nice, but it lacks a certain star power.

THERE WAS NOTHING WORSE FOR GORE IN 2000 than to raise memories about his fundraising in 1996. He had a pretty good record of proposing campaign finance reform when he was a legislator—in his first term in Congress he had called for full public financing of all federal elections. And he had a good reputation for being clean. But by 1996, fundraising was out of control, and Gore couldn't or wouldn't say no to climbing down in the muck to do it. In the Clinton White House, being willing to raise the big bucks was about more than money. It was a rite of passage, it showed you were a real guy, a real player, the kind of guy who "pissed standing up." Perhaps to show that he was not some goody-goody wimp or perhaps because he really believed big money could secure victory, Gore threw caution and his reputation to the winds. "There's going to be a major scandal," Bill Daley had told me a few months before the 1996 fundraising scandal began to break. "The public is going to revolt. Fundraising has gotten out of hand."

How far out of hand? Well, the United States Secret Service has more than 2,000 agents and an annual budget in excess of half a billion dollars. Two of its highest priorities are to protect the president and vice president of the United States. The precautions taken are elaborate—from heavily armored limousines that can travel on steel rims should the tires be shot out to bulletproof glass panels occasionally set up around the armored presidential and vice presidential lecterns, each known as the "Blue Goose." In risky crowd situations, agents will hold portable Kevlar panels around the president and vice president. Agents equipped with night-vision goggles and rifles with telescopic sights are positioned atop the White House. Crash barriers, fences, motion detectors, iron gates with anti-ram devices, and video cameras guard the White House perimeter, one side of which fronts on a street Clinton closed to all traffic for security reasons. And inside the White House, Secret Service agents armed with 9mm Sig Sauer pistols stand outside the Oval Office whenever the president is there. The point of all of this is to ensure that nobody who is a potential threat gets close to the president or vice president. Unless, as it turns out, that person contributed a large sum of money to the president's political party.

We know this to be true because Eric Wynn did it on December 21, 1995. Wynn attended a coffee in the White House Map Room, which attracted a star-studded cast including Erskine Bowles, then deputy chief and later chief of staff at the White House; Democratic National Committee co-chairs Christopher Dodd and Donald L. Fowler; Thomas "Mack" McLarty, counselor to the president; and, of course, Bill Clinton. It was only Wynn's credentials that were somewhat less than stratospheric: According to the *Washington Post,* Wynn had been sentenced to three years in the slammer after a 1989 guilty plea for theft and tax evasion. He reportedly was an associate of the Mafia's Bonanno family, one of the so-called Five Families that control organized crime in America. And, the *New York Times* reported, just five months before sitting down with Clinton, Wynn was convicted on 13 counts of conspiracy, securities fraud, and wire fraud, and was sentenced to 52 months in prison. At the time he was sipping java with the leader of the free world, Wynn was out on bail. According to a close associate, Wynn was also trying to obtain a pardon.

Two days before his audience with Clinton, a Florida firm that Wynn reportedly had partial control of donated $25,000 to the Democratic National Committee. The *New York Times* ran a Nexis search on him—which the DNC, the White House, or the Secret Service was equally capable of doing—and found this in a 1989 issue of *Forbes* magazine: "Federal documents say Bonanno family capo Frank Coppa, his associate Eric Wynn and other friends paid a visit to a stock promoter and bashed him on the side of the head with a telephone." This might have been considered significant because even though we can assume that Wynn had to pass through a metal detector before entering the White House, it appeared that Wynn knew how to use such common household objects as bludgeons. Why was this man allowed in the same room as the president? Because he had money to donate to the Democrats.

But Wynn was only one of a remarkable list of thugs, hoodlums, and lowlifes who were able to get access to Clinton and Gore. There was a piece of work named Jorge "Gordito" Cabrera, who did time in 1983 for conspiracy to bribe a grand jury witness, and again in 1988 for tax evasion, both convictions related to narcotics trafficking. But Cabrera donated $20,000 to the DNC and was invited to attend a fundraiser for about 60 guests in Cocoplum, Florida, in late 1995. The guest of honor was Al Gore. Cabrera got his picture taken with Gore and got a set of vice presidential cufflinks. In 1996, Cabrera was sent to prison to serve a 19-year sentence for transporting 6,000 pounds of cocaine into the country. The DNC returned his $20,000 donation (though, presumably, Cabrera was allowed to keep the cufflinks). The list went on and on.

Then there was the Buddhist temple fundraiser in April 1996. At first Gore said he did not know the temple event was a fundraiser, even though a staff memo made that clear. He said he thought the event was one of "community outreach." That statement later proved to be inoperative. In January his spokeswoman said: "He knew it was a finance-related event." Then came the revelation that

Gore had sat in his White House office and dialed for dollars, phoning big Democratic donors and asking for money.

On Sunday, March 2, 1997, a front-page story by Bob Woodward of the *Washington Post* revealed that Gore had "played the central role" in raising money for the Democratic Party in scandal-ridden 1996, that he made phone calls from his vice presidential office soliciting money that were "heavy-handed and inappropriate" and that he was known as the administration's "solicitor-in-chief." One donor said Gore's call to him was "revolting" and another called it a "shakedown." Gore would call large corporate donors, the story said, and tell them, "I've been tasked with raising $2 million by the end of the week, and you're on my list." He would discontinue the practice, Gore said at a news conference in March, even though he had broken no law.

"On a few occasions, I made some telephone calls from my office in the White House, using a DNC credit card," Gore said. "I was advised there was nothing wrong with that practice."

But there was something wrong with Gore's statement: It was not correct. The day after the news conference, the vice president's office hurriedly announced that Gore had not used a DNC credit card, but a Clinton/Gore campaign credit card. The Associated Press then reported, however, that "contrary to his original assertion" that all the calls went on a credit card, in 20 cases Gore did not use a credit card at all and the taxpayers got billed. The Democratic Party quietly reimbursed the government for the calls.

Gore also seemed to be taking on Clinton's famous ability to redefine common words in the English language (like "sex" and "is"). Gore said he made fundraising calls from his office "on a few occasions" and made only "some" calls. But that depends on your definition of "a few" and "some."

In fact, Gore made 71 calls in 10 sessions. In 46 cases, Gore spoke to the person he was calling, asking for between $25,000 and $100,000. In the other cases, Gore left phone messages.

By 2000, however, Gore was a changed man. Nor was there a need to look under every rock to find rich goons with ill-gotten gains to put the squeeze on. The wealth of America was incredible and there was a huge pool of honest, upright citizens who could be squeezed just as well.

"I made a mistake going to the Buddhist temple," Gore said in March on the day he announced that he wanted a ban on soft money. "I made a mistake in making telephone calls from my office. And I have learned from those mistakes. And I am passionate about the need for campaign reform. . . . I have a passion for campaign finance reform that is fueled in part because of the pain of those mistakes. . . . I had a passion for this before, but the passion became stronger in the wake of the '96 campaign, when both parties pushed the limits. I don't want to see any other campaigns conducted like that."

In that case, a reporter asked Gore, why not refuse to accept soft money right now? Why not refuse to go to these fundraisers? Why not stop making the same mistake over and over?

"I am not," Gore said, "going to unilaterally disarm."


THOUGH IMMEDIATELY AFTER SEWING UP THE Democratic nomination, Gore had announced he would make passage of the McCain-Feingold bill banning soft-money contributions his No. 1 priority as president, he never stopped raising soft money. His polls were showing what public polls were showing: Ordinary people didn't care that much about campaign finance reform. In late January when the campaigns of John McCain and Bill Bradley were making it a hot topic, a Fox News/Opinion Dynamics

Poll asked voters which issues were most important to them. Campaign finance reform came in last. A *Newsweek* poll conducted that same month had campaign finance reform coming in second to last, just above gay rights. And perhaps that is why Gore was not deterred from immediately going out and raising tons of soft money. In fact from March, when he locked up the nomination, to the end of September, Gore raised $60 million for the Democratic Party. In May, he and Bill Clinton raised $26.5 million at a single event at MCI Center in Washington. These figures, the *New York Times* editorialized, were "so outlandish that they numb the mind and threaten to dull the capacity for outrage."

But who was the most outraged by soft money? The politicians getting and spending it. Just ask them.

The New York event for Charlie Rangel is unusual because it raised a huge sum of money at the behest of somebody who did not need money. Charlie Rangel, who got to the House in 1970 by beating Adam Clayton Powell Jr., often gets more than 90 percent of the vote at election time and almost defines what having a safe seat means. In 1994 he got 97 percent of the vote, in 1996 he got 91 percent, in 1998 he got 93 percent and in 2000 he would get 91 percent. So why should people give money to Rangel? Because, as David Jones and others emphasize when they call potential givers, it is one of the few ways you can show gratitude to Rangel. "This is a way of showing thanks, of saying, 'I am doing something for you,'" Jones says. Rangel is the ranking Democrat on the House Ways and Means Committee, which controls tax policy for the nation. And if the Democrats ever retake the House, he will become chairman and there will be many, many people who will want to have done something for him. In politics, you never have to ask the question: What do you get a man who has everything? The answer is always: money.

Is this system bad? You bet! Just ask some of the people gathered together for Rangel.

"We're in a pickle," David Bonior, the House Democratic whip, tells me. "We need to fix the system. And we need to fix it before people start going to jail."

"It needs reform," Dick Gephardt agrees.

(In late 2000, Patrick Kennedy decides not to serve another term as DCCC chairman and he is replaced by Nita Lowey of New York. She tells the *New York Times,* "Let's face it, the amount of money that has to be raised is obscene, and so I'm very vocal in saying we need campaign finance reform." She also announces she hopes to raise roughly $100 million for the 2002 election cycle.)

And if you ask Rangel, be prepared to hear more than you wanted about the evils of soft money.

"I think this is a threat to Congress as we know it," he says. "It is a disease and it is not restricted to one party. Who would know better than I how potentially dangerous it is for large sums of money to be coming into the party? Someone some day could come to me and say: 'I represent the Democratic Party and let me tell you how much we've raised and here is how much you got to get elected and this is what it will take for you to remain chairman.'

"If and when we get a majority, will I be scared to speak out then as I speak out now? Will I have to put our thin majority on the line? I am just saying that reporters and do-gooders are missing the boat when they talk about buying off a member of Congress— [contributors] are buying off the Constitution! Big contributors are outbidding each other! We need to take a deep breath and stop this madness!"

The system is so mad, Rangel says, that he has to ask himself whether he encouraged Hillary Clinton to run for the Senate because she could raise the money that native New Yorkers could not.

"I don't even like the idea that subconsciously I reached out to Hillary Clinton not because I thought we didn't have qualified people in this great state, but who else could raise money to run? You want to run today, they ask: How much money can you raise? Not how well qualified you are. Rick Lazio? Can he raise the money to compete? That's all they ask. That is sad."

The party swirls on around him. The Harlem Boys Choir sings and the Lionel Hampton Orchestra plays. And, like boats against the current, borne back ceaselessly into the past, envelopes full of money change hands.

"So, anyway," Rangel says. "I'm just trying to raise some money. And isn't it ironic? Goddamn people want to give it to me."

7

# DENY, DENY, DENY

"IF BILL CLINTON WERE THE *TITANIC*,
THE ICEBERG WOULD HAVE SUNK."

—Popular joke, 1998

A L GORE IS A HIGHLY DISCIPLINED AND serious man, a man who loves to study things and the systems of things, who loves to see where and how they fit in with the big picture and with his constantly evolving and maturing world view. He is systematic and substantive and loves nothing more than to assemble experts and talk to them at breakfasts, lunches, dinner, panels, study groups, and symposia. His eldest daughter, Karenna, who had worked in his vice presidential campaigns and is the Gore most likely to follow him into public life, once said that her father was an introvert who was most comfortable living inside himself. She meant it as a compliment. His wife, Tipper, said, "He is shy. He's always been shy. He was reserved when he was a teenager." Only after long study and only after Gore had settled on a proper course of action did he become a strong advocate for bold action, and he repeatedly urged Clinton into undertaking more daring initiatives than Clinton, at first, was willing to consider. But, unlike Clinton, Gore is not a man of impulse, rarely a man of inspiration, almost never a man of public passion. (In private, his passion is another matter. His smoldering embraces of Tipper are a constant source of mild embarrassment to his children, who were the least surprised people in America when Gore gave

Tipper that lingering kiss in front of the TV cameras at the Democratic convention. "He's always doing stuff like that," Karenna sighed.) The consultants and aides brought in at the start of Gore's presidential campaign who wanted to change Gore did not really know Gore very well, did not understand that Gore looked upon campaigns as a learning experience, and that he always got better as the campaign went along. But his advisers saw polls in the spring of 1999 showing Gore losing not only to George W. Bush but also to Elizabeth Dole—Liddy Dole, for cripe's sake!—and, perhaps understandably, they panicked. Gore was handsome, friendly, and bright, but when you saw him standing there in his blue suit and white shirt and solid tie, you didn't think "president," you thought "airline pilot." They knew from their meetings with him that Gore could be funnier, more charming, and more relaxed in private, and they wished the public could see the private Gore. So they hit upon the not very original tactic of "letting Gore be Gore."

"All we need to do is to get him to act in public like he acts in private," aide after aide would say.

It was a profoundly bad idea. Few people can act in public as they do in private. Privacy is a time to escape from our public selves. And Gore is not, at the heart of things, an outgoing, funny, relaxed man, though he could certainly be those things when he wanted to. Joe Klein put his finger on it best in a piece he wrote for *The New Yorker* in 1997. After an interview in which Gore started off as sometimes giggly, sometimes rowdy, sometimes joke-cracking, and monumentally insincere, Klein noted that Gore "seemed to be searching for the right . . . attitude to strike, something that wasn't defensive or rectitudinous; something casual." The interview finally got around to nuclear strategy, a subject that Gore said he had studied for 8 to 10 hours a week for 13 months. And then, Klein noted, Gore "changed, suddenly" and was "engaged and enthusiastic." Gore went to a white plastic blackboard and began drawing in Magic Marker a "metaphoric diagram of the meaning of fear" and, using plastic cups, he demonstrated how putting fewer warheads on more missiles would bollix the Russians. "He seemed more like the world's best Ph.D. student, attacking his orals," Klein wrote. "But there was no awkwardness about it: this was, palpably, the real Al Gore."

(Only once on the Bush plane did I see the same kind of moment. Bush was coming up the aisle, not making much eye contact because the reporters were still new to him and he was still leery of "gotcha" questions, which, in those days, was any question. But when a reporter handed him a baseball magazine and asked him about a trade in the news, Bush straightened from his usual slouch and his voice took on a firmness and certainty that I had never previously heard from him. Finally, he was on solid ground, ground upon which he could relax and be authoritative and himself.)

Which was the problem for Gore. The real Al Gore, the private Al Gore, could not be sold to the public. At first he simply did not or would not grasp this. (Who wants to be told his essential self is unpalatable?) "I am who I am," he told Diane Sawyer in June 1999. "And I'm old enough now to know that there are some things that are not—not going to change. There are a lot of things I just don't want to change. And I'm just going to be who I am. And that's— that's all I can do."

He would later change his mind about that. He would later have to. He would learn what the public really wanted. The public wanted someone who understood them, connected with them, and—this was often overlooked—needed them. Someone like Bill Clinton, who felt their pain, *was* their pain. Clinton's life was one of constant need to love and be loved, which in the modern era of television meant the constant need to communicate. "When Bill Clinton wants to relax, he'll invite 20 friends in, play some hearts, talk about books," a Gore staffer said. "When Al wants to relax, he'll go off alone somewhere with his laptop. I think he has the potential to be a great leader, a visionary; he sees things before other people do. But I worry that he tends to make intellectual rather than emotional connections with people."

Making an emotional connection with strangers—in essence what campaigning had become in America by the year 2000—is no easy thing, even though Bill Clinton made it look easy. Clinton, though, had spent his whole life perfecting the art. Clinton had been making speeches before civic groups since he was in high school. He had reached out to people emotionally since he was in grade school. His boyhood friend David Leopoulos recounted the day when a 9-year-old Clinton walked into the playground of his elementary school, stuck out his hand, fixed him with a penetrating blue-eyed stare, and said, "Hi, I'm Billy Clinton." Clinton did that when he was the new kid in the playground and then, in the following years, he did it again when others were the new kids in the playground and needed a friend. Talk about sympathy and empathy. Talk about someone running for president since he was nine. But Clinton also had that actor's ability, like Ronald Reagan, to believe utterly in what he was saying when he was saying it, to be the role he was playing. "He is like an improvisational actor," Michael Sheehan, his speech coach and a graduate of the Yale Drama School, told me. "You feel the part and you see what comes out. For me, working with Clinton is like Kazan getting to work with Brando." Bill Clinton never had to worry about appearing caring or concerned. It was a role he had immersed himself in since childhood. Maybe it was like the old, cynical joke: "The public wants sincerity?" the candidate says. "Hell, I can fake that." Or maybe, if you immerse yourself in being concerned about other people since childhood, maybe you really are concerned, maybe the repeating of it makes it genuine and second nature.

Al Gore was a serious and committed man who had to learn to be more charming and casual in public. George W. Bush was a casual and charming man who had to learn to be more serious and committed in public.

In other words, the presidential campaign was about seeing who could be Bill Clinton.

A L GORE IS ON THE FAR SIDE OF THE ROOM looking at Bill Clinton with the awe and envy that a flounder might feel for a shark. The occasion is yet another bill-signing ceremony in the Roosevelt Room of the White House, where staff members fill what look like gold-painted kitchen chairs and applaud lustily at whatever boilerplate is being mouthed. But Clinton has, as usual, transformed the moment. Draped over the lectern, his hands grasping its corners, he speaks slowly, easily, movingly, his eyes locking onto each audience member in turn, persuading them that only they and he share the planet at this wondrous moment in time. Virtually every time they shared a podium, you could see Gore studying Clinton, deconstructing him, trying to break him down into replicable bits, trying to get the rhythm of him, even going so far as to study Clinton's deft use of pauses (which Michael Sheehan attributed to Clinton's early musical training). And Gore could sometimes get it right. He actually wowed audiences on occasion. He had been trying out his raspy, guttural, "Preacher Al" voice for years, dropping it into a speech here or there. It always got good, if somewhat shocked, notices from the press. Gore was proud of it and had (like everything he did) worked and worked on it. He always remembered his first political speech when he was in his twenties and his father was running for reelection in Tennessee. They were in a black church and young Al was nervous to be facing a crowd and to be giving a political speech in a church. (He would get over this in time to visit the Buddhist temple in 1996.) So, being Al, he got up and gave this dense, but perfectly reasoned, speech about the separation of church and state in America. When it was over, the congregation sat in stunned silence until the preacher got up and shouted, "What the boy means is: Vote for his daddy!"

Gore worked on his speaking style and tried to hit a rhythm that reminded him of the preaching he had heard in black churches. He used it sparingly, but not sparingly enough to suit Bill Clinton. Gore's mistake came when he tried out Preacher Al with Clinton at his side. Because whenever Clinton heard Gore become less Gore-like (and more Clinton-like), Clinton always did the same thing: He put Gore down to the crowd. At least that was the way Gore viewed it.

Take Cleveland on election eve 1996. It was the last joint campaign appearance for Gore and Clinton. Elizabeth Shogren of the *Los Angeles Times* wrote about how "President Clinton watched with slack-jawed amazement as Vice President Al Gore delivered an animated, rapid-fire introduction that filled the field house at Cleveland State University with chortles and applause."

When Gore had finished and Clinton got up to speak, he said: "I do not know what the vice president ate for breakfast this morning, but if he had two more bites of it, he would have blown the roof off."

At the end of January in 1998, a few days after the Monica Lewinsky story broke and the day after Clinton ignored the scandal in his famous "save Social Security first" State of the Union speech,

Clinton and Gore ventured outside Washington and before a crowd of real people for the first time. The White House did not know what to expect. The advance work had been good—crowds don't just happen; crowds are created—but the crowd that showed up at the University of Illinois in Champaign was enormous. Some 12,000 people filled every seat in the cavernous flying-saucer-shaped Assembly Hall and 8,500 more were stuffed into two overflow locations. "It's like Elvis," one senior White House official said, gazing in awe at the seemingly endless line of students and other citizens snaking back and forth in front of the building where they had been waiting several hours to get in. Of even greater interest to the White House was the lack of protest signs. Americans were supposed to be furious over allegations that the president had sex with a young intern and urged her to lie about it. But except for one man who positioned himself on Clinton's motorcade route and carried a large sign that said "Repent," there was virtually no protest to be seen. (When later that day, Clinton got to La Crosse, Wisconsin, the only protest was the word "Impeach" that someone had stamped out in the snow on the west bank of the Mississippi River.)

I was covering the White House for the *Chicago Tribune* then and I noted in my story for the next day that "The only unexpected thing to happen to Clinton at the Assembly Hall was that his speech was overshadowed by that of Vice President Al Gore." Gore did Preacher Al, this time pumping his left fist into the air and dropping his "g's" (which he usually did only in the South), saying: "I'm tellin' you, we're movin' in the right direction! He is the president of the country! He is also my friend! And I want to ask you now, every single one of you, to join me in supportin' him! And standin' by his side!" There was enormous cheering and applauding and whistling, and when Clinton took to the lectern, he said: "When he really got going, I wish I had people walking down the aisle passing the plate. It was amazing. . . . I can't do as well as the vice president—he must have gotten 30 more minutes' sleep than I did last night."

A year later after another State of the Union speech, a crowd of 22,000 in Buffalo braved more than four feet of snow and sub-freezing temperatures to hear Bill and Hillary (the first handmade "Hillary for NY Senator" signs appeared in the crowd) and Al and Tipper speak. Gore did Preacher Al again. "We've got the LEAD-er-ship! Last night we were given the ag-EN-da! We have the VIS-ion," he rasped. "When anybody brings about as much POS-i-tive change in such a short period of time as President Bill Clinton has brought, it's bound to dis-com-BOB-u-late some people! It's bound to SHAKE them up."

And when Clinton marched up to the microphone, he turned in Gore's direction and said, "I think you got so excited that you melted the snow for a mile around this arena." Then, turning to the crowd, Clinton said, "Let me ask you, have you ever seen the vice president so fired up in your life? I want you to know that just before we came in here, we went off into a little room and he had a quick hit of buffalo wings and Flutie flakes, that's what he did!"

Everyone assumed such exchanges were light humor and a sign of mutual admiration. Everyone was wrong. Gore saw them as a sign of what he called Clinton's "competitive nature" and Clinton's inability to admit that Gore could possibly be a good speaker without doing something extraordinary (like getting extra sleep or eating "Flutie flakes," a cereal named for Doug Flutie, quarterback of the Buffalo Bills). And though Clinton realized on an intellectual level that some day Gore would have to step out from Clinton's shadow to run for president, on an emotional level Clinton couldn't help putting off that day. And when you got right down to it, they had always been rivals as much as friends. Though Clinton was 19 months older, Gore saw little reason to feel like Clinton's junior. In 1988, when Clinton was cooling his heels in Little Rock as governor of Arkansas and worrying if bimbo eruptions would always keep him from the presidency, Gore was running for president at age 39. (It was a disaster of a campaign. Mario Cuomo denounced Gore's slash-and-burn attacks on his fellow Democrats as "terribly dangerous.") Clinton and Gore did have several similarities: they came from bordering states, were of the same religion, and both in the center of their party. Gore was a man who was running for president in part because he needed to be loved by his parents; Clinton was a man who was running for president in part because he needed to be loved by everybody.

But Clinton noticed the little things like newspapers saying Gore had overshadowed him, and in January 1997 Dan Balz of the *Washington Post* reported that Clinton had been overheard to complain about Gore's "puffy profiles" in the newspapers. Balz also quoted a senior administration official saying, "There's a little whiff of competition between the two." When Clinton chose Gore as his vice president, Clinton liked Gore's seriousness and substance and expertise, but he also had to make the secret assessment that all first-time presidential candidates make but never talk about: If I lose this time, will I have elevated my running mate so high that he will challenge me in four years? Clinton decided Gore would never challenge him.

To outsiders, the rivalry seemed trivial and silly, especially considering how much Gore had done for Clinton and Clinton had done for Gore. But it would have a profound effect on Gore's presidential campaign in 2000 and how much he would call upon Clinton for help. And the tensions between the two men ran deeper than any but a small group in the White House inner circle knew.

. . .

THE DAY AFTER THE 1996 FUNDRAISING SCANDAL broke in March 1997, White House spokesman Mike McCurry was fielding questions in the White House briefing room about the story when Al Gore made the decision to go and confront the press himself. All his advisers, Gore admitted later, told him not to. But Karenna reportedly pressed him to do it. Her father was an honest, good, and decent man, and surely the reporters would see that. Karenna had a lot to learn.

Gore faced the White House press corps, holding one hand over his heart and gripping the lectern with the other. Then as if he were holding up a cross in front of vampires, Gore told reporters seven times that his lawyer had informed him that "no controlling legal authority" said any of his telephone activities violated the law, though he would never do it again. Even before it ended, Gore knew that his performance had been a debacle, but it was the last question that really rocked him. A reporter asked if he had been aware that President Clinton had refused to make the phone calls that Gore had been making.

"No, I was not," Gore said.

Now Gore knew why God had made vice presidents: to take the fall for presidents who were too smart to take falls themselves. Gore knew he had a lot to learn from Bill Clinton, and he learned even more when Clinton had his own news conference a few days later. The differing responses of the two men were not only instructive, but also critical to understanding them.

At his March 3 news conference, Gore had said: "I also made phone calls to ask people to host events and to ask people to make lawful contributions to the campaign. On a few occasions, I made some telephone calls, from my office in the White House, using a DNC credit card. I was advised there was nothing wrong with that practice."

Four days later, at his own news conference, Clinton was asked about the phone calls. His answer was a little different than Gore's:

"I can't say over all the hundreds and hundreds and maybe thousands of phone calls I've made in the last four years that I never said to anybody while I was talking to them, 'Well, we need your help or I hope you'll help us,'" Clinton said.

"I simply can't say that I've never done it. But it's not what I like to do and it wasn't a practice of mine. And once I remember in particular I was asked to do it, and I just never got around to doing it.

"I don't want to flat-out say I never did something that I might, in fact, have done just because I don't remember it."

Which is one difference between a flounder and a shark.

Essentially, however, Clinton and Gore shared the belief that making calls to people whose giant corporations depended on the government for this regulation or that law was just fine. Deep down, they both believed in the prevailing rule of politics known as the Staszek Rule: Joe Staszek was a Baltimore tavern owner and state senator who assiduously sponsored legislation that would help the liquor business. When asked if that constituted a conflict of interest, Staszek replied: "How does this conflict with my interest?"


GORE ALWAYS SAID THE MOST IMPORTANT LESSON he learned from Clinton was "Never give up!" But it became abundantly clear to Gore from early on that to Clinton never giving up had a special meaning: It meant never stop lying. Perhaps Clinton's greatest political gift was to know when to confess and when to keep silent, when to bare his soul and when to hide the truth. Perfectly in touch with the temperament of his times, Clinton has always known what his fellow citizens would admire and how much they would tolerate.

His career rarely had been free of accusations of sexual misconduct, but through a combination of public confession, obfuscation, and denial, he managed to emerge as the dominant figure in American political life, so dominant that by the time he left office, there was really nobody in second place.

To Bill Clinton, everything, including the English language, was negotiable. The past did catch up with him, time and time again, but it seemed to do him no harm. When Clinton ran for president in 1992 and was asked several times if he ever had used drugs as a youth, he replied, "I never broke the laws of my country." Reporters took that to be a blanket denial. What they found out later, however, was that Clinton had tried marijuana while attending Oxford University in England. Some reporters did ask Clinton why he had not answered a simple question with the simple truth. But that was before reporters really knew him. "That's not the specific question I've been asked in the past," Clinton said. "If anybody had asked the question, I'd have answered it." Running for president in the crucial New Hampshire primary, Clinton's draft history came up. He was of draft age during the Vietnam War and some wondered how Clinton had finished college, gone off to Oxford and never been called up for the draft. "I wound up just going through the lottery, and it was just a pure fluke that I was never called," Clinton told the *Washington Post*. But reporters later discovered that Clinton had in fact been called, he had been sent an induction notice in April 1969. So had he lied to the *Post* about never being called up? No, Clinton said. He didn't think getting an induction notice was the same thing as being called up for the draft, because "it just never occurred to me to make anything of it one way or the other, since it was a routine matter."

Millions of American males who had lived through the Vietnam era knew that getting an induction notice in 1969 was not "routine." It was a life-changing—and to some a life-ending—experience. But not to Bill Clinton.

Then there was the case of Gennifer Flowers, who said she had a 12-year affair with Clinton. Clinton, appearing in a televised forum stage-managed by his TV producer friend Harry Thomason during the New Hampshire primary in 1992, said, "The affair did not happen." A few days later, appearing on "60 Minutes," Clinton said Flowers was just a "friendly acquaintance."

Interviewer Steve Kroft said, "I'm assuming from your answer that you're categorically denying that you ever had an affair with Gennifer Flowers?"

"I said that before," Clinton said. "And so has she."

"You feel like you've leveled with the American people?" Kroft asked.

"I have absolutely leveled with the American people," Clinton replied.

Six years later, on January 17, 1998, Clinton admitted in a sworn deposition in the Paula Jones sexual harassment suit that he had sex with Gennifer Flowers on one occasion. So was he lying to the American people at a crucial time in his 1992 election campaign?

A reporter asked White House spokesman Mike McCurry, "Mike, why should the American people believe the president's denial with regard to this [the Monica Lewinsky accusations] when in 1992 he told us that he did not have an affair with Gennifer Flowers and apparently has now testified under oath that he did?"

McCurry gave the official response, one that had been carefully crafted earlier that day: "The president knows that he told the truth in 1992 when he was asked about that relationship, and he knows that he testified truthfully on Saturday, and he knows his answers are not at odds."

The press persisted. "Mike, you're saying there was no affair with Gennifer Flowers?" a reporter asked.

"I just gave the answer that I gave," McCurry said.

After the public briefing was over, reporters were privately told what Clinton meant in 1992: He did not have an "affair" with Flowers, because he had had sex with her on only one occasion. (Though that, in itself, seemed quite likely to be another lie.) Whether sex on one occasion is the definition of a "friendly acquaintance" and whether Clinton was "leveling with the American people," as he told Steve Kroft, seemed very much in the eye and ear of the beholder.

McCurry later went to Harvard University's John F. Kennedy School of Government to appear at a seminar. After he made a presentation and had answered several questions, one student asked: "How do you reconcile Gennifer Flowers?"

"I would never attempt to do anything with Gennifer Flowers," McCurry replied.

There was laughter and there was applause, and nobody asked another question.

A T THE BEGINNING OF 1998, AFTER THE MONICA Lewinsky scandal broke, Clinton's job approval ratings were in the 70s, the highest numbers in polling history for a second-term president. His chief accuser, independent counsel Kenneth Starr, had an approval rating of 12 percent.

If Bill Clinton had a working theory about these things it could be summed up in three words: deny, deny, deny. In a telephone conversation with Flowers, Clinton was taped telling her, "If everybody's on record denying it, you've got no problem," and "They can't run a story like this unless somebody said, 'Yeah, I did it with him.'"

Lewinsky said Clinton had told her, "There is no evidence, so you can deny, deny, deny," and "If there are two people in a room and something happens and they both deny it, there is no way to prove it."

And then, of course, there was the famous Roosevelt Room appearance when, with Hillary and Gore standing behind him, Clinton wagged his finger at America—the finger wag had been stage-managed once again by Harry Thomason—and said: "I want to say one thing to the American people. I want you to listen to me. I'm going to say this again. I did not have sexual relations with that woman, Miss Lewinsky."

So what was the nation, what was Al Gore, to believe? Gore knew four things: One, Clinton was a twister of truth—you only had to look at what he said about his draft history to see that.

Two, Gore also knew that Clinton would cling to the most strained legalisms and outrageous definitions to maintain that he was at least technically a truth teller. Clinton stalwart James Carville even had a joke about it: A man appears in court and is ordered to swear to tell "the truth, the whole truth and nothing but the truth."

"Judge," the man says, "which one do you want?"

Three, Gore also knew that Clinton's first tactic was always to deny, deny, deny. So what was Gore to believe when Clinton addressed his statement directly to the American people and denied having had sex with Lewinsky? And what was Gore to believe when Clinton put his arm around him outside the Oval Office and assured him personally that the story simply was not true?

Four, Clinton did have enemies, and these enemies were not above spreading the most vicious lies about him in an attempt to bring him down. It was like Hillary said: There was "a vast right-wing conspiracy" out to get Clinton. (Even the White House admitted that Clinton engendered deep negative feelings among people, deeper than past presidents. As Mike McCurry said to me, "One-third of the American people have a deep, visceral dislike for this president.") Sitting in a train station in Baltimore, waiting to return to Washington after giving a speech on the day after the Lewinsky story broke, Hillary said of the new allegations: "Certainly, I believe they're false. Absolutely. It's difficult and painful any time someone you care about, you love, you admire, is attacked and subjected to such relentless accusations as my husband has been." She went on to say "there has been a concerted effort to undermine his legitimacy as president, to undermine much of what he has been able to accomplish, to attack him personally when he could not be defeated politically." She concluded confidently: "He'll deal with it and continue to fulfill his responsibilities as president."

She clearly believed him. So why shouldn't Al? Still, the Lewinsky accusations disturbed Gore on a deeper level, especially since in the beginning few knew that Monica had been other than a blushing, innocent victim seduced by an older man who was technically her boss. Gore's reaction was that of a father, a father who had three daughters, aged 24, 20, and 19 and who could imagine the rage he would feel if some supervisor had tried that with any of his girls.

It was just easier for Gore to believe it had never happened, that Clinton was, this time, telling the truth. And Clinton had assembled the Cabinet on January 23 and told them the accusations were untrue. "There was no sex of any kind. I told the truth. There is nothing to worry about," Clinton told his Cabinet, blinking back tears, biting his lower lip. "I'll be fine and you will be, too, and let's all hang in there." Then he went on and asked each in turn about highly specific matters concerning their departments and what they thought should be included in the upcoming State of the Union speech. He seemed not the least bit distracted.

It was the performance of a lifetime.

"He went into a 45- or 50-minute Cabinet meeting dealing with very detailed stuff," Bill Daley, his commerce secretary, told me later. "And I sat there looking at him thinking, 'The story mustn't be true, because nobody could do this.' You know, just smiling and laughing, and he had all this detail. I forget what the subjects were. But it was remarkable."

Afterwards, four Cabinet members walked out of the West Wing into a chill rain to tell America that they believed their president when he said it was all a lie.

"I think what he thinks. . . . I absolutely do," Education Secretary Richard Riley said.

"I believe that the allegations are completely untrue," Secretary of State Madeleine Albright asserted.

"I'll second that, definitely," echoed Daley.

"Third it," chimed in Health and Human Services Secretary Donna Shalala.

Later, they all felt like asses.

# 8

# EXEMPLAR

BILL CLINTON'S TACTIC OF DENY, DENY, deny looked as if it were going to work just fine in the Lewinsky scandal—it was the word of the president against the word of an obviously ditzy young woman—until the little blue dress brought reality into the picture.

In the White House, the staff was divided between those who were merely disappointed that Clinton had lied to their faces and those who were appalled by it. Nobody had been a bigger supporter of Clinton than Al Gore. He had gone out of his way to praise him, out of his way to stand by his side, out of his way to be loyal. This had earned Gore exactly nothing. Clinton had lied to him just as he had lied to everybody else. But now Gore had a new concern, one that he never talked about in public and almost never talked about in private: What if Clinton really were removed from office for perjury and obstruction of justice? The Republicans certainly had the votes to impeach him in the House, but could they really muster two-thirds in the Senate? It seemed highly unlikely, but now, with Clinton's admission, nobody knew what was going to happen, nobody knew how the public was going to take this. And Gore, a methodical man to say the least, started doing what he did best: He planned. Not plotted, he insisted to himself, but planned. He had to prepare for the day—a day he did not want to see come—when Clinton was removed from office and Al Gore became president. The first thing he had to do, Gore decided, was pick a vice president, and he knew whom he was going to pick. Every passing week confirmed his choice: He wanted a man of honor and decency, a man whose political beliefs were close to his own, a devout man whose private life could not be questioned, a man who yielded not to the temptations of the flesh, but to the power of a higher being and without embarrassment could quote the Bible as well as Al Gore could. He also wanted a man who told the frigging truth for a change. It would become his deepest secret, but way back in 1998, Al Gore decided that if Clinton were removed or resigned and Gore became president, he wanted Joe Lieberman as his vice president. In other words, he wanted a Jewish Al Gore.

Joe Lieberman had been typing a speech into his laptop for several days. He had started it after Clinton had called him as part of an "outreach" to key Senate Democrats who could either save Clinton or hang him if the House impeached him. Although his aides had hoped Clinton would use the phone calls to apologize, Clinton instead used them to portray himself as the victim of evil, right-wing forces. Lieberman thought the president's behavior had been reprehensible and now intended to say so on the floor of the Senate. Word of this leaked out, and Clinton's chief of staff, Erskine Bowles, called Lieberman and begged him to hold off until Clinton returned from a trip to Russia and Ireland so that Clinton would not be embarrassed in front of world leaders. Lieberman agreed to wait at least until Clinton left Moscow, but when he saw Clinton's news conference with Boris Yeltsin and Clinton's refusal, once again, to forthrightly apologize for his affair, Lieberman decided to let him have it. He was no longer sure that Clinton was capable of being embarrassed.

* * *

LIEBERMAN STOOD IN A MOSTLY EMPTY SENATE chamber and called Clinton's behavior "disgraceful" and "sordid." Lieberman, a longtime friend and political ally of Clinton, said that contrary to the president's brief national address after his grand jury appearance, this was not a private matter solely between him and his family. And he said Clinton's deceptions were not just a "reflexive" attempt to protect himself and his family, but "intentional and premeditated." Then he hit his central theme: The president was supposed to hold himself—and be held—to a higher standard of behavior than ordinary citizens.

"We all fall short of the standards our best values set for us. Certainly I do," Lieberman said. "But the president, by virtue of the office he sought and was elected to, has traditionally been held to a higher standard." Then he quoted presidential scholar James David Barber, who wrote: "The president is expected to personify our betterness in an inspiring way, to express in what he does and is, not just what he says, a moral idealism which, in much of the public mind, is the very opposite of politics."

Clinton learned of Lieberman's speech when he woke up in Dublin the next morning. His first public event was a photo opportunity with Irish prime minister Bertie Ahern. And in Ahern's elegant, wood-paneled office filled with red upholstered armchairs, a towering oil portrait of Irish patriot Eamon de Valera, and a bust of John Fitzgerald Kennedy, Clinton said he had no problem with Lieberman's castigation. "Basically I agree with what he said," Clinton said. "I can't disagree with anyone else who wants to be critical of what I have already acknowledged was indefensible. I've already said that I made a bad mistake, it was indefensible, and I'm very sorry about it."

. . .

THERE WOULD BE ONLY TWO CABINET MEETINGS
in 1998, the one on January 23, in which Clinton lied to his
Cabinet, and the one on September 10, in which he was supposed
to make everything all right. Instead of using the Cabinet Room
in the West Wing, this time Clinton assembled the Cabinet in the
private residence portion of the White House, in the Yellow Oval
Room, just behind the Truman Balcony. Clinton sat in front of the
fireplace; Gore arrived late. Clinton quoted the Bible and thanked
the Cabinet members for their support, saying he realized he had
put them in a difficult position. "It's more important to be a good
person than a good president," he said. "And I'm going to spend the
rest of my life trying to atone for this." Everybody was there except
Bill Daley. Daley had a speaking engagement in New Hampshire.
He could have canceled it, but Daley didn't want to go to the Cabinet meeting. After it was over, Daley called Bowles and said: "Look,
I'm glad I didn't go. I don't quote scripture, I don't cry, I don't hug.
What would I have done at this thing?"

PEOPLE ARE PRAGMATIC, NOT IDEALISTIC," WHITE
House spokesman Mike McCurry told me. "Our judgment of
what is exemplary has changed. People want someone who will get
the job done. They want someone who will protect a strong economy and a strong country."

From the very first decades of the American republic, presidents
have struggled with a dual role—to be a moral exemplar who
stands above ordinary citizens and to be a man of the people. Few
presidents had done a better job in the latter role than Clinton.

In the eldest bracket of the Baby Boomers, he came of age in an era when the birth control pill was readily available but AIDS was not even on the horizon. He entered middle age in an era when popular television sitcoms make sex an open joke. It wasn't just new standards of sexual tolerance and openness that Clinton grasped and benefited from. He also understood that as Boomers aged and started families, they wanted safer streets and better schools for their kids, better health care for themselves, and someone to make sure Social Security would still be there when they were old enough to collect it. Sexual morality? Well, that was pretty far down on their lists.

"He has turned the country around economically and socially," senior White House aide Doug Sosnik said. "He is the only person on the political scene who is defining in positive, future-oriented terms where he wants to lead the country. The Republicans are not even close. They are not even on the field when it comes to ideas."

But what about the traditional role of president as moral exemplar? Most Americans, seemingly, had made a split decision. Most citizens, at least if the polls were to be believed, were saying a president could descend from the moral pedestal as long as he got the job of the presidency done. The presidency was no longer about values, but about policy. Clinton might be a sleazebag, but he was a sleazebag when the Dow Jones Industrial Average was booming and wealth was increasing dramatically. Maybe the presidency really wasn't about character. Maybe presidents could have reprehensible private lives as long as they had laudable public ones.

There was something more. The sinner was easier to love than the saint. The sinner we could understand—all our flesh is weak, after all—but the saint arouses our suspicions. The saint pretends to be better than us, but the saint, we feel, is hiding something. Michael

Kinsley, writing in *Time* on April 29, 1996, had said: "In every presidential election from 1968 to 1988, the Democrats nominated a goody-goody (Hubert Humphrey, George McGovern, Jimmy Carter, Walter Mondale, Michael Dukakis). And they lost every election during those decades except 1976, when the Republicans also nominated a good-goody (Gerald Ford)." But in 1992, Democrats nominated a "slippery politician" who "is also morally flawed," Kinsley wrote. And they found a winner.

AL GORE WAS DEFINITELY A GOODY-GOODY. AN impatient goody-goody. At 28 he was a congressman, at 36 a senator, at 44 the vice president. (Which seemed uniquely impressive until you considered Dan Quayle's career: At 29 a congressman, at 33 a senator, at 41 the vice president.) The last time Gore had to wait for something, he didn't like it. It was 1970. He had just graduated from Harvard and faced the draft. Al Gore Jr. was opposed to the Vietnam War, as was his father, Al Gore Sr., a senator from Tennessee locked in a brutal reelection campaign. And though his mother offered to go to Canada with him, young Al decided to enlist and fight in a war in which he did not believe in order to serve his father's political career (as well as his own). After his induction, he donned a uniform and cut a TV commercial with his father, one in which his father said, "Son, always love your country." And then young Al waited, but his orders for Vietnam did not come. His family blamed it all on Richard Nixon, who, they believed, did not want Al Jr. to become a live hero or a dead martyr. "All I know is I was not allowed to go until the first departure date after the November election," Gore said later. By then, his father had lost. But in his future campaign pamphlets, Al Jr. was able to use pictures of himself in uniform and carrying a rifle—though, oddly, in his 1988 presidential campaign pamphlet, the rifle butt is planted on the ground and Gore seems to be very unwisely staring down into the barrel. Which was another wonderful comparison of the flounder and the shark: Gore was faced with a tough choice and chose risking his own life at least partly in order to advance his political career. But Bill Clinton, the shark, didn't bother making such a choice: He dodged the draft and *still* advanced his political career. Leave the agonizing calculations to the flounders of the world. The shark moves forward! Breathe! Move! Win!

But Al Gore was no force of nature. He was no natural at all. When he was in Congress and used to play basketball with the other lawmakers, he was observed late one night all alone, flat on his back on the gym floor throwing the ball over his head toward the hoop again and again. Al Gore knew a cool trick shot would make him look fun and loose and impulsive. Which is why he practiced it for hours. Now, he was practicing being Al Gore, practicing him over and over again until he could make him look spontaneous.

Until the 1996 campaign Gore had an almost unblemished record of personal rectitude. Sure, he would exaggerate a little, but nobody made a big deal out of it, not on a national level, anyway. In 1987, Gore told the *Des Moines Register* that an investigative series he did as a reporter for the *Nashville Tennessean* "got a bunch of people indicted and sent to jail." In reality only two men were indicted. One was acquitted and one was convicted, but his three-year prison sentence was later suspended. So big deal.

Gore's misrepresentations about his infamous visit to the Buddhist temple and the fundraising calls he had made from his office were more serious missteps. But Gore was not overly worried. Look at the massive lying Clinton had done and gotten away with. At every step, Clinton had twisted, massaged, and mangled the truth, and the American people had elected him, reelected him, and given him high approval ratings. So how big a deal could they make out of Gore's misstatements?

Quite a lot, as it turned out. Once he began running for president, even his mildest exaggerations of the past—that he and Tipper were the model for *Love Story*—and even his obvious jokes—his mother had sung "Look for the Union Label" to him as a child—were treated as the deadliest, darkest, and most foul of lies. On October 11, 2000, William Bennett began a commentary in the *Wall Street Journal:* "Albert Arnold Gore Jr. is a habitual liar . . . The vice president lies reflexively, promiscuously, even pathologically."

The sheer unfairness of it wounded Gore to the quick. He realized something odd was going on here. You could try to be like Bill, but nobody was going to get treated like Bill. And Gore was not the only one who was worried. In September of 1998, after Clinton admitted the Lewinsky relationship to a grand jury and the American people, George W. Bush told the *Austin American-Statesman* that he was so downcast by all the personal scandal reporting that he was wondering if he still wanted to run for president. "This has been a very depressing time for me," Bush said and then decried the "bubble" of constant scrutiny that candidates had to live in. "I think running for president is a commitment to the bubble, and I've got to make up my mind at the right time if that's what I want to do. Is this something I want to put my family through?"

BARBRA STREISAND MAY HAVE PUT IT BEST WHEN she spoke about Bill Clinton and the remarkable resilience of his appeal. Standing behind a microphone set up on a lawn at an October 24, 1998, Democratic fundraiser (on a Beverly Hills estate so large that guests were ferried from their cars to the main house in golf carts that resembled miniature Cadillacs), the singer and longtime Clinton supporter threw a diamond-draped arm in his direction and said in a strong, clear voice: "Lo and behold this weakened president, this president who is unable to govern!"

The audience giggled nervously. Clinton was weakened, was he not? Weakened as almost no other president had been in this century. After all, an independent counsel, a former judge, had carefully laid out his case as to why Clinton should be impeached and in a few weeks Clinton's fate could be decided by the most divided and partisan committee in Congress, the House Judiciary Committee: 21 Republicans (all white; all male except for Mary Bono, who got there through the death of her husband; all Christian; and nearly half from the South) outnumbering 15 Democrats (five African Americans, three women, six Jews and a self-avowed homosexual and geographically skewed to the Northeast). A simple majority vote by that committee followed by a simple majority vote in the Republican-dominated House was all it would take to impeach Clinton and send him to trial in the Senate.

"Weakened?" "Unable to govern?" That should have been putting it mildly. Except . . . except that it wasn't. Streisand, reflecting the same sentiments as Joan Didion, writing in *The New York Review* two days earlier, had hit on a simple truth, one constantly overlooked by the talking-heads and the elite who lived in the echo chamber that is Washington, D.C.: Bill Clinton had, in fact, never had more support.

"Lo and behold this weakened president, this president who is unable to govern, who has strong-armed the Republican Congress and wrestled them to the ground," Streisand said to the $10,000-a-plate guests sitting at little white tables under a starry sky. And it was true. Rather than risk being blamed for another government shutdown, the Republicans had given Clinton virtually everything he wanted in his new budget. "They were out to get him from Day

One," Streisand continued, "with partisan attacks that observe no limits of decency or even legality. But guess what? The ... people ... are ... too ... smart! The president's job approval rating is 65 percent! They have elected Bill Clinton twice to be their president, not to be their pope! A president's private life historically has never affected his ability to lead! We must stop this attempted coup on our government!"

She brought down the house. It was not exactly as if Streisand was unused to bringing down houses, but even she was momentarily stunned by the response. The audience was up on its feet applauding madly, shouting, defending the judgment of the "people" (with whom they had as little contact as the power brokers in Washington) and there was Clinton, on his feet, too, beating his beefy hands together, mouthing, "Thang-kyew, Barbra, thang-kyew" above the din. Who could deny the truth? In the face of a mountain of damning evidence, Bill Clinton had never been stronger.

And he had never been stronger because no president in modern times—perhaps no president ever—had been in such close touch with the ethos, the rhythms, the feelings of his time. Let the power elite blame the public for not caring enough about perjury, abuse of power, and sin. Let them try, in Didion's words, to make the public "the unindicted co-conspirator" in the Lewinsky saga. The public knew (or thought they knew) Bill Clinton and what they knew of him they liked, when it came to running the country, anyway.

Clinton's response was fumbling at first, but then he found his groove, the perfect message for America's twelve-step culture: His "sin," for which he now had "atoned," had made him "stronger," and he encouraged other couples in America to talk more openly. In fact, when you got right down to it, he had done America a favor.

• • •

A T THE SAME MOMENT ON THE AFTERNOON OF
December 19 that the House of Representatives was voting
the first article of impeachment against Clinton, a Saturday afternoon, Clinton was in the Oval Office talking with one of his spiri-
tual advisers, the Reverend Tony Campolo, a Baptist pastor from
Pennsylvania. Earlier, the two had prayed together. Clinton's new
chief of staff, John Podesta, and top aide Doug Sosnik entered the
Oval Office and told the president that he had just been impeached.

With Campolo exiting, the president, Podesta, and Sosnik moved
into the small study next to the Oval Office, where Clinton had had
encounters with Monica Lewinsky. They watched the next three votes
on television. As the last article was being voted on, Gore arrived.
"It's not fair what they've done to you," the vice president said.

Outside the White House, a small band of highly organized protesters put down their "Impeach" signs and picked up signs that
said "Resign."

"I think the results of a meteor strike are more likely than the
resignation of the president," Gore said later in the day. "He is just
not going to do that."

Heavenly objects seemed to be the theme of the day. "I'm just
waiting for the asteroid to hit," a dejected White House aide said.
"And then maybe the meteors."

There was a chill in the air and the sky was low and gray as reporters assembled on the South Lawn. Like everything else at the
White House, the event had been heavily stage-managed. Buses and
cars had brought 101 Democratic members of Congress to the White
House, and now they arrayed themselves on the lawn, behind where
the president would speak.

At 4:06 P.M., Clinton and Hillary walked out of the Oval Office and onto the lawn. They were holding hands. The press corps did not know it at the time, but Hillary had not been scheduled to show up at the event. She did it on her own, her way of saying that the punishment of her husband had gone too far.

Gore and Dick Gephardt walked out behind them. Gephardt spoke first. "We've just witnessed a partisan vote that was a disgrace to our country and our Constitution," he said. "Despite the worst efforts of the Republican leadership in the House, the Constitution will bear up under the strain, our nation will survive."

Gore spoke next. "I do believe this is the saddest day I have seen in our nation's capital because today's vote in the House of Representatives disregarded the plain wishes and goodwill of the American people," he said.

Clinton looked on impassively as Hillary nodded.

"What happened as a result does a great disservice to a man I believe will be regarded in the history books as one of our greatest presidents," Gore said.

Gore aides winced. That was so Al. He was so competitive. He needed to outdo Gephardt and get a gold star from the teacher, and so he went too far and called Clinton one of our great presidents. The president might be grateful to him, but so what? Gore needed to get out of Clinton's shadow, not firmly plant his lips on Clinton's fanny. No, it was a bad moment, they agreed. A moment that was going to hurt them in the presidential campaign.

SOME THINGS WERE CLEAR: BILL CLINTON HAD, IF only incrementally, changed the face of politics in America, the way candidates had to run, the way they had to get elected. Connection, likability, authenticity (real or imagined), call it what you wanted, now had to be there. George W. Bush recognized it first. In an article in the *New York Times* on May 23, 1999, reporter Rick Berke described Bush as having "the raffish charm of Bill Clinton" and said he made the case "for a President who connects with voters."

"People want to know you care," Bush said. "People want to know you relate. People know if you're uncomfortable around them. People know if you don't like them. People are smart."

But something else had changed, too. Nobody was going to catch the breaks Clinton caught. Nobody was going to get the same slack. Fool me once, the public was saying, shame on you. Fool me twice, shame on me.

Clinton himself had a very clear idea of what he meant to America.

"If I could have run again," he told Dan Rather on December 19, 2000, "I'd have done fine."

# 9

# USE AND LOSE

"VOTING AGAINST GORE WAS THE
LAST WAY OF GETTING CLINTON."

—Bill Daley to author,
December 27, 2000

I T IS TWO DAYS BEFORE THE DEMOCRATIC
National Convention, two days before Bill Clinton is to make
his farewell address to the party faithful, and Bill Daley still
has not seen the speech. Clinton knows that he is supposed to submit the speech so Al Gore's people can vet it, look it over, make
sure it doesn't duplicate the vice president's speech and make sure
everybody is on the same page of the hymnal. That is the way it is
done. Clinton knows this. And you can bet everybody had to do it
for Clinton's two conventions in 1992 and 1996. But he still hasn't
done it. And he doesn't intend to. Why? *Because Elvis has not left
the building, that's why!*

He is still the president, and Al Gore is still just the vice president, and Clinton intends to treat him that way. It is petty, silly, nar-
cissistic. It is Clinton. Two years earlier, when Gore stepped up to
the plate and vigorously defended Clinton during the Lewinsky disaster, Clinton press secretary Mike McCurry said, "Gore went out of
his way to defend the president. And the president was incredibly
grateful. I sense increasingly that Clinton is willing to take a half-
step sideways and let Gore step into the spotlight."

Sure. You bet. There has never been a soul in American politics
less likely to step out of the spotlight than Bill Clinton. It would

take a very large hook to drag him out of the spotlight. During the 2000 Democratic convention—Al Gore's convention—Clinton has 24 events scheduled and Hillary has 28. Clinton is not taking half-, quarter- or even eensy-weensy steps to get out of the spotlight. "Why won't he give it up?" says Bill Daley. "He won't give it up because he won't give it up. This is all he's ever done. Why wouldn't he keep doing it?"

IN HIS NEARLY EIGHT YEARS IN OFFICE, BILL Clinton visited California many more times than Ronald Reagan did as president—and Reagan's house was there. To Clinton, California in general and Hollywood in specific is the home he always wanted: glamorous, glitzy, fun. He was a movie buff as a kid and he has admitted to a kind of unabashed joy in meeting movie and entertainment stars. And the stars like him. So it was only natural that they would throw a "Hollywood Tribute to William Jefferson Clinton" when he came out for the convention.

About 1,400 people, each paying $1,000—that's $1.4 million, which will go to Hillary Clinton's Senate campaign—sat in green and beige directors chairs on the lawn of the Brentwood estate of radio mogul Ken Roberts. There was a live orchestra and a stage and huge TV screen set up. Clinton, Hillary, and Chelsea sat in the audience, surrounded by the stars, who ranged from Milton Berle to Rob Reiner to Brad Pitt and his new bride, Jennifer Aniston. Pop culture icon Stan Lee, who invented Spider-Man, began the tribute to Clinton by saying: "I'm a guy who's dealt with superheroes most of my life, and you, sir, have great potential. I think if you would learn to climb the side of buildings and wear Spandex tights, I think I could make you famous."

Over the next two hours, praise for Clinton builds up in great heaps. "You and I will forever be linked historically, because it was after your first inauguration that I decided to come out publicly," Melissa Etheridge says. "I just want to say thank you so very much for inviting us into the house and to the table and we'll never, ever have to go back into the closet again." She then sings a song with words that go "Come to my window, I'll be home soon," and Clinton can be seen wiping away tears.

She is followed by actress Alfre Woodard, who says: "May you take your new freedom of movement and speech to cry foul, to save lives, and to get the barbecue sauce all over your face. And to dance." Cher says: "I have a confession to make. Sir, I didn't vote for you. But if you were running again, which I wish you were, I would vote for you." John Travolta says: "If I were hungry, you'd sit right down and eat a cheeseburger with me, not even suggesting holding the fries. And if we were playing golf and you were better than me, you'd let me win. . . . We will miss you." Whoopi Goldberg says: "You kicked ass and even when they tried to kick yours back you stood up and you didn't falter. . . . The last eight years have been a great gas. You're not going anywhere. You're going to be here."

But Shirley MacLaine says it best of all: "You are a mirror for all of us."

It was an interesting notion that people look at Clinton and see themselves. Maybe this is where his ability to connect comes from. Actors certainly connect with him. They know a kindred spirit when they see one. Clinton gets up to speak and says, "Franklin Roosevelt once said it was necessary for the president to be America's greatest actor. When I read that, I had no clue what he meant. Now I understand that all too well."

TV producer Harry Thomason, Clinton's Arkansas buddy, knows all about the affinity. "TV shows and movies and political events are *all the same*," he once told me. "They are all designed to move people. People in Washington try to make politics some sort of deep secret, like a Masonic handshake. It's not."

B ILL DALEY SHOULD BE THE PERFECT MIDDLE MAN between Clinton and Gore. He is Clinton's friend and was his commerce secretary. He's the man who got the North American Free Trade Agreement through Congress for him. He is also Clinton's golf partner and they golf alone, which is about as inner circle as you can get.

"When you're golfing with him, how do you address him?" I once asked Daley.

"You say, 'Nice shot, Mr. President,'" Daley said.

"Isn't that a little weird?" I asked.

"It's not weird when you have 30 guys standing around with guns," Daley replied.

He wasn't as close to Gore, but Gore knew his skills and liked him: Daley was smart, but he wasn't slick. He was frank, which is why the media liked him, and he believed politics sometimes demanded that you do something and hope for the best rather than dither endlessly over developing the perfect plan. He was 7 years old and the youngest of seven children when his father became mayor of Chicago. He was more interested in politics than the other kids— Rich, the eldest son, was already a teenager and didn't hang out that much with his youngest brother—and when he was old enough he would go to wakes, parades, and political events with his father. It was, he admits, a sheltered life. The searing, all-seeing, all-intrusive eye of the media did not yet exist, at least not for the young children of big-city mayors. He grew up in Bridgeport on Chicago's South Side and went to elementary school at Nativity of our Lord, two blocks from his house. "The only difference between us and the other families in the neighborhood was that in the summer, we went to Michigan; very few people in the neighborhood could do that," he says. "In the '60s, there was a focus on the riots, on media coverage, but we were always really protected. We saw a different Richard Daley. We knew it was a *business*. He stressed that. It was no big deal. 'Don't let it bother you,' he would say. He didn't pace the floor at night. He slept very well. I wish I could say that."

Bill liked to hang out at Democratic headquarters in the Loop, his father being both mayor and chairman of the Cook County Democratic Party. "In 1975 or 1976, I think over at the Sherman House or the LaSalle Hotel, they kept moving the Democratic headquarters, and I'm there one day and General Somoza walks in."

General Anastasio Somoza Debayle was elected president of Nicaragua in 1967. He resigned in 1972, but was reelected in 1974 and imposed martial law when civil war broke out. "The State Department had asked my father to show him a good time in Chicago," Daley recalls, "so we take him to lunch and it's Stephen Douglas's birthday, so we have to go out to his statue at 35th and Lake Shore because we go out there *every* birthday and *every* anniversary of his death. Douglas was our father's hero, and we had to read every fucking book on Stephen Douglas that ever came out."

Stephen Arnold Douglas, born April 23, 1813, in Vermont, nicknamed "The Little Giant," came to Illinois at age 20, became a wealthy Democratic lawyer and land speculator, helped make Chicago a railroad hub, became a member of the Illinois legislature, a judge of the Illinois Supreme Court and a member of the U.S. House of Representatives and the U.S. Senate. He debated Abraham Lincoln up and down the state in the U.S. Senate election of 1858. He ran against Lincoln for president and lost. He died of typhoid fever in 1861, and he is buried in the Douglas Tomb State Historic Site in Chicago, a tourist attraction tourists stay away from in droves. Few know of its existence. The site is on the wrong side of Lake Shore Drive, meaning it is on the railroad track side, not the lake side. A statue sits atop a very tall column, overseeing some housing projects, rumbling trains, and eight lanes of traffic, remembered by almost no one except Richard J. Daley, who might have been the only person in America to still honor Douglas's name on a regular basis.

"We had to go out every birthday without fail," Bill Daley is saying, "and so here we are at the statue, I'm looking around and it's me, my father, and General Somoza of Nicaragua. It was like a Fellini movie." He did not know it at the time, but there would be many more moments in the life of William Daley that resembled a Fellini movie, with several of them coming during Al Gore's campaign for president.

Gore wanted Daley as his campaign chairman from the beginning, but Daley didn't want to do the primaries. Primaries are about appealing to the party base. That meant labor, and labor was still smarting over NAFTA, which Daley personified. Daley also knew that first campaign chairmen never last. Things go wrong, somebody has to take the fall and you can't fire the candidate. "It is much better to be the second or third chairman," Daley said. So when Gore Campaign Chairman Tony Coelho resigns in June 2000 for reasons of health—to say nothing of continuing investigations into his past financial dealings—Daley takes the job.

Now it is the Sunday before the convention, and Daley is taking a behind-the-scenes tour at the massive Staples Center in Los Angeles. He is checking out the seats, the stage, the skyboxes, and the speech rehearsal room, and it occurs to him there is one thing he hasn't seen yet. He takes out a cell phone and calls Steve Richetti, Clinton's deputy chief of staff. "Can I get a look at the remarks?" Daley asks. There is a pause. "Thanks, buddy," Daley says.

They are going to send him Clinton's speech, he says. Sure they are.

It is all a bit of a surprise. Daley knew Clinton, and Daley knew Gore, and he thought they were genuinely close. There had been all this talk about how it was the closest relationship between a president and his vice president in history, their weekly lunches, etc., etc. "I thought it was genuine," Daley said later. "Clinton had often said to me that on the bus tour [after the 1992 convention] he thought they really connected as friends and as colleagues in arms. That's why, to be frank with you, when I got into the campaign and found out that there had been this kind of estrangement, I was really surprised. I really was." And Daley soon realizes that the Lewinsky matter did not open up a rift between Clinton and Gore; it widened a rift that was already there.

WHICH BECOMES APPARENT WHEN IT COMES time for Gore to choose a vice president. It is just after the Republican National Convention, Gore is way down in the polls, and now it is time for him to pick a running mate, preferably one that will generate a little good publicity, a little heat, someone who might help turn around the bad numbers. A small group gathers in Nashville at the Loews: Gore; Tipper; Frank Hunger, Gore's brother-in-law; Warren Christopher, who heads the selection process; and Daley. It is Sunday night and they are basically down to Senator John Edwards of North Carolina, Senator John Kerry of Massachusetts, and Senator Joseph Lieberman of Connecticut, in that order. (Dark horses like Dick Gephardt, Bill Bradley, and Bob Kerrey have been eliminated.) Edwards, 47, is dynamic, a good speaker, and a self-made millionaire. He has been in the lead for the vice presidency all weekend, but the Gore people are now getting down to the politics, the personalities, and the imponderables. Edwards may be too dynamic, too good a speaker. He might overshadow Gore. Kerry is a Vietnam War hero and was one of the organizers of Vietnam Veterans Against the War, which would give the Democrats two Viet vets vs. a guy who went into the Air National Guard and a guy who got deferments. That's not bad. But does Kerry really generate much news if he is selected? Lieberman is a centrist, son of a liquor store owner (though he often can't bring himself to say that, instead saying his father owned a "package" store), and an Orthodox Jew who criticized Clinton for the Lewinsky affair. True, Gore would have wanted Lieberman to serve as vice president in 1998, when it looked like Clinton might be forced from office, but that was different. Gore would have selected Lieberman under the terms of the 25th Amendment, which states "whenever there is a vacancy in the office of the vice president, the president shall nominate a vice president who shall take office upon confirmation in a majority vote of both houses of Congress." A Lieberman nomination would have sailed through Congress. But 2000 is another matter: Lieberman has to face the American public, he has to help the ticket get elected. The discussion is vigorous, and Lieberman's religion is talked about. Daley wonders whether a Lieberman nomination will bring anti-Semites out of the woodwork. He doesn't know that it will or even how to determine that in advance, but it is on people's minds. And how will it play with black voters? Interestingly, Lieberman and Gore are getting the same kind of reaction to rumors that Lieberman is a finalist: Some Jews are against it. "I hope he doesn't pick you," a Jewish voter tells Lieberman in Connecticut. "Why?" Lieberman asks. "I don't know," the voter says. "I'm nervous about the reaction." Some Jews are afraid that Gore is doomed to defeat and that a Jew on the ticket will end up a scapegoat. "Joe Lieberman would be a bold and courageous choice, maybe the finest person in politics," Ed Rendell, who is Jewish and the general chairman of the Democratic National Committee, announces publicly, but then adds, "I don't think anyone could calculate the effect of having a Jew on the ticket. If Joe Lieberman were Episcopalian, it's a slam dunk." That angers Gore, though Gore has to admit that some Jewish supporters are telling him the same thing. But there are pluses to selecting Lieberman: His name would attract some big money, and his selection would be seen by the media as bold and dramatic. There is also Florida. It would not hurt to have a Jew on the ticket if they want to carry Florida. And pretty soon, it is looking like Lieberman.

Whatever the downside of Lieberman, it could be worse. The president of the United States came up with worse. Not long before, Bill Clinton had called Daley and suggested Leon Panetta for vice president. It certainly would be an audacious choice. In the same sense that jumping off a cliff is an audacious choice. Panetta was Clinton's chief of staff during the Lewinsky affair. Lewinsky was in the West Wing because she was an intern for Panetta. There are all sorts of Panetta references in the Starr Report, such as: "During the [government] shutdown, Ms. Lewinsky worked in Chief of Staff Panetta's West Wing office, where she answered phones and ran errands. The President came to Mr. Panetta's office frequently because of the shutdown, and he sometimes talked with Ms. Lewinsky. She characterized these encounters as 'continued flirtation.' At one point, Ms. Lewinsky and the President talked alone in the Chief of Staff's office. In the course of flirting with him, she raised her jacket in the back and showed him the straps of her thong underwear, which extended above her pants."

And the media wouldn't make too much of that, would they? That wouldn't fill the papers and the airwaves day after day if Gore picked Panetta, would it? But wait, it gets better: Panetta is the guy who possibly ties Gore to alleged illegal activity in the White House. Gore said there was "no controlling legal authority" banning his raising of funds from his White House office in part because he thought he was raising only "soft money" for the party, not hard money for the Clinton/Gore campaign. The raising of hard money would have been a violation of the 1883 Pendleton Act. But during an investigation, Panetta testifies that Gore had "listened attentively" during a meeting in which the raising of hard money was discussed. Gore later claims to an investigator that he might have missed the talk about hard money because he drank a lot of iced tea and had to go to the bathroom a lot.

In other words: Is Clinton completely out of his mind? Leon Panetta? Why not Vernon Jordan? Why not Betty Currie? "During the selection process, we put Panetta's name under 'others,'" Daley said dryly. A few weeks later, after Lieberman is announced, I see Panetta standing, unrecognized, inside the Staples Center and we chat. "My view is that the president represents a real strength and he, frankly, has to be part of the strategy for Gore to win in November," Panetta says. "I wouldn't put him to the side. If I were Gore I would build Clinton into the strategy. I think Al Gore will need him in November to win." So you can see why Clinton likes the guy. On the other hand, Panetta's strategy is exactly what Gore has decided against.

It becomes the central question for the Gore campaign: how to use Clinton. Which begs the larger question: How do Americans view Clinton and Gore's relationship with him? It first comes up when Gore is trying to figure out how to get credit for the booming economy. Critics keep writing that Gore is failing to get credit, but nobody is writing about how he can manage this. Surveys are showing that few citizens see any connection between Gore and boom times. It is what keeps them smiling down in Austin. "The current prosperity is considered a force of nature," Ari Fleischer, Bush's spokesman, says. "People give more credit to the private sector. He [Gore] is perceived as taking too much credit. He's [just] the vice president. He really has the worst of both worlds: He's not getting credit for the good things, and the bad things seem to stick to him." Another senior Bush aide tells me, "They [Clinton and Gore] didn't create the economy; it's not believable. The average person busting his buns doesn't believe it. Gore and Clinton didn't have anything to do with the stock market." Bush is excellent on the stump at exploiting this feeling. One of his standard lines is about how his opponent took credit for the economy just like he took credit for inventing the Internet. It always gets a big laugh.

Unfortunately for Gore, his private polls and focus groups show the same attitude. "When Gore stood up and said, 'We created 21 million jobs, we did this, we did that,' people just went off the charts with anger," Daley tells me. "People said, 'Oh, bullshit.' Gore would run an ad stressing the prosperity, and people would say, 'Fuck him! He doesn't know what he's talking about!' Great, OK. So the problem was, how can we take credit for the economy? And so some people told us, 'Well, get Clinton out there more and have him do commercials.'"

The trouble was, however, that even though Clinton's job approval was now around 60 percent, his personal approval rating was around 27 percent. And in swing states, especially with white voters, Clinton's numbers were far worse. Further polling showed that even African Americans, those voters most loyal to Clinton, wanted to hear from Gore rather than hear from Clinton. From the first day of campaigning to the last, Gore's polling showed the same thing: Clinton was a loser. Use him and lose. Move close to him and lose big. (Clinton's pollsters showed just the opposite, but Gore and Daley didn't believe Clinton's pollsters.) And it's not like the media hadn't noticed the same phenomenon. A story by Katharine Q. Seelye in the *New York Times* on September 4, 2000, noted: "The central concern is that while voters appreciate the good times, there is lingering resentment toward Mr. Clinton over his personal behavior, creating a complex web of emotion that still seems to ensnare Mr. Gore." Allan J. Lichtman, a political analyst at American University, said: "The fundamentals are in Gore's favor. Peace, prosperity, tranquillity at home and a united incumbent party. Why has the race even been close? The Clinton scandals."

Daley understood this perfectly. "And it was tough for me because I like Clinton so much and for me to be in that position and to say to Tom Harkin [a Democratic senator from Iowa] when he's yelling at me to send Clinton to Iowa, 'Tom, the people in Iowa who are swing voters, who we need to get this ball over the line, it's not going to mean shit to them. If anything, it may work as a negative.' And Clinton understood that. He didn't like to hear it. You wouldn't like to hear it either. But I think he understood it." In one respect, Clinton's scandals had been good for Gore. With the exception of Bill Bradley, who was not in public office, the Lewinsky affair kept Democratic office-holders from running against Gore in the 2000 primaries. "The scandal froze people like Gephardt and Kerry and Tom Harkin," Daley said. "For them to go out in 1998 and explore a run for president would have looked disloyal to Clinton, would have looked like they were siding with the Republicans." On the other hand, the scandals and eight years of intense partisanship did take their toll on Gore's chances for election. "I think people had just had it," Daley said. "They wanted it to end. In some people's minds, Gore's candidacy was a continuation of that, a continuation of the stress. And they didn't want that. And if you were a conservative, voting against Gore was the last way of getting Clinton."

•  •  •

DOWN ON THE FLOOR OF THE DEMOCRATIC convention, thousands of delegates are packed like hogs in a pen, sweatily rubbing up against each other and craning their necks to see what is happening on the huge projection screens overhead. Somewhere up front there is an actual human being speaking from behind an actual lectern, but human beings are really pretty darn small when you get right down to it, and it is so much easier to just watch the whole thing on the screens.

High above the floor, up in skyboxes, the Gods of the Convention are relaxing, sipping drinks, watching TV, and wondering how anybody—even if they were from Wisconsin—could run around wearing a large wedge of cheese on their heads. Conventions aren't about excitement or mysteries or floor fights anymore. They are about programming and entertainment and persuading the networks to cover as much of the show as possible.

Bill Daley is up in Skybox 51, with a magnificent view of the proceedings. Ted Kennedy and Caroline Kennedy Schlossberg have just entered and have taken seats in the first row of the box. In a few minutes, Bill Clinton will give his speech, but before we get to that, a law enforcement official would like to give Bill Daley a little briefing: "We got a problem outside. Anarchists are cutting the fence. Ten thousand of them are trying to get in here." Daley seems to take this news in stride. Hey, it's a convention. There is supposed to be rioting, isn't there?

I try to be helpful and take his mind off things. "Have you seen Clinton's speech yet?" I ask.

He shrugs. "It's not worth it," he says. He has bigger problems. Down on the floor, the worst thing possible is happening, worse than 10,000 anarchists cutting through the fences: the show is going long. Clinton has been guaranteed prime time, and he must be finished with his speech by 11 P.M. Eastern time, when the networks will cut away for local news. But Blanche Lambert Lincoln of Arkansas keeps yapping about Social Security and by the time Senator Patty Murray of Washington comes on, the show is running 17 minutes late. There are a lot of other women to hear from, both on the podium and on the floor, and that is where the planners have screwed up. On the podium, the director can signal people to stop talking. But far away on the floor, the speakers can speak as long as they want and you can't control them. Which is what is now happening. The show is now running an incredible 40 minutes late, which means that Hillary, who precedes Clinton, will get prime time but that her husband won't. Daley's phone rings. It is Clinton. Down in the bowels of the Staples Center, he is waiting to go on. He has kept secret the dramatic long walk to the floor, which Harry Thomason has cooked up in order for Clinton to look like Gary Cooper in *High Noon*. But the walk is a long one, something like 35 strides, and it takes time, and now Clinton and his people are worried there will not be time and they are really, really pissed. Who cares about these women talking about issues! Get them the hell off TV so the president can go on!

Daley rushes down from the skybox and walks into the holding room where Clinton and his aides would like to kill him. Forget that they never gave him the speech, never told him their plans, forget that he's got 10,000 anarchists cutting through the fence. They are pissed because the president will have to finish his speech out of prime time. And they blame Daley. Daley, they are convinced, is screwing them on purpose because he now works for Al Gore.

"When I walked in there, I was like the turd thrown on the table," Daley says later. The only guy taking it well is Thomason. Thomason knows TV and he knows star power. "Forget it," he tells Daley. "The networks are going to stay with Clinton. They're going to stay with Clinton as long as he speaks." Which, of course, is true. Because nobody cuts off Elvis.

And Clinton goes out and makes this great speech, and the networks stick with him and delay the local news. Weeks earlier, Daley had asked Clinton to do one thing in his speech: Talk about the past. Make people feel good about what was accomplished. Gore could not do that. "We could never get credit for the past," Daley said. But Clinton could. "We asked him to do the 21 million new jobs, yadda, yadda, everything great that happened in the eight years," Daley said. Clinton came through. The next day, the Gore campaign carefully watched the response to the poll question: Is America headed in the "right direction" or "wrong direction"? Clinton's speech caused an increase in the "right direction" figures, and Gore picked up 5 points in his private polling.

IN AUSTIN, IN THE FANCY OFFICE BUILDING WHERE Bush headquarters sprawls behind a wall of security—you have to surrender your driver's license before you are allowed inside— they know they have a secret weapon: Their candidate has no Clinton baggage. "The moral direction of the country is a problem for Gore," Ari Fleischer says. "Bush talks about that in a subtle, sweet way."

Bush tells crowds: "I want to restore honor and dignity to the Oval Office." Very subtle. Very sweet. Gore, on the other hand, is irrevocably tied to Clinton. When you think of Gore, you think of Clinton. When you think of Bush, you think of his father, his mother, maybe Millie, but you do not summon up controversial, let alone negative, images. It is, the Bush aides feel, their ace in the hole. Though the official line from the Bush people is that a "sitting vice president in a time of peace and prosperity" should be running away with the race, in fact, they know better. "It is tough being a leader when you're the vice president," a senior Bush aide admits and goes on to say that Gore's very intelligence is a drawback. "People don't want a person who has the answer to everything. They want a person whose judgment they can trust." Bush, they tell me, is "a big thinker" and a "sponge when it comes to information."

What about likability? "Likability is important," a senior aide says. "I think you have to like the people you put your trust in." Bush thinks so, too. In late August, he gives an interview to the *Milwaukee Journal Sentinel* in which he says voters ultimately will cast their votes based on what they think of a candidate's "judgment and heart" rather than on specific issues. It is a theme his team stresses. Issues to them are not mere issues, positions that the American people will judge. Rather they are insights into the soul of the candidate. "The No. 1 issue will be a feeling about the candidate and leadership," an aide says. "People won't decide based on Gore's 401(k) plan vs. our Social Security plan. A middle-class person will say, 'I like them both.' Instead, they will ask, 'What do these plans say about the candidates? It shows Bush is courageous.'"

"People view Bush as real, authentic, funny," says Fleischer, who will later become White House press secretary. "Giving access to the press paid off in likability and made him a stronger candidate."

I ask a number of Bush's aides about his management style, and they paint the same picture: a strong, though somewhat detached, chief executive officer: "Gore is a smart guy who has buried himself in the details for 25 years," one says. "Bush focuses on the details when needed. He hasn't been doing it for 25 years. That is not his style. He has the best quality of leadership: He knows what he needs to know and leaves the details to others. He very rarely looks back and rethinks. Once he makes a judgment he almost never looks back." He does not want to see polling questions, raw data, that kind of stuff. He does want to see all TV commercials in which he or his wife appears. "He always wants to see what he and Laura look like in the ads," an aide says.

I ask what happens when the staff gives conflicting advice.

"He first likes to make sure people giving conflicting advice have talked to each other," the aide says. "He would rather the staff come to him with a consensus, if it's a real consensus."

In Bush focus groups the words that people associate with Gore are "alpha male," "disconnect," "attack dog," and "Elián pander bear," a reference to Gore's support for keeping Cuban refugee Elián González in the country. The words associated with Bush are "optimistic," "cheery," "bold," and "likable."

But what do the American people think of when they think of Bush's qualifications for president of the United States? I ask a top aide.

"Adequacy," he says. "They ask: 'Does this person have the qualifications for office?' Gore can't relate. Americans want a strong, sensible person with convictions that won't change, not a guy who has plans to colonize Mars. People don't think you become the nominee of a major party after being elected and reelected the governor of a major state by being dumb."

Just before Gore announces his vice presidential choice, another Bush aide says: "I'll tell you Gore's weakness in picking a vice president: Trying to find a guy as smart as he thinks he is."


BUT LIEBERMAN IS NAMED AND PEOPLE ARE REALLY excited. How excited? Even Gore looks excited, that's how excited. While it is playing well overall—an ABC News poll indicates that 72 percent of Americans "think more favorably of Lieberman when they're told he was one of the first Democratic lawmakers to criticize Clinton publicly"—Lieberman plays less well at first with the most loyal of Democratic voters: African Americans. They stood behind Clinton during the Lewinsky affair, and some have publicly attacked Lieberman for upbraiding him. On the day Lieberman is named, Dallas NAACP President Lee Alcorn says on the radio, "If we got a Jew person, then what I'm wondering is, I mean, what is the movement for, you know? . . . I think we need to be very suspicious of any kind of partnerships between the Jews at that kind of level because we know that their interest primarily has to do with, you know, money and these kind of things." Kweisi Mfume, national president of the NAACP, immediately condemns the remarks as "repulsive, anti-Semitic, anti-NAACP, and anti-American." Alcorn is suspended and later resigns.

But Lieberman has to address the concerns of blacks, especially his past questioning of affirmative action, and so before his nomination he goes to the Bonaventure Hotel in Los Angeles for a meeting of "African-Americans for Gore/Lieberman 2000." There are hundreds of empty seats and the mood is unsettled. Eleanor Holmes Norton, the delegate to Congress from Washington, D.C., tries her best to reassure the crowd. "This man has already done wonders for the Gore/Lieberman ticket," she says. "His faith forms his values, and ours is a faith-based community. Where one barrier is broken, we cannot be far behind." But Representative Maxine Waters of California, who is sitting near the front row, is refusing to endorse Lieberman, which is a bad sign. A real split in the black community would almost certainly doom the ticket. No group gives its votes to Democrats with more loyalty than African Americans, and, in fact, no Democratic presidential nominee since Lyndon Johnson has won the white vote. Jimmy Carter and Bill Clinton managed to get to the White House by staying alive among whites and rolling up huge figures in the black community. But as Lieberman begins to speak to the group, you can see that this is going to be his day. "I am so proud that the first group I am seeing is this one," he says. Then he points to Waters and says, "It's Maxine's birthday!" The applause is thunderous and Waters smiles. "You are looking at not just a senator and vice presidential candidate, but a frustrated preacher," Lieberman goes on and then lists his *bona fides:* How he marched with Martin Luther King Jr. in 1963, how he went to Mississippi where he "registered voters and brought them to the polls," and the pantheon of civil rights heroes that he knows and has worked with. "I come not to boast because the work is not finished," he says. And this affirmative action thing? "I have supported affirmative action, I do support affirmative action, I will support affirmative action," he says. "Why? Because history and current reality make it necessary." Then he concludes with: "We are not only citizens of the same great country, but we are children of the same awesome God. Don't let the press or the critics divide us." This brings down the house. Waters leaps up and hugs him and tells reporters she is endorsing him. "He has said enough, he has done enough, and he has demonstrated his willingness to deal with issues of concern to the black community," she says.

The Gore campaign is way beyond happy. They knew Lieberman was good, but they didn't know he was going to be this good. Maybe, just maybe, they are going to get to the White House after all.

# 10

# MEDIA APERTURES

A T BUSH HEADQUARTERS IN AUSTIN they cannot quite believe it. "We keep going around saying to each other, 'We're not really this smart, are we? We are not really geniuses, are we?'" The senior aide laughs and slaps his desk and his little countdown clock jumps a little. All the senior Bush aides have digital countdown clocks that count the remaining months, days, hours, minutes and seconds to Election Day. The clocks are supposed to keep everybody focused on the task ahead, but now they send a different message: It is only a matter of time. We have got this thing in hand, sewn up, put away. Because deep down they believe either, yes, they are geniuses, or, shucks, this national campaign thing is not as tough as everybody makes it out to be. Although the top three members of Bush's senior staff lack any Washington experience, they have produced a juggernaut, a well-oiled, finely tuned machine that has raised $100 million, won the nomination, and produced a double-digit lead for Bush in the polls. And they are giddy with delight. Right up until Labor Day.

By Labor Day, Bush was behind in several national polls and the staff in Austin was not so giddy anymore. Except for a week here and there, Bush had never trailed Gore. Claiming they didn't care about polls, the campaign staff, in reality, cared very much. Forget all this crap about how polls are a "snapshot in time." That is not the true value of polls. Good polls inoculate candidates against media attention to their gaffes, missteps, and bobbles. When Gore threw batting practice with the Detroit Tigers in early September and hit first baseman Robert Fick on the leg, it did not make big news. A few months earlier, this would have been portrayed as yet another example of how nothing was going right for the "hapless" Gore campaign. Now, with Gore up in the polls, the media laughed it off, and when Gore was mobbed by autograph seekers afterward—and, typically, spent time signing every piece of paper— he said, "Here I was, worried about throwing my arm out. I'm gonna throw my wrist out!" The stories about Bush were not filled with such amusing quips. Instead they were filled with examples of his disarray, including a first: Bush campaign people attacking the Bush campaign. An unidentified "Washington-based adviser to the Bush campaign" told the *New York Times:* "Today, I think anybody forced to wager on the race would have to bet on Gore." This was followed the next day by a "high-ranking" Republican official blasting Bush's campaign team in Austin for arrogance and stupidity. On September 3, the *Austin American-Statesman* began a front-page story with "Vice President Al Gore may have found a groove in his race for the White House. . . ." Two days later, Reuters would begin a story, "George W. Bush just can't seem to get his groove back." All because of the polls.

Polls drive, shape, and color coverage, and Bush saw his poll numbers dive at the worst possible moment: Labor Day. While in reality there is nothing magical about who leads in the polls on Labor Day, the media generally believe that whoever is ahead at that point is likely to win, and so the day has become extremely important. Taking a look at the polls for every presidential election since 1936, the Gallup Organization announced in a news release in early

September: "If a candidate is substantially ahead around Labor Day, the odds are high that he will cruise to a victory." That had happened three times: In 1984, when incumbent Ronald Reagan led Walter Mondale by 19 points and went on to win by 18. In 1972, when incumbent Richard Nixon led George McGovern by 28 points and went on to win by 23. And in 1964, when incumbent Lyndon Johnson led Barry Goldwater by 36 points and went on to win by 22. And in the last three elections, the leader on Labor Day had gone on to win: Bill Clinton in 1992 and 1996 and George Bush in 1988. The one big exception to the rule was when Thomas Dewey led Harry Truman by 8 points on Labor Day 1948 and Truman went on to win by 5 points. Actually, the sample size is really not large enough to draw firm conclusions—there have been only 16 presidential elections between 1936 and now—but the disproportionate attention the media pay to Labor Day polls threw the George W. Bush campaign into something close to panic.

A *Newsweek* poll taken August 30 and August 31 showed Gore leading by 10 percentage points, which was 6 points beyond the margin of error. What had happened to the 17-point lead Bush had carried into the Republican convention? Dick Cheney helped erode some of that. Not that Cheney had looked like a bad choice at the time. The selection of Cheney as Bush's running mate was supposed to have a calming effect. Cheney was supposed to allay fears about Bush's lack of experience in conducting foreign affairs, in dealing with Congress, and in managing the White House. As it turned out, however, Bush and his campaign staff immediately had to spend a great deal of time allaying fears about Cheney. The Bush forces had to run around assuring people that, contrary to what his voting record in Congress might seem to suggest, Cheney did *not* want Nelson Mandela to rot in jail for the rest of his life, did *not* think cop killer bullets were a swell idea, and *did* think that if you *are* going to buy a plastic handgun you should *not* be an assassin. And the late-night comics found Cheney's history of heart attacks downright hilarious. ("This is what the Republicans are calling the 'Wizard of Oz' ticket," Jay Leno said. "Cheney needs a heart; Bush needs a brain.") A few weeks before Cheney's selection, when I was in Austin, a top aide said: "The governor does not care if [the vice presidential nominee] comes from a big state, because vice presidents don't usually attract many votes even in their home state. And he does not have to provide ideological balance. But this will be seen as Governor Bush's first presidential decision, and all Bush has to do is look presidential in making it."

What the decision seemed to show, however, was how little care Bush sometimes took in making decisions. A good clue was provided by New Jersey Governor Christie Todd Whitman, who, in a meeting with the political staff of *U.S. News & World Report* on the Sunday before the Republican convention, said, "When Governor Bush called me and told me it was Cheney, I mentioned his legislative record, and Bush said, 'You know, I really wasn't looking that closely at it.'"

Here was George Bush picking a vice president, the person who is supposed to be ready from Day One to become the president and the person who is supposed to make Bush look presidential by virtue of his selection, but Bush "wasn't looking that closely" at how Cheney had voted? Why? The Rangers were on TV that day? Not that Whitman thought Cheney was a bad choice. Not at all. Whitman said the selection of Cheney was Bush's way of saying, "I know I need some help" and Cheney "can get my agenda moving right away."

"I've known Cheney for 30 years," Whitman said. "I've always known him as balanced. [In Congress] he could work both sides of the aisle. Do I share all his beliefs? Of course not." Whitman did say she was a big, big fan of Cheney, even though she also said, "He's got to explain these votes" and "I think we were all surprised what came out on the voting record." But why the surprise? Wasn't Cheney vetted? Well, that was the problem. Cheney was the guy in charge of picking the vice presidential candidate, he was the vetter and obviously he couldn't vet himself. And so Bush said he vetted Cheney personally. But when I asked a top Republican operative and Bush supporter who had really vetted Cheney, he sighed and said, "Obviously, no one." And day after day, there were stories about Cheney's votes, Cheney's business dealings, and Cheney's heart.

There was also the problem of what Cheney brought to the ticket. Nobody questioned he would bring something to the White House once he got there—and that certainly might be important to the nation—but how did he help the ticket get to the White House? By guaranteeing Bush Wyoming? Some thought Bush needed an edge in a battleground state such as Pennsylvania, and he could have selected Pennsylvania governor Tom Ridge as his running mate to obtain it. But Ridge was pro-choice and Bush did not want to push that hot button and, even more, did not want to piss off the religious right. Bush had already reached an accommodation with the right: If they would stay below the radar screen, he might just get into office and be able to help them with their agenda, including channeling public funds into faith-based organizations, and picking a cabinet they could live with. (The right would claim that it had vetoed Bush's first, more moderate choice for attorney general, Montana governor Marc Racicot, though Bush would deny it. In any case, when Racicot withdrew his name, the religious right was ecstatic to get John Ashcroft and felt it had gotten just reward for saving Bush's neck in South Carolina.) The Republican convention was an exercise in altered reality. Leaders of the religious right such as Jerry Falwell and Pat Robertson were not invited to speak, while so many black people were paraded on stage, critics dubbed the convention a "minstrel show." (The results in November would indicate that more black people were offended by the parade rather than impressed by it.) There was one African American missing on stage in Philadelphia, however: Alan Keyes, who had won 21 delegates to the Republican convention but was not allowed to address them. He would certainly have wanted to talk about abortion, and Bush did not want that divisive issue to be highlighted. Cheney did, however, warm slowly to campaigning, even though a wickedly funny story was written by David Von Drehle of the *Washington Post,* who began: "There's a line in Dick Cheney's stump speech that doesn't exactly ring true. It comes at the beginning, when he says, 'I'm delighted to be here.'"

The other reasons for Bush's nose dive in the polls were largely beyond Bush's control. Gore—of all people!—began doing startling things: He took a risk and selected Joe Lieberman as his running mate. And even though Lieberman had years of votes to explain, just as Cheney did, that is not what the media focused on. The stories done on Lieberman were all about his being the first Jew to be selected as a running mate on a major ticket, and how Lieberman had criticized Clinton on the Senate floor over the Lewinsky affair and what a courageous act it was for Gore to pick him. Then Gore planted a big, wet kiss on Tipper, gave the speech of his life at the Democratic convention, and the polls began turning his way.

And as the polls went, so went the media coverage. Not even a charm offensive can save you from the effect of bad polls, and reporter after reporter suddenly pointed out Bush might be mortal after all. On August 24, the *New York Times* took an unusually tough jab at Bush in a story that suggested he was both lazy and "not entirely coherent." (Though it was buried at the bottom of page 21, it ran ominously under a story headlined "Gore and Company Making a Serious Play for Florida.") The Bush story, by Frank Bruni, listed Bush's light campaign schedule: "On Friday his one public event was over by midafternoon, and the high point on his remaining schedule was a run along one of his favorite routes in Dallas. On Monday, after a day at home, he told reporters that one of the pleasures of his break was taking a nap. In addition, he added: 'I went to bed relatively early.'"

Bruni pointed out that in the next few days, Bush would take three days off, travel three days, and take three more days off and observed that this "does not exactly portray him as a ball of fire." Further, Bush seemed unable to explain or defend his huge across-the-board tax-cut proposal. "When he departs from the scripted eloquence of a stump speech, and, sometimes when he mangles the words within it, he can seem fuzzy on specifics, less than forceful in his thinking, tired," Bruni wrote.

On the same day, the Associated Press ran an equally pointed story that began: "George W. Bush doesn't seem to break a sweat on the campaign trail, unless he's jogging." Again, there was a list of Bush's very light schedule and his preference for naps and jogging over campaigning. "The Texas governor likes to be in bed by 9:30 P.M., and when campaign events keep him out late he tends to jumble his words," wrote Laurie Kellman. "On Monday night, he bewildered Iowa campaign donors by stumbling repeatedly during a 7:45 P.M. event, mistaking 'hostile' for 'hostage.' . . . Gore is following Clinton's almost fanatical footsteps [in terms of campaign pace]. On just about four hours' sleep and not quite finished with three weeks of nonstop campaigning, Gore did a round of early morning talk shows Monday and pushed through soggy weather into Hannibal, Missouri. 'I don't care how hard it rains, I don't care if the lightning comes down, I'm going to stay here and shake hands with y'all and talk to you,' he told voters there."

Kellman quoted Bush as saying: "I like the pace I'm on."

Bush's staff had no illusions about his energy level, but now the media were beginning to catch on. Early images of Bush plunging into crowds and chatting up voters to show how much he loved campaigning were just that: images. The reality was somewhat different. He had been doing this for 14 months and he is now sick of it. It is hard, boring work, and he is lugging around a press corps that is starting to snipe at him. (The *Boston Globe* will run a story in a few days, stating: "He prefers to sleep in his own bed, so recent campaign swings have called for no more than three days on the road. When he travels, he takes along his favorite feather pillow and eats peanut butter and jelly sandwiches that airplane caterers make especially for him.")

One genuine trait of Bush's, however, is his optimism. Things almost always work out for him. People always come through for him. And why should running for president be any different? So, at first, Bush could laugh at the downturn in the polls. And he suggests to reporters that maybe he ought to change the name of his plane from "Great Expectations" to "Shaky Wheels" or "Lost Momentum Two." In Austin, they are not quite as jolly. The Bush campaign had based its endgame strategy on being ahead by 6 to 8 points on Labor Day. But one national poll has him trailing by 6 points, another has him trailing by 3 points and a third has him tied with Gore. So the campaign does what everybody knows it will do— what it did in South Carolina—and goes negative. The Republican National Committee puts together a negative commercial blasting Gore for his Buddhist temple fundraising in 1996 and his alleged claim to have invented the Internet. And Bush readies a speech for Labor Day that will be a real barn-burner. "It's time to get rid of all those words like 'no controlling legal authority,'" Bush will say. "We need plain-spoken Americans in the White House."

But just before he says it, he calls a reporter for the *New York Times* an asshole. And that dominates the news a little.

·  ·  ·

KNOWING THAT BUSH NEEDS A LITTLE EGO BOOST to counter all the negative stories, his staff books him into a "preaching to the choir" event on Labor Day in Naperville, Illinois, 35 miles west of Chicago. Naperville is in DuPage County, the most Republican county in the state, and the parade he will march in after his speech—the area is so anti-labor that they don't even call it a "Labor Day" parade but "The Last Fling" parade—is a tradition, which means a large crowd is guaranteed without the campaign's having to put it together. It is a rainy morning, with gray thunderheads building up in the sky, when Bush and Cheney arrive outside Naperville North High School and at 9:10 A.M. take the stage. Bush is wearing a long-sleeve dark blue shirt and Cheney is in a blazer and navy golf shirt. They wait to be introduced. Next to the stage, a local band is blaring "The Washington Post March" at earsplitting volume, and Bush makes a classic mistake: He assumes the noise of the band will drown out any comments he makes to Cheney and, as Bush scans the crowd, counting the house, checking out the press stand, he leans over to Cheney and says . . . what does he say?

I am standing on the press riser several yards in front of him, but I hear him over the loudspeakers and I write in my notebook: "Bush—'There's a major league asshole over there from New York.'" It seems like such an unlikely thing to say in front of a crowd that I turn to Dan Balz of the *Washington Post,* who is standing next to me, and ask, "Did Bush really say 'asshole'?"

"I think he did," Balz says. "We'll have to check the tape."

We both had minicasette recorders, but those just picked up what the loudspeakers were broadcasting. Most people had missed what Bush said either because they couldn't really hear it or they couldn't really believe it. Bush and Cheney were still smiling on the stage, and there was no visible crowd reaction. But Balz and I knew we could get the exact quote from any reporter who had plugged a recorder into the "mult box," that suitcase-size piece of electronic equipment present at each event so the media could get "clean" sound directly from the microphones on the stage. As it turned out, Bush had said: "There's Adam Clymer, major league asshole from the *New York Times.*" And Cheney had responded: "Oh, yeah. He is, big time." Bush made the comment not so much because he didn't like Clymer's coverage of him but because Bush thought a recent story had been unfair to Cheney. Fierce loyalty is one of Bush's hallmarks, and he was trying to buoy Cheney's spirits. But the microphones on the lectern were live, and now his comments were part of history. Neither Bush nor Cheney yet knew it, however. So as the wind began whipping up a light rain, Cheney gave a short speech, saying, "We've all gotten tired of the Clinton-Gore routine, and it is time for them to go. We will restore honor and dignity to the White House." Then Bush spoke, saying "It's time to elect people who mean what they say and say what they mean"—words that would be tinged with irony this day. He spoke for 11 minutes, ending with a mini-Bushism: "Collectively, we can come together."

I was a member of a small pool of reporters who would stand in a cattle truck directly in front of Bush as he walked along the parade route. We were made up of print, radio, TV reporters, camera crews, and still photographers. Bush would walk behind us and the cameras would capture his every movement.

On each side of the route, a few Gore supporters disguised as Bush supporters were holding up signs that read: "Me and My Concealed Weapon Are Voting for Bush" and "I'm Voting for Bush Because I Hate Minorities, Too" and "Vote Bush Because Gay People Have Too Many Rights." It was very confusing. Some members of the crowd came up and tried to rip their signs away. Others came up and congratulated them.

Bush lined up with Cheney in the middle of the street to begin the mile-and-a-half parade. The crowd that lined each side of the route several deep was large, happy, and demonstrative. They were delighted Bush was here. But from the cattle truck, I saw Karen Hughes, Bush's communications director, walk up to Bush and whisper in his ear. Bush then whispered to Cheney, and the two men stepped off down the street. Bush was visibly upset, however. His face took on a frozen smile that seemed to radiate cold instead of warmth. While aides walked down both sides of the street holding a rope that Bush was supposed to lean over to shake hands with people, he instead stayed on the center stripe shaking no hands, not even when the parade made temporary stops. He just stood about eight feet behind a truck carrying photographers and reporters, smiling into the cameras for block after block.

The people along the route reached out their hands and called out his name, but Bush would not go over to them. He was furious. He was sick of the whole thing: the long days, the stupid rope lines, the "gotcha" reporters who were trying to make him look bad and who now would beat him to death with the "asshole" quote. Bush was politically savvy: He knew what the coverage was going to be the next day. He knew that his attack on Gore would go unnoticed. He knew it was going to be all about what he had called Adam Clymer, who was, in his considered opinion, when you got right down to it, a major league asshole. Karen Hughes walked over to the press truck, and we called questions down to her. She confirmed that the audio tapes had clearly recorded Bush making the comments. She tried to joke her way out of it, saying, "The message of the day was plain spokenness, and I think he delivered!" But she knew what Roger Ailes, who was the media guru for Bush's father, always said: "There are four things that media care about: pictures, mistakes, attacks, and polls. A guy plays a wonderful symphony, and at the end he falls into the orchestra pit. What will be the story? The wonderful symphony or him falling into the pit?"

George Bush had just fallen into the pit. But could he get up? Not for at least 24 hours. Everybody knew that. No matter what he said this day—and he still had to fly to Michigan and Pennsylvania—nothing was going to make news. "I wish I had known about the asshole remark earlier," one weary TV cameraman said at the end of the day. "I wouldn't have bothered to shoot the parade."

A S IT TURNED OUT, BUSH STAYED IN THE ORCHESTRA pit for longer than a day. First came the "major league asshole" stories, and the next day came the stories about the stories. The *Washington Post, Los Angeles Times, USA Today, Boston Globe* and *Baltimore Sun* printed the word "asshole," while the *New York Times* would not, referring to it as an "obscenity." (Though it was technically a vulgarity.) And the *Washington Times* proved that a euphemism could be worse than what it was replacing by saying that Bush had used a euphemism "for a rectal aperture." The *Chicago Tribune* called it an "expletive" that was "reflective of the newfound aggressiveness" in Bush's rhetoric. The evening news on ABC, CBS, and NBC bleeped it out, as did CNN. Then the press committed sociology, quoting all sorts of experts about the use of vulgarities in modern times, how popular culture was becoming more crude, etc., etc. Then, inevitably, came the goody-goodies, who were shocked—shocked!—that such words could be uttered by an American presidential nominee. "It would be better if no person in the United States spoke about others in that fashion," said Bush's fellow Republican, Charles Grassley, a senator from Iowa. "In every respect, from the youngest to the oldest person, we are seeing a lack of civility."

But reporters had now found a theme. They didn't really care about words like "asshole" or about civility, but they seized on Bush's quote as a way of showing how he was getting down and dirty to claw his way back up in the polls. And also—and this was always the media's favorite point of attack—it showed how he was being a hypocrite by demanding "dignity" in the White House but not providing any on the campaign trail. "Increasingly, Governor Bush is seen to be falling behind in the polls, which may test his often-stated desire to bring a new tone of civility to politics," ABC reported that evening. "Well, today, he was caught on tape with a decidedly uncivil comment, the kind that can get in the way of what the Bush campaign would rather talk about." The *Wall Street Journal* reported that Bush "wasn't where he wanted to be on Labor Day" and that not since Bush lost the New Hampshire primary to John McCain "has his candidacy been in this much trouble." Down in Austin, they knew a fall into the orchestra pit when they saw it, and they didn't even try to put a positive spin on it. "We've hit trouble before and plowed through," Karl Rove, Bush's chief strategist, said. "And we'll plow through this."

Rove was far more worried about the candidate than about a few days of negative publicity. The campaign was the candidate. For all the support, the strategies, the maneuvers, the surrogates and the staffs, the need for a single, strong visual image day after day, night after night, had made a continuing, strong performance by the candidate indispensable. Rove knew what Bush was doing by refusing to shake hands during the parade, by standing in the middle of that street and just staring at the camera truck: He was sending a "fuck you" message to his own campaign. He was telling them it was their fault that the microphones had been live and that if they were going to screw up like that, hang him out there like that, embarrass him like that, then he would just stop campaigning. Did they think this was easy? Let them try it. Let them go out and campaign five days a week, existing on only eight hours sleep a night. It's not like he enjoyed it. You'd have to be nuts to enjoy it. He endured it. And if he was going to be made to look like a fool by his own staff, well, just screw it. "If he wasn't winning, he would quit. He would just walk off," Doug Hannah, Bush's boyhood friend, told *Vanity Fair*. "It's what we called Bush Effort: If I don't like the game, I take my ball and go home." Bush did not need to win. He wasn't some campaign machine like Al Gore. He was a human being! And he could just go back to Kennebunkport and pick up the old boy, and they could go fishing.

CLEARLY, SOMETHING HAD TO BE DONE, AND the next day the campaign did it: They plucked Laura Bush out of Austin, put her on a jet and got her to her husband's side. "Finally my wife caught up with me on the campaign trail," Bush said the next morning in Scranton, Pennsylvania. "I feel like a better candidate when Laura is with me." He *was* a better candidate when Laura was with him. She was calm and strong and disciplined and no-nonsense. He never would have pulled that stunt in Naperville if Laura had been there. So getting Laura on the trail was Step One. Step Two was letting reporters know that if they were going to treat Bush like just any other candidate, he could treat them like any other press corps. So even though Bush had come back and schmoozed with reporters on virtually every flight, calling them by the nicknames he had given them—"Pancho," "Stretch," "Gazelle," "Carlos," "Barney"—on the flight following the parade, Bush stayed up front. By the next leg, he was back to semi-normal, walking down the aisle, stopping to playfully slap a reporter on both his cheeks. But there was a difference: from now on, the plane was going to be off the record. No TV pictures of Bush; no microphones, no quotes. Let the press learn that the charm offensive wasn't called offensive for nothing.

In Scranton—Bush was spending a huge amount of time in Pennsylvania in a high-stakes gamble to win the state—he once again stepped up his attacks on Gore and the Clinton White House. "All this 'no controlling legal authority' or what the definition of 'is' is, is going to end with Bush/Cheney!" he said. "I don't need polls. I don't rely on polls or focus groups to tell me what to think!" Which is a good thing, because the polls stayed lousy. On September 19, the Gallup Organization released a poll showing a stunning reversal of fortune: "After the Republican convention this summer, Bush was perceived as the probable victor by a two-to-one margin: now Al Gore is ahead on this projective measure, 54 percent to 33 percent, the first time Gore has been viewed as the likely winner by the public this year." Further, Gallup said, after the Democratic convention, Gore's favorable rating increased to his high point of the year (61 percent) and has stayed there. But Bush's rating has continued to fall and is now at its low point, 52 percent.

Which was always the danger of going on the attack and why the "asshole" comment, which was essentially harmless, created a dissonance: Bush was supposed to be the nice guy in the race. Gore was the mean, attack guy. Bush was the likable one; Gore was the say-anything, do-anything one. By shifting Bush into attack mode, the campaign knew it was risking Bush's good-guy image, but it saw no other way of stopping Gore's soaring poll numbers.

On the flight from Scranton to Milwaukee, where Bush would deliver a major defense speech, I asked for and was granted an interview. As I sat down in the window seat next to him, Bush looked a little relieved to have an excuse to put aside the speech he was supposed to be studying. Across the aisle from us one row up and sitting backwards so that she faced us, Laura sat quietly reading a newspaper. Throughout the interview, as he spoke, Bush would look across and stare at Laura as if to say, "See, I am doing this just fine. I am answering these questions just fine." Otherwise, a remarkable calm radiated from the candidate as he cut into the cotton wool pancakes the flight attendant brought him. "I am a disciplined and focused and patient candidate right now because I believe that people are going to come my way," he said, holding a forkful of pancakes in midair. "After it's all said and done, after all the polls and surges and ads and the debate on the debates and all that, they'll come my way."

I asked him once again if he wanted victory less than the vice president wanted it.

"No, I don't," he said. "I think I want it in the right perspective. I'm a tough competitor. I hope they underestimate my competitive nature, because I'm a competitor. I'm a competitor, Roger; I want to win. But I don't want to win to the point where I'm going to try to be somebody other than I am. I'm not going to fake."

I ask him how the campaign had changed him.

"Well, it's made me in some ways tougher," he says. "I was thinking about it the other day when I was driving through a crowd of people, 90 percent of whom were cheering, 10 percent of whom were booing. I'm sure in the past I would have been concerned about the fact that 100 percent of the people weren't for me. Now it's just part of the routine. And I think that's a sign that I'm steeling for the process. Let me rephrase it: The process has steeled me, and I'm a better candidate for that."

Bush does feel steeled, as if he has gone through the worst that the press can throw at him and he has survived. But he is wrong. The worst is yet to come.

On September 12, a story by Rick Berke on the front page of the *New York Times* begins: "At first glance, the Republican television commercial on prescription drugs looks like a run-of-the-mill attack advertisement.

"The announcer starts by lauding Texas Gov. George W. Bush's proposal for dealing with prescription drugs and criticizing Vice President Al Gore's plan. Fragments of the phrase 'bureaucrats decide'—deriding Mr. Gore's proposal—then dance around the screen.

"But then, if you watch very closely, something else happens. The word 'RATS,' a fragment of the word 'BUREAUCRATS,' pops up in one frame.

"And though the image lasts only one-thirtieth of a second, it is in huge white letters, larger than any other word on the commercial. The tagline of the advertisement declares, 'THE GORE PRESCRIPTION PLAN: BUREAUCRATS DECIDE.'

"As might be expected, though, in a tightly contested presidential race, the Democrats have given the 30-second advertisement more than a quick glance. After being alerted by an eagle-eyed Democrat in Seattle, aides to Mr. Gore examined the advertisement frame by frame, spotted the suspicious word, and gave a copy of a slowed-down version to the *New York Times*."

The rest of the story deals with "subliminal advertising" and quotes Jim Ferguson, president of Young & Rubicam, who heads the Bush campaign's group of Madison Avenue advertising consultants, as saying, when told of the ad: "Are you serious? That's unbelievable. . . . I hope we haven't stooped to that. That's pretty bad. I thought that was illegal anyway."

The story causes another tsunami of negative publicity for Bush, who digs himself in deeper on "Good Morning America" by admitting he doesn't know anything about the ad or the story, even though it was on the front page of that day's *New York Times*. "The first I've heard of it was sitting here this morning," Bush says, as if he were living in some kind of hermetically sealed vault. "Campaigns take bizarre twists. This has got to be one of the more bizarre accusations. We don't need to be, as far as I'm concerned, our campaign—or in this case, the Republican National Committee—doesn't need to be manufacturing kinds of subliminal messages to get my message out."

Then it gets even worse. The RNC says it is not going to change the ad, because the RATS accusation is nuts and there is no subliminal message. But later in the day, Bush says he is pulling the ad.

And all those phrases that used to be reserved for the Gore campaign are now applied to the Bush campaign. "I think the questions are going to be about the competence of this campaign and is it becoming the gang that can't shoot straight," George Stephanopoulos says on ABC.

Over at Gore headquarters, they are jumping up and down with delight. The RATS ad will be remembered as one of the most successfully planted stories in campaign history. It was pulled off by Gore spokesman Chris Lehane, who was Gore's answer to the Bush charm offensive. Let Bush be charming; Gore had Lehane working 24/7 to kick his butt.

It all began when Gary Greenup, a retired technical writer for Boeing, was watching his 21-inch television in the living room of his Ballard, Washington, home and saw the word RATS fill the screen during a Republican commercial attacking Gore. According to the *Seattle Times,* Greenup alerted the TV station and state Democratic Party officials, but nothing happened for about three days until a party official sent to Nashville the videotape that Greenup had made. And that is when Lehane heard about it. From then on, as usually happened when Lehane got involved, things expanded explosively.

Lehane didn't hesitate for a second in pitching the story to the *New York Times.* "You know if you make the front page of the *Times* that it's going to be a huge story," Lehane told me. But Lehane also knew the story couldn't be pitched like any other story because it was too, well, odd. And so he created an aura of great mystery about it. He called the *Times*'s Rick Berke at home on a Sunday. Berke was one of the two or three most respected political reporters in the country. He also had a great deal of clout within the *Times*. If Berke agreed that RATS was a story, it stood a good chance of getting to the front page, which, in turn, would make the story a legitimate news item around the world. Technically speaking, the Gore campaign had Berke listed as a "hawk." The Gore press operation ranked all reporters as either hawks, doves, or in-betweens. "A hawk was a reporter who was much more aggressive, somebody trying to make a story, trying to make something out of everything that happens," a senior Gore aide told me. "Someone down the middle is someone who basically just calls it as they see it. And a dove is someone who is sort of Democratic leaning." Berke, in their view, was a hawk, but he could get them the front-page bounce they needed.

"Look, I got news that I think is stunning," Lehane tells Berke. Berke asks what it is, and Lehane says, "I can't tell you. I'll only show it to you." Lehane can imagine Berke rolling his eyes at this, but continues, "Look, believe me, it's worth it. I'm going to show it to you. It's totally off the record. If you decide you don't want to do it, you can't breathe a word about this to anyone."

Now Berke is intrigued and asks where he can meet Lehane.

"No," Lehane says, "I need to come pick you up." Lehane says it's like Woodward leaving the flowerpot on the windowsill as a signal to Deep Throat that he needs to see him. Berke agrees to be picked up.

Lehane takes him to the office of Bill Knapp, a Gore consultant, where a technician plays the GOP commercial for Berke at different speeds. Another technician explains to Berke that such a thing cannot happen accidentally in the making of a campaign commercial, that the words are typed in frame by frame. Berke is very interested.

An ordinary campaign would stop there. But this is a Gore press production. "So we give him the tape and we had put together supporting background documents about subliminal advertising, the law, the FCC, and all this stuff," Lehane says.

I interrupt him with a question. "Didn't anybody at your end, before you went to Berke, say, 'This is crap and the *New York Times* will never go for it?'"

"Yes," Lehane said. "Half of our people thought they were going to laugh us out of town."

About 9:30 on Sunday night, word that Berke's story was going to appear in the *Times* the next day appeared on an Internet site, and so Lehane gleefully called the networks to tell them what was coming. "But I was very somber, very serious," Lehane said.

"Look," Lehane told the network reporters traveling with the campaign. "I'm going to have to talk with you guys late tonight. I can't tell you exactly when." By this time, Lehane and the campaign were in Dayton, Ohio, so Lehane set up a hotel room where each TV reporter in turn could view the commercial. "I had a video, a Betamax tape for each of them," Lehane said. "Beta is important for these guys. And I had a packet of all the background material. Oh, and some cheese. And I showed them in one by one. They were in a very pissy, sullen mood until they saw the tape and then they were very excited. I had gotten Berke's story off the *Times*'s website by then, it was 12:30 A.M. or something, and that obviously legitimated it."

But that was not enough stagecraft to suit Lehane. Each time a network reporter left the room and went to the elevator, Michael Feldman, the traveling chief of staff, pretended to be just wandering by and said in a low, serious voice, "So, what do you think?" Feldman did this after each viewing, acting as if some very serious moment in campaign history was playing out.

The next morning, the Gore campaign got not only its front-page story in the *New York Times,* but also huge TV coverage. Neither Bush nor his staff had any idea of what hit them. To them it was just an insane, goofy story that nobody could really believe, but somehow everyone was treating very seriously.

"It sounds like happy hour over at the Gore campaign. It's a bizarre allegation. It's ridiculous and it's not true," said Ken Lisaius, a spokesman for the Bush campaign in Austin.

Alex Castellanos, who produced the 30-second commercial for the RNC, said the use of "RATS" was "purely accidental," and added: "We don't play ball that way. I'm not that clever."

But Scott Reed, who had run Bob Dole's disastrous 1996 presidential campaign and had used Castellanos back then, said he could not believe the word had been inserted accidentally or inadvertently. "Someone ought to have the grace to resign," Reed said. And Greg Stevens, a veteran Republican admaker, added: "There is no way that anything Alex Castellanos does is an accident."

The story had spun out of control. Castellanos tried humor— "If you play the ad backwards, it says, 'Paul is Dead'"—but that didn't work, and reporters barraged Bush with questions about it.

"We don't need to play cute politics," Bush told reporters during a plane-side news conference in Orlando. "We're going to win this election based upon issues. . . . This is hardly a conspiracy. But nevertheless, to put people's minds at ease, I will say loud and clear, this kind of practice is not acceptable."

It was a full-fledged disaster. Lehane was very pleased. He had the Bush campaign exactly where he wanted it every Monday: on the defensive. Lehane and many others had noticed the "echo effect" of the news media, especially in Washington: A major story would break in one outlet, it would be picked up by another, taken over by the 24-hour cable channels, which would fill the air with "experts" and talking heads, which led to network coverage, which led to an examination of the story as a media phenomenon. It was all reverberation, all repetition, all echo, and the Gore campaign each week wanted to be the first one to hit the gong.

Lehane called his stories "Bush Whacks" and he tried to arrange a major one every Monday beginning right after the Democratic convention and lasting until Election Day. Each week was a zero sum game to him: Either you won it or you were the loser. And the entire week was dictated by what happened on Mondays. "Our whole point was that someone's up and someone's down, so whoever is driving the news is by definition up and whoever is having the news driven down his throat is down," Lehane told me. "We wanted to move on Bush; we wanted to get him off track and we wanted to set it up each week." The Gore campaign even measured it. Each week, in its private polls, it asked people, "Did you hear more good news or bad news about Bush? Did you hear more good news or bad news about Gore?"

"And we won every single week by very decent margins from the convention on, except for the three weeks of the debates," Lehane said. "We killed them. Every week, we zinged Bush on something. It was the same approach we had used on Bradley, literally, which is you go out and you do your positives but you make sure you have something keeping those guys off balance."

With the RATS story coming so soon after "major league asshole" and accompanied by bad polls, the Bush campaign was way off balance. And Austin continued to put its foot down the only place it could: On the necks of the reporters. From here on out, it said, no more Mr. Nice Guy. From here on out, no more daily press availabilities with Bush. From here on out, Bush would stop speaking to reporters on the record. The charm offensive was over. At least as far as press access was concerned. In other words, George Bush had become Al Gore.

# 11

# SIGHS AND LIES

"I THINK THAT ITSELF IS
AN EXAGGERATION."

—Al Gore
after Larry King asks him about
his tendency to exaggerate,
September 28, 2000

GOING INTO THE FIRST DEBATE WITH George Bush, Gore's private polling is showing him 5 points ahead in the race for the presidency, but Gore is doing his best to blow the lead. After naming Lieberman, after the kiss, the speech, a 400-mile boat trip down the Mississippi with a lot of good publicity, Gore runs into a buzzsaw of his own making. On September 11, Gore makes a big splash on front pages everywhere by saying he will give the entertainment industry six months to clean up its act and stop marketing violent entertainment to children. If Hollywood doesn't respond, Gore vows, he will force the change through legislation or regulation. It is a very tough, gutsy stance considering how much money the Democrats suck up from Hollywood. During the 2000 election cycle, Democrats have received $13.6 million from individuals, companies, and political action committees associated with the entertainment industry, while Republicans have received $8.6 million. In addition, Gore's campaign has received $928,000 from the industry compared with $725,000 given to Bush. Lieberman joins Gore in his denunciation, and it is all playing very, very well with married voters, a demographic group Democrats usually lose but now could be on their way to winning.

There is only one problem: Eight days after the announcement,

Gore and Lieberman head to the Beverly Hills mansion of super-market magnate Ron Burkle to scoop up $4.2 million from the entertainment industry. The grounds of the mansion come complete with a carousel and a doghouse larger than some human abodes. Wolfgang Puck caters. Carl Reiner emcees, and in attendance, among many others, are Dustin Hoffman, Tom Hanks, Rob Reiner, Jeffrey Katzenberg, Paul Reiser, Heather Thomas, and Quincy Jones.

Lieberman does his borscht belt shtick—"Lox and load!" he tells the crowd. "Ask not what your country can do for you, but what you can do for your mother!"—and then says, "Al and I have tremendous regard for this industry. We're both fans of the products that come out of the entertainment industry. . . . It's true from time to time we will be critics or *noodges,* but I promise you: we will never, never put the government in the position of telling you by law, through law, what to make." Gore gives his regular stump speech, but the event gives Bush an opportunity to thrash the Democrats for hypocrisy. Speaking at a town hall meeting in Pittsburgh, Bush says, "I noticed my opponent went out to Hollywood yesterday. It seems like he must be auditioning for a Broadway play because he keeps changing his tune. At the beginning of the week he sounded awfully tough on Hollywood. He talked a tough line. After a couple of fundraisers, he's changed his tune. Go out there to Hollywood, collect some money." It may not have been the most articulate attack, but people got the point.

Two days later, with oil prices at a ten-year high, Gore proposes tapping the nation's Strategic Petroleum Reserve to increase supply and reduce prices, a plan Clinton quickly adopts, making it all seem a little too cozy and a little too political. Bush hits back by saying that the petroleum reserve "should not be used in an attempt to drive down oil prices before an election . . . for short-term political gain."

Meanwhile, the *Boston Globe* breaks a story saying that when Gore was campaigning in Florida in August, he told seniors that "his mother-in-law pays nearly three times as much for the same arthritis medicine used for his ailing dog, Shiloh." But, according to the paper, Gore aides could not say with certainty that Shiloh or Gore's mother-in-law actually takes the brand-name drug, Lodine, and even if they do, "the Gore campaign admitted that it lifted those costs not from his family's bills, but from a House Democratic study." It will come to be known as Doggie Gate and like the Hollywood pander and the petroleum release, it will not stay in the news long. But, months later, when the campaign is over and its operatives are deep in self-analysis, Gore aides will talk about these three events in September as the turning point, the point at which Gore could have put Bush away, but instead was forced onto the defensive and began losing ground. "It was the same old story," a Gore senior aide said. "It all confirmed that Gore was a guy who would do anything for politics." But there was still hope: There were the debates.

With the debates Gore has a chance not only to expand his lead but to put the election out of reach. And the expectations for Gore are extremely high. Bush's strategist Karl Rove says his side's debate strategy "can be summed up in one word: survive. We are facing the world's most preeminent debater." After all, Gore is the guy who made Ross Perot look like a loony in their NAFTA debate (not all that hard, when you think about it) and Gore convincingly beat Jack Kemp in their vice presidential debate in 1996. Gore's people figure the debates will be their killing ground, their opportunity to expose Bush's lack of experience and knowledge. But they are well aware that they must not overdo it. "We have to find a way to engage Bush on the issues in a way that does not require our candidate to be excessively negative," Gore deputy campaign manager Mark Fabiani says before the debates. "That is one of our biggest challenges."

The Gore campaign has decided that the task for Gore in the debates and the rest of the campaign is to be likable, show leadership, and portray himself as the only safe steward of America's prosperity.

The Bush campaign has decided that the task for Bush in the debates and the rest of the campaign is to be likable, show authenticity, and demonstrate a certain "threshold" mastery of the issues.

The debates are hugely important and hugely risky. Ever since the first televised presidential debate in 1960, debates have been remembered for embarrassments and disasters, not for serious exchanges of ideas. In 1960, Richard Nixon's makeup made him look like a corpse. In 1976, Gerald Ford stumbled badly when he assured the world there was "no Soviet domination of Eastern Europe." In 1988, Dan Quayle fell into a trap and compared himself to Jack Kennedy. The same year, Michael Dukakis failed to show sufficient passion when talking about a fictitious rapist and murderer of his wife. And in 1992 George Bush was caught impatiently looking at his wristwatch. (Which is why neither Gore nor Bush will wear wristwatches for their debates.) That's the downside. The upside is that debates can attract a huge number of viewers compared to other campaign events. About 25 million Americans watched Al Gore and George Bush give their acceptance speeches at the conventions. About 12 million people watched each of them try to be warm and fuzzy on "Oprah." But the presidential debates average about 64 million viewers, which is about 12 million more than watched the last episode of "Survivor." True, some 88 million people watched the Superbowl in 2000, but the last presidential debate in 1992 drew an audience of 97 million, just 4 million shy of the most-watched show in TV history: the last episode of "M*A*S*H." (As it turns out, the first Gore/Bush debate will draw 46.6 million viewers, the second will draw 37.6 million, and the last will draw 37.7 million.)

A few days before the first debate, I interview Gore in a very weird holding room in the bowels of McCormick Place in Chicago. It really isn't a room at all. On a vast concrete floor—so vast it could have swallowed up several football fields—four temporary walls had been thrown up, a carpet thrown down, a few couches dragged in, and a couple of lamps plugged into sockets on the floor. In a few minutes Gore will give a speech to the United Brotherhood of Carpenters and Joiners of America about his favorite subject: protecting working families from the evil forces of wealth and power. While party strategists will argue over whether this is too "populist" and not "centrist" enough, the Gore campaign has broadened the definition of "working family" to mean anyone who is not "the idle rich." Gore seeks to portray himself as a protector of mainstream America and seeks to portray Bush as a protector of special interests, greed, and despoilers of the planet. Gore also intends to use the debates to expose Bush's allegedly weak grasp of issues. Gore is very much aware, however, that very little is expected from Bush— "If he doesn't drool, Bush will be declared the winner" is the joke that everyone on the Gore campaign repeats—and so Gore's job before the debates is to raise expectations for Bush.

"I think that he is a much better debater than the conventional wisdom would have it," Gore tells me. "He was seen as the clear winner of the debates in the Republican primaries with some extremely capable people like John McCain. He is a very able debater, and I think that, as they have acknowledged, he has been practicing almost every day, which means that he'll be extremely good in the debates. There's no question about that—no question."

I don't believe Gore believes a word of it, and he knows I don't believe that he believes a word of it. But that is the way the expectations game is played.

But do you think you'll win the debates? I ask him.

"You know, it's for the American people to decide. . . . I think that the gladiatorial elements of these things are way overdrawn," Gore says. "Their real value is in their unique ability to provide the American people with a chance to learn more about the positions of the candidates on the issues and the kind of individuals the candidates are."

He is right, but most Americans will watch the debates to see if anybody crashes and burns. Gore has made one big improvement to his image preceding the debates. His kiss of Tipper and speech at the convention have humanized him. "According to the polls, the whole world now knows you're not wooden," I say.

He laughs. "That may be an overoptimistic reading," he says.

IN AUSTIN, THEY ARE LOOKING FOR A SILVER lining in the cloud of bad poll numbers, and they think they have found it: The possibility of losing the election, which really hasn't occurred until now, will force Bush to concentrate and work hard at debate prep. Bush always begins to work hard when he thinks he might actually lose. "Gore had the best three weeks he's going to have after he came out of his convention," Joe Allbaugh, Bush's campaign manager, says. "People are nervous and that's good. Your head is always in the ballgame when it's close. It's not whether you get knocked down that matters. It's how you pick yourself up."

Aboard Bush's campaign plane, I ask Bush if he is watching videotapes of his debate prep to learn from them.

"No, I haven't watched myself," he says. "I've been critiqued by the people who've watched. But I know what I believe, and I know what I stand for. I'm looking at how Vice President Gore has conducted himself on TV."

We talk a little bit about 1996 and how the Clinton campaign demonstrated an almost maniacal attention to detail before the debates: In practice sessions, Clinton aides drew a grid pattern on the floor to replicate the debate studio and mapped out exactly where Clinton should be standing at each point of the debate.

"They got into the *theatrics* of the race," Bush says.

And that's bad?

"Well, one of the things that I hope we'll able to do is to convince people that debates are important formats and forums to exchange ideas, not practice theatrics," he says.

I ask him if he thinks the debates will be decisive.

"I think they tend to confirm support," he says. "More importantly it's going to be, when it's all said and done, people walk in that booth and they're going to say, 'Who do we trust to lead the country?' And in this case, do they want the same four more years of really the same type of politics? And that's the ultimate deciding factor in this election."

JESSE JACKSON STANDS BEHIND A FOOSBALL TABLE in the Budweiser tent just a few yards from the converted hockey rink at the University of Massachusetts in Boston, where more than a thousand members of the news media have gathered to watch the first presidential debate.

The debate won't begin for a few hours and in the meantime Jackson is watching the Chicago White Sox play the Seattle Mariners on a large TV provided by Budweiser, which is also providing free soft drinks, chicken, roast beef, salad, and, of course, Budweiser. Many members of the Fourth Estate are scarfing down these free goodies without a twinge of guilt—the same reporters who say politicians ought to clean up their act see no reason to examine their own—but Jackson is standing and watching the TV screen and is neither eating nor drinking. Various TV crews are begging for a few moments with him, but he waves them off as the Sox come to bat in the ninth.

"I'm having a sacred moment," he says, and the TV crews back away a respectful few steps.

But Jackson being Jackson, he sees more than a mere baseball game. He sees a metaphor. "Blacks in Seattle are cheering for a white pitcher to strike out a black man playing for the White Sox," he says, "just as whites in Chicago are cheering for a black hitter to get a hit off a white pitcher. Why are we able to overcome race in sports?"

I first interviewed Jackson when I was a reporter for my college newspaper, and I have learned he does not expect replies to his questions. He provides both the questions and answers. "It is because the playing field is equal," Jackson says. "In the projects not far from White Sox park, the educational playing field is not equal. But in White Sox park it is equal.

"White players in football do not get a first down by gaining eight yards," Jackson continues, effortlessly switching sports, "while black players are forced to gain twelve yards. They each must gain ten yards. The playing field is equal. You don't hear about affirmative action in sports because the field is equal."

I can find nothing to argue with in any of this, and so I just nod and watch the White Sox strand a man on second and send the game into extra innings (where they will swiftly lose).

There is a surreal quality to the press rooms at presidential debates. Reporters have flown here at great expense to sit in a room and watch the debate on television. They could have stayed home and watched the debate on television or they could have stayed in their hotel rooms and watched the debate on television, but they have chosen to schlepp out to the University of Massachusetts in south Boston to watch the debate on television. The excuse is that if we do not show up at the event, we will miss the "spin," almost all of which is worthless. The forces of Al Gore have printed up elaborate signs with the names of their spinners on them—senior campaign aides, elected officials, and Cabinet secretaries—and the forces of George Bush have made similar signs for their spinners. And guess what the spinners will say? The Gore spinners will say Gore won the debate, and the Bush spinners will say Bush won. So what's the point? The reporters really show up at the debates because they are another part of the extended summer camp that is the presidential campaign season. And better than summer camp, we are all on expense account. But to justify my presence, I ask Jackson: Got any spin for me?

He doesn't hesitate. "Bush's résumé begins at age 45," Jackson says. "Everything before that was a youthful indiscretion."


JUST BEFORE THE DEBATE IS TO BEGIN, GORE LEAVES his trailer, where he had been engaging in a series of rapid-fire questions and answers with aides, and sits in a small holding area behind a curtain in the debate studio, studying some handwritten notes. His aides have given him the same last-minute advice that the Bush aides have given their man: "Just be yourself." (Though it might be refreshing if, just once, an aide told a candidate, "Be someone else for a change.") When word comes that it is time to begin the debate, Gore falls silent for a moment as if in prayer, stands and walks out to the stage.

Hours beforehand, George Bush had toured the site and made fun of the frigid temperature Gore had insisted on so that he would sweat less. (Gore's sweat glands were downright Nixonian, and he had to consciously remind himself not to keep wiping his upper lip as he had done repeatedly during his announcement speech.) "Who's got my parka?" Bush said. Then, walking out onto the stage he said, "Laura, get up here! Let's practice that kiss." Just before the debate, Bush walks into the curtained area and, just as Gore has done, falls silent as if in prayer and then strides onto the stage.

The first debate will be remembered as the "sighs and lies" debate. Gore, who never sighed in debate rehearsals, now sighs audibly as if to point out what a dummy Bush is being. The debate will also be remembered for Gore's makeup, which looks as if it has been applied by trowel. There is too much rouge on his cheeks and his lips look an unnatural pink. It looks as if he is running for First Hooker and not president. (And, of course, his makeup generates dozens of stories and late-night jokes the next day.) Just as when campaign signs blocked his face at his announcement, every now and then basic stagecraft seems to elude the Gore campaign. But his biggest problem is an aside he makes when answering a question about fires in Texas. Gore says he visited the area with James Lee Witt, head of the Federal Emergency Management Agency. In reality, though Gore had taken 17 trips with Witt, he had not gone on that one with him. Who cares? Nobody, except that by the end of each presidential campaign, the candidates are reduced to cartoons—a simple image the public can grasp that sums up each person—and Gore's cartoon is Pinocchio (Bush's is Dumbo). Anything that feeds those images will become news. And so the bobble or exaggeration or lie—depending on your point of view—about Witt becomes the news of the debate.

"He made up the story," Karen Hughes tells reporters afterwards, her voice registering high on the outrage scale. "The president of the United States cannot do that . . . the president cannot go to a meeting with a foreign leader and simply make things up that aren't true." And to emphasize how they possess the classy, responsible candidate, the Bush campaign now changes the name of its airplane to "Responsibility One."

But news often does not just happen. News is driven. And this time, the Bush campaign is in the driver's seat. "I didn't pick up the sighs during the debate," Ari Fleischer said after the election, sitting in the large and elegant White House office reserved for the press secretary. Fleischer said Bush's private polling had him 6 points down going into Boston (almost exactly what the Gore polls were showing), and Bush realized the importance of the debates. "We knew that Bush was classically underestimated, so we felt good going in, but no one knew how they would turn out. What I picked up was the question of going down to Texas with James Lee Witt. I was told at two A.M. that it was not true, and I woke up at six A.M. and heard that Gore was going to be on morning shows, so I started calling into the control rooms and spoke to the producers and said Gore had acknowledged it wasn't true and he is continuing this pattern of exaggerating. After 'Good Morning America' challenged Gore on it and Gore indicated he had misspoken, I went onto the press buses before they left for Logan Airport at eight in the morning and began the day by saying, 'Here is the vice president's pattern of exaggeration.' And that drove the news for several days. Bush understood the importance of it. He felt good."

The sighs become equally big news. Psychologist Robert Lefton, CEO of Psychological Associates, finds a world of significance there. "He created an atmosphere of arrogance and hostility," Lefton says of Gore. "When he is in that kind of condition, he is not a nice person. . . . I'm not sure Gore is terribly insightful about the kind of reaction that his behavior produces in others. He is possibly lacking in self-awareness." But there are plenty of others around willing to be aware for him. Both campaigns are doing focus groups, and the news from Gore's group is bad. People didn't like the sighs, and they didn't like Gore's aggressiveness. Gore foolishly believed his aides when they told him to be himself. What they really meant was: "Be yourself, but much more likable."

NOT THAT THE REVIEWS FROM THE BUSH FOCUS groups are anything to cheer about. "He needs to connect his ideas with how they will improve people's lives, and he hasn't done that yet," a Bush confidant says.

At the end of the first debate, Gore's private polls drop from 5 percentage points up to 1 percentage point up. The Gore aides are genuinely nervous. Daley tells them to get over it. "Two and a half months ago, we were supposedly 15 points down, a year ago he was 25 points down," he says. "If two and a half months ago somebody told us we'd be, essentially, even, we would have said, 'Hey, great!'"

So to prepare for the second debate, Gore's aides show Gore the devastating parody of him and Bush on "Saturday Night Live." Gore laughs and vows to drop the sighs and preachiness. After 25 years in public office, Gore has knowledgeable down cold. But likable he is still learning. The campaign staff adopts a new tone. They no longer claim Gore won the first debate. "Did you see 'Saturday Night Live'?" Lehane asks reporters. "It portrayed Gore as a boring asshole and Bush as an idiot. I think that's how most people see the race."

Flying to Winston-Salem, North Carolina, for the second debate aboard Air Force Two, Lehane tells me, "We're going to let you do his makeup tonight."

"Great," I say, "is it paint-by-numbers?"

As it turns out, Gore is so un–made up for the second debate that his 5 o'clock shadow is showing and his forehead is glistening with sweat. Like the makeup fix, the entire second debate is a repair job for the damage done at the first debate. Gore is humble, laid back and so polite that he is almost comatose. "It seems like we're having a great lovefest tonight," Bush says during the debate. Bush gets through 40 minutes of foreign policy questions without a major mistake and even though he does goof up the number of men he is itching to execute in Texas for the murder of James Byrd Jr., the black man who was chained to the back of a pickup truck and dragged to death—it's two, not three—the media make almost nothing of it. And Bush's response to Gore's challenges to his Texas record, especially health care for children, is everything the Bush campaign hoped for. "You can quote all the numbers you want, but we care about people in Texas," Bush says, a wounded look on his face. "If he's trying to allege I'm a hard-hearted person who doesn't care about children, he's dead wrong." It is likable, it is warm, and it oozes with sincerity. Gore has gone for the facts—Texas rates dead last among the states on a number of critical measurements—while Bush has gone for the emotions: I'm a good person, trust me, I would do nothing to harm kids. And TV is better at transmitting emotions than facts.

Television has profoundly changed presidential debates to make them more "watchable," though they are now less informative. When the League of Women Voters ran the debates, they were plodding affairs with long (i.e., five-minute) answers and little opportunity for candidates to launch attacks and counterattacks. Also, a panel of journalists—dominated by print reporters—asked the questions. When TV grabbed control in 1988, answers began to get shorter until they shrunk at one point to just 90 seconds. TV wanted things faster, snappier, more exciting. Candidates were encouraged to attack each other, and the panel of print journalists was eventually replaced with a single TV superstar doing all the asking. Debates became theater, and the instant postdebate criticism, masquerading under the guise of press analysis, became theatrical. Candidates were now judged on how they answered questions. Was the candidate properly emotional? Self-assured? Likable? And how was his makeup and his body language? The plethora of instant polls and focus groups also served to make citizens feel inadequate or "wrong" if they didn't feel the same way about the debaters as the polls said most people did. By 2000, debates were not about issues as much as they were about debating.

FOR THE THIRD DEBATE IN ST. LOUIS, THE GORE people give up on likability. "Sure Bush is likable," says Gore adviser Tad Devine. "And he may have a higher favorability than Gore on Election Day. But that doesn't mean he's going to get more votes than Al Gore on Election Day."

Ari Fleischer wanders among the press doing what is called pre-spin. "If the public were giving the government credit for prosperity, Al Gore would be winning and he's not," he says.

Gore is aggressive in the last debate, and the Bush forces scramble to hit back afterwards. "I don't think Americans want bitterness and bickering," Bush said primly. Even Bush's 75-year-old mother, Barbara, just three weeks out of a hospital bed for back surgery, is pressed into the attack on Gore. "I don't like lying," she tells a reporter and says that when Gore walked across the stage during the debate and loomed over her son, "I thought he was going to hit him. I really did."

Later, Daley tells me: "We underestimated the impact of the first debate. But people only reacted like they did because of the kind of foundation that was laid down before that about Gore: He's not a nice guy, he's always trying to be the smartest guy in the class, he's this and that." Gore knew he had to do repair work in the second debate, which wiped out his chance to gain much ground in that debate. "I think most people would say we lost all three debates," Daley says. Aside from not projecting a strong, solid, consistent image for Gore, the debates also did not paint Bush as dumb. And Daley was not surprised. "The perception of Bush as dumb is nowhere near as strong as people think," he says. "People don't think he's dumb. By virtue of who he is: A Bush. A governor. A guy running for president with all the Secret Service around him. It all gives him stature." Gore's private polling is now showing Gore 3 points down. The numbers will bounce up and down a little bit, but essentially from now until Election Day, the race will stay at just about dead even.

The campaigns are now at endgame. Bush sums up his campaign in just eight words: "Me trusting people and my opponent trusting government."

Gore sums up his campaign in just nine: "Fighting for working families against wealthy and powerful interests."

Gore now knows that he is not going to win this campaign on superior intelligence. He now knows he is not going to win it on traditional likability, on being the voters' pal. Instead, he will be the voters' champion, their defender, the good steward of their prosperity. He will go to his strength: He will try to win the election on fear.

IN THE END, CAMPAIGNS ARE USUALLY ABOUT FEAR. If voters make the wrong decision, good times will turn bad (or, if they are already bad, they will get worse). Peace will turn to war, wealth will turn to want, hope will become despair. Only through the right choice can there be salvation, only through the right man deliverance.

So when Al Gore talks about prosperity in the last weeks of the campaign, he is really talking about the fear of losing it. He is really talking, as he tells a crowd in an airplane hangar in Everett, Washington, about ending up broke, alone, and afraid in a county poorhouse. "Sixty-five years ago, we began the Social Security system in America," he says. "Prior to that time there were county poorhouses." There are murmurs from the crowd. Though few can remember when such things existed, all can summon up mental images, mostly drawn from Charles Dickens, of what county poorhouses must have been like.

"And those seniors who had lost the ability to earn their own way had to throw themselves on the mercy of the local government," says Gore.

Local government? Local government can't fix potholes, audience members are thinking, but it's going to take care of me in my old age? Gore, with his shirt sleeves rolled up above his elbows, continues. "There was no way to assure they were treated with dignity. Social Security changed all that. And now my opponent is proposing to privatize Social Security."

The audience can see it, smell it, taste it: a Republican presidency, a Social Security system in ruins, seniors shuffling forward in the dank basement of a poorhouse, their bowls held up for a ladle of gruel. "For me," Gore will say later, "that's really kind of what this whole race is about: It's important that nobody takes our prosperity for granted."

Those opposed to Gore also believe in fear itself. Bush tells his crowds that Gore is a "partisan, big-spending Washington insider," who will leave this country "trillions in debt." Poorhouses? We may not be able to afford poorhouses under Al Gore. Seniors may have to graze the countryside in herds, seeking their sustenance like cattle.

Not that all is gloom and doom on the campaign trail. On the

Gore campaign, anyway, there is also, well, lust. Lust worked at the convention, so Gore figures it will work now.

He flies into Shreveport, Louisiana, where the tarmac crowd is hot and happy under a blazing autumn sun. Gore is in a playful mood. At most stops, he is introduced by Tipper, who goes through a list of concerns designed to appeal to women while also raising the fear of what will happen if Republicans gain the White House. "We have to protect the right to choose," she says. "We need more money for breast cancer research. They will take us backward into the Dark Ages." She then points out how her husband volunteered for military service in Vietnam and, while running for president this year, also managed to attend all of their son's football games. At the end, she introduces Gore, who hugs and kisses her.

This time, however, as Tipper is speaking, Gore steadily creeps up on her from behind to the enormous delight of the audience. "I'm ready!" he shouts.

Tipper turns around and gives him both a startled and bemused look. "Oh, yeah?" she says.

Gore plants an open-mouth kiss on her as the crowd goes wild. Tipper breaks away from his clinch to turn back to the microphone, and Gore shouts, "It wasn't long enough!"

Tipper wisely leaves that straight line alone and says to him, "We don't have time! We need every vote!"

And they do. The Gore campaign has finally started to take Ralph Nader seriously, feeling Nader could cost them five or six states. Asked whether he would like Nader to drop out, Gore wisecracks, "I'd like Bush to do that."

The solution? There are many people with many ideas (mobilize the base vote, reach out to women, solidify the hold on seniors), but there is one thing the Gore campaign is adamant about: Bill Clinton is not going to be the solution. He is the problem, and Al Gore is not going to change his mind about that.

Clinton is hurt and complains to intimates, but he also goes along with the plan. "He did everything we asked and didn't do what we asked him not to do," Daley says.

"What did you ask him not to do?" I ask.

"We asked him to stay out of the news, and he did," Daley says.

Clinton aides would call Gore aides and say the president would like to campaign here and there for Gore, and the Gore response would be no.

"And they'd say, 'fine,'" Daley says. "And Clinton would go and do a fundraiser in New Jersey and that was it. If he did a campaign event for Gore, he would big-foot us. If he went out on the loose, he would big-foot us. If he was doing foreign travel, it didn't matter. But if he went out and did an official event in this country, he'd make television and he'd be the news that day, not us."

By the final weeks of the campaign, Al Gore figures the presidential race is his to win or lose.

In the end, he will do both.

# FLORI-DUH

I F THE NEARLY INEXCUSABLE FAILURE TO carry his home state of Tennessee would prove fatal to Al Gore's presidential ambitions, then the half-baked job the Bush campaign did in Florida was a near-death experience for him. And the importance of Florida was far more predictable than the importance of Tennessee. Everybody knew from the beginning of the campaign that Bush needed Florida to get to the White House. Democratic presidential candidates had to carry New York and California, and Republicans had to carry Texas and Florida, if they were to win in the electoral college. Yet by September of 2000, the media were already doing stories about how Florida was slipping away from Bush, and all the fingers were pointing in the same direction: At his brother Jeb, the popular governor of Florida, the "smart" brother, the one that many had assumed would end up in the White House.

Nor was Florida that tough a state for a Republican to win convincingly. True, younger and more independent-minded voters had been migrating there, and, true, Bill Clinton had won it in 1996. But Clinton was the first Democrat to take Florida in 20 years, and many thought it a fluke, the result of a weak Republican challenger, Bob Dole, and the anger of the Cuban American community toward Republican immigration policies. Now, four years later, Cubans had come back to the Republican Party because of the forcible return by the Clinton administration of Elián González to his father in Cuba. And even though African Americans were angry with Jeb Bush over elimination of affirmative action in university admissions and state government contracts, they usually did not vote for Republicans anyway. Besides, the GOP was spending a fortune in Florida. Until the last three weeks of the campaign, when the Democrats opened up their own cash spigots, the Republicans were outspending them by about $700,000 a week on TV alone.

But Jeb was the real key to winning the state. Jeb was not only a good campaigner, but he also had a real state organization. And he had plenty of motivation. "I would never live it down if my brother didn't carry Florida," Jeb said in August. "Imagine all the family gatherings for the next 20 years when he looked at me every time and said, 'What happened in Florida?'"

A good question. So why was Jeb doing such a half-assed job for his brother? ("If I was the governor of a state and my brother was running for president," Bill Daley said, "there's no way he'd lose in that state.") When George came to Florida, Jeb usually campaigned with him. But when George was not there, Jeb did not make speeches for him on his own. Stung by media criticism that he was not doing enough, Jeb said on October 10, "I'm busting my hump. I've raised a lot of money; I've campaigned when my brother has come to the state." Except the month before, that is, when Jeb failed to appear at a Sarasota rally for George, and George said to the crowd, "I'm a little disappointed the chairman of my campaign is late." The simple fact was that Jeb was less prominently supporting his brother than some other Republican governors such as John Engler of Michigan, Tommy Thompson of Wisconsin, and Tom Ridge of Pennsylvania. Jeb would not go on network talk shows, for instance, and turned down interview requests from national publications.

His explanation? Well, it was in code: "I have a different relationship with Governor Bush of Texas than Governor Engler. I'm his brother, so I have to be a bit more careful about how I help. Because of the comparisons that might not help George in some cases."

Translation: I might overshadow him. I'm brighter; I'm more articulate; I'm a better campaigner. And he might suffer by comparison.

The media noticed that Jeb would tone himself down considerably when he was with George. In one campaign swing through Tampa, Miami, and Orlando in September, Jeb introduced his brother in one or two sentences, called him a "decent and caring man," and then turned the microphone over to him. It did not exactly bring the crowd to its feet.

The *Wall Street Journal* noted that Gore was gaining ground on Bush in Florida in part due to the "improved performance by Mr. Gore, who has emerged from Clinton's shadow. . . ." There was also the presence of Joe Lieberman on the ticket. Jewish voters make up 6 percent of the electorate in Florida, which is double the national average. Traditionally they went for Democrats anyway, but Lieberman was pumping them up, they were volunteering in droves to work in the campaign and though Jewish turnout was already so high it was hard to improve upon, the Gore campaign was squeezing every vote out of the community. And it wasn't hard. Some Jewish voters entered into an advanced state of awe when Lieberman was around. I was with Lieberman in Tamarac, Florida, in the fall at a retirees center when a woman grabbed his hand after a speech, kissed it, and said, "It's like kissing the Torah, kissing you." She left a bright red lipstick smear on the back of his hand. Another resident, Rosalind Kaplan, tugged on the suit of the Secret Service agent beside Lieberman and said, "Take good care of him!" (On Election

Day, in the predominantly Jewish precincts of Broward County, the turnout was already 82 percent by 10 A.M.)

"Bush should be up 6 to 12 points, and he's not," Jim Kane, editor of the independent Florida Voter Poll, told me in mid-October. "Jeb is acting like he's a nonpartisan. He could be getting tremendous TV coverage by campaigning for his brother, and he's not. What he is doing is really taking his job as governor seriously. He's a serious young man. He's the governor of all the people." And he would have to face election in two years, and he wanted to build up his image as governor, rather than his image as his brother's Florida campaign chairman.

Both campaigns' private polls were showing Florida as a tossup. Gore's last poll, taken four days before Election Day, showed him up by a statistically insignificant 1 percentage point. His campaign decided that unless it could significantly boost African American turnout, Gore would lose. Back in the spring, when Gore made the decision to contest Florida, victory was not the goal. Gore could get enough votes in the electoral college to win without Florida. But Gore could pin Bush down in Florida and make him spend money and time there. (Bush tried to use the same gambit in California to ensnare Gore there, but Gore never went for the bait.) "If you can force Republicans to spend three or four dollars for every one or two dollars you're spending, it's obviously to our benefit," a Gore strategist said in April.

But that was April. Six weeks before Election Day, Nick Baldick was sent to run Florida for Gore. Baldick had done the same job for Clinton four years earlier and had won the state fairly easily, but his first marching orders for Gore were just to remain competitive. The campaign was not going to spend the big bucks there; it just wanted to make Bush nervous. Then, two weeks before Election Day, that changed. With polls in other states tightening up, with Tennessee,

New Hampshire, and Arkansas slipping away, Gore strategists decided their best chance of getting to the White House was winning Pennsylvania, Michigan, and Florida. By strategist Michael Whouley's count, if they could get Florida and its 25 electoral votes, they would end up with 292 electoral votes, 22 more than they needed. So Whouley called Baldick and delivered the news.

"Nick, you're no longer just screwing around with making them spend money," Whouley said. "Now you have to actually win Florida."

"It was," Baldick remembers, "a sort of disturbing phone call."

To achieve a Florida victory, Whouley started pouring real money into the state via the Democratic National Committee, and in the last two weeks the Democrats believed they might be outspending the Republicans in the state. Baldick directed $700,000 into buying black media and directed a huge get-out-the-vote effort in black neighborhoods. The result was that not only did black turnout shoot up by an incredible 60 percent over four years earlier, but while blacks gave Gore 90 percent of their votes nationally, in Florida it was 93 percent. Similar efforts were conducted in other communities. The Gore campaign made literally millions of phone calls and put thousands of people on the street on Election Day to check with the poll watchers to see who hadn't voted and then went to their homes, knocked on doors and got the people out, directing them to hundreds of vans if need be. The Republicans were doing much the same thing, but the Democrats were concentrating on boosting their numbers by bringing out hundreds of thousands of first-time voters. And though nobody worried about it much at the time, this meant that hundreds of thousands of people were going to the polling places in Florida unfamiliar with the varied and mysterious ways of casting a ballot there.

"We turned out a lot of new voters who'd never voted before, black or white," Baldick said later. "This wasn't a race thing. These new voters were more likely to screw up the ballot. They're more likely to be intimidated by the ballot, more likely to get something wrong, especially in places using an arcane punch system. And, to be honest, some of our voters are less educated than their voters. Their voters are rich people; our voters are working people." Later, this would be fodder for the late-night comics. People can mark six Bingo cards at a time in Florida, but they can't mark a ballot? Talk about Flori-duh!

After the final presidential debate, Bush kissed several of his family members, including Jeb. "It looked like I was kissing him," Bush explained later, "but what I was really doing was whispering in his ear, 'We better carry Florida, buddy.'"

By the end of Election Day, with his brother at his side in Austin, Bush could not tell if he had won Florida or not. But by the early morning hours of November 8, Jeb had to confront the disappointment of his family and the possibility of national humiliation. And now he was sure of one thing: Maybe he couldn't win the election for his brother, but he sure as hell could try to win the post-election.

THE GORE CAMPAIGN MOUNTED AN IMPRESSIVE and dramatic let's-hit-the-beaches effort in the hours following Election Day. A planeload of operatives left Nashville for Tallahassee at 6:30 on the morning after the election—there were 85 volunteers but only 72 seats on Lieberman's DC-9, and some of those left behind openly wept. But for all their energy and acumen, the Democrats soon found they had flown into a meat grinder. On paper, Gore's position did not look that bad. He had won the popular vote, he was leading in the electoral vote 267 to 246, and he had, at

most, maybe a couple thousand votes to make up in Florida to sur-
pass Bush. How tough could that be?

Very tough, was the answer. As if suddenly awakening from several months of slumber, Jeb started taking a very active role in saving
his brother's campaign and political future. While staying out of the
public eye, he provided detailed advice to his brother's legal team
and asked his own campaign lawyer, Barry Richard, to be the chief
Florida lawyer for George. And within 24 hours, six of Jeb's senior
political operatives took unpaid leaves to go work for George. "The
state Republican Party, which is run by Al Cardenas, a lawyer who
has been a close ally of Jeb Bush's for 22 years, turned overnight
into a full-fledged operative arm of the Bush effort," the *New York
Times* wrote. Thirty employees of the party, who were supposed to
have been laid off after Election Day, were put at the disposal of the
Bush election team 24 hours a day, seven days a week, and Cardenas
recruited lawyers with ties to the party in at least 42 of Florida's
67 counties. Nor was all the work centered on the legal effort. Both
Bush and Gore were keenly aware of the role that public opinion
could play in a crisis (they had both seen it save Bill Clinton). And
so Bush operatives set up a statewide network, connected by phone,
e-mails, and faxes, to establish daily "talking points" and to call
radio stations and other media to emphasize how Bush had won
and how Gore was now trying to steal the election.

In addition to the state's governor, George W. Bush could count
on the chief state official in charge of elections, Secretary of State
Katherine Harris. She had been a Bush delegate to the Republican
convention and was the co-chairperson of his state campaign.
Though Harris repeatedly portrayed herself as an impartial enforcer
of election law, in fact every decision Harris made over the next 36
days, the *New York Times* noted, "without exception helped Mr. Bush
and hurt Mr. Gore."

If that were not enough, Bush had the Florida legislature to fall back on. With both houses controlled by Republicans and with Bush lawyers determining that Article II of the U.S. Constitution gave final authority over selecting electors to the state legislatures, Bush had his fire wall: If he lost in the recount, if he lost in the manual counts, if he lost in the courts, he still had a legislature willing to seat 25 Bush electors no matter what.

The seven weeks that followed were so confusing and contentious that the two sides could not even agree on the meaning of the word "count." The Bush campaign would continually say that the votes had been "counted and recounted" in Florida and that Bush had won both times. The Gore campaign would continually say that the votes had never been counted and that its whole purpose was to "count every vote" to determine the will of the people.

What was each side saying? After people voted in Florida, their ballots were run through voting machines and counted. Some ballots, however, could not be counted by the machines. Typically, they either had no vote for president because the little rectangle, or chad, on the punchcard had not been completely punched through (which was called an undervote) or because two votes were indicated for president (which was called an overvote). If there was sufficient reason, undervotes could be examined by hand in Florida to determine the intent of the voter—which led to discussions over hanging, dimpled, and pregnant chads. Overvotes were usually disqualified because there was no way of determining who the voter really wanted. The Gore campaign found, however, that on some ballots, confused voters had voted for Gore and then written in Gore's name in the write-in portion of the ballot. Those votes were disqualified as overvotes, but the intent of the voter seemed clear. The Florida voting system was the typical melange of different voting methods including punchcards, optiscan ballots in which voters had to color in ovals on paper ballots, and what would become infamously known as the butterfly ballot, so confusing that thousands of mostly Jewish voters thought they were voting for Gore but ended up voting for Pat Buchanan. "It was heartbreaking," Whouley said. "You would have these Holocaust survivors coming into the headquarters saying, 'My God, what did I do? What did I do?'"

The Gore position was that just because a ballot had gone through a machine didn't mean it had been counted. In the cases of thousands of ballots, Gore contended, only a manual count could determine the true intent of the voter. The Bush position was that manual counts were "chaotic" and subjective.

"Our general strategy for the 36 days was to convince people that the election count had already taken place," Bush spokesman Ari Fleischer later told me. "As people watched TV and saw people holding up microscopes to ballots and peering into light, it raised questions as to the accuracy of the ongoing process. Our position was that after everything went through those machines once and then went through twice, that was the best our system could deliver."

In other words, the people had voted once on Election Day, and those votes had been counted. Then, because the results were so close, it triggered an automatic recount that meant the ballots were fed through the machines once again. (Though Nick Baldick contends that in 20 Florida counties, the recount never took place.) After the recount in Florida, Bush's total had nose-dived to 327 votes and Gore would spend the next few weeks struggling to gain the lead even for a single day through manual vote counts to erase the image of him as a challenger and Bush as the president-elect. Both campaigns faced a deadline of December 12, the date electors could be seated without risk of later challenges.

Knowing that, the Bush forces had two strategies: Slow down the vote count while at the same time hurrying up the process of establishing Bush in the public mind as the legitimate winner. As it turned out, neither proved that difficult. Harris instituted delay after delay, and the courts provided others. And the same low-key, easygoing approach that Bush had assumed during the campaign now served him well. He looked like a relaxed and confident winner, going about the task of picking a government.

"That Thursday night, Bush held an event outside the governor's office on the second floor of the state capitol and announced he was appointing Cheney to run the transition," Fleischer said. "We moved [and here he snapped his fingers] fast. I'll bet the Gore people will now tell you that was one of smartest moves we made."

Bush made another smart move. He immediately dispatched James A. Baker III to Florida to head up his efforts there. Though it seemed like a logical choice—Warren Christopher, a former Democratic secretary of state, was running Gore's operation, so why not have Baker, a former Republican secretary of state, run Bush's?—it turned out to be even more: It was inspired. It was widely believed that in 1992, Baker had let Poppy down in his reelection campaign. Wanting to run for president himself someday, Baker was angered at being forced to give up his secretary of state post to run the Bush campaign. Many thought he did a lackluster job. The relationship between Baker and the Bush family had been strained. But Baker would view this opportunity in Florida as a chance to redeem himself. He would do for the son what he had not done for the father: He would get him to the White House. (And the first thing Baker did upon landing in Tallahassee was to head for the state capitol and a 90-minute meeting with Jeb.)

The Gore people, however, were not concentrating on the smart moves that Bush was making. They were more concerned about the dumb moves Gore was making.

. . .

FROM THE BEGINNING, GORE WAS THE CHALLENGER, trying to take Florida away from Bush. That's how the public saw it and that, to the consternation of some in the Gore campaign, is how Gore saw it as well. Every decision that Gore made was balanced against his perception that the public was impatient with him for dragging out the final resolution of the election. Yet it didn't have to be that way. Gore led not only in the popular vote but also in the electoral vote, and it was obvious that Florida would determine the winner. But who said Florida should be put in Bush's column? Television, that's who. In probably the most abysmal night in the history of the medium, the TV networks first gave Florida to Gore, took it away, gave it to Bush and then, in the wee hours of the morning, took it away again, declaring the race too close to call. Most people had gone to bed with Bush having been declared the winner, however, and what stuck in their minds was Bush's face on the screen with the words "43rd President of the United States" beneath it.

If the networks had just reported that Florida was too close to call all election night, however, would that have made any difference? The Gore campaign firmly believed so. "The psychological impact of 'Bush Wins' on the screen and some newspaper headlines [the *New York Post, Austin American-Statesman, St. Louis Post-Dispatch, Miami Herald, Dallas Morning News* and *Philadelphia Inquirer,* among others, ran Bush victory headlines the next day] totally made us fight for legitimacy in spite of winning the popular vote," Bill Daley said. "Had all of the networks held off, had they all been announcing all night that it was 'too close to call' and not 'Gore refuses to concede,' the dynamic would have been totally different—totally different.

Totally. Because Bush would have had to prove he won, not us having to prove that he didn't win, and that he would not have been able to delay and stop things. Everyone would have said, 'Well, let's just find out who won this thing.'"

Others in the Gore campaign put some blame on Gore himself. "What put us in the hole," one top aide said, "was that, No. 1, the news media declared Bush the winner. But, No. 2, there was Gore's phone call of concession. That was sort of a second strike. The third strike, which would have been Gore going out and giving that concession speech, that did not happen."

Daley knew the tone had been set when on November 8, the day after Election Day, he went before reporters, and one of the first questions asked was: "Bill, do you feel that you're undercutting the next—possibly the next president—by challenging this, dragging this out?" Less than 24 hours after the polls closed, the press already felt the process was being dragged out. Little did they know what lay ahead.

FOR THE NEXT 36 DAYS, GORE ALWAYS FELT HE WAS balancing on a knife edge: attempting to get the victory he felt was his, while not straining the patience of the public and members of his own party. Gore always had to worry about the Democrats in Congress. If they broke ranks with him and publicly pressed him to concede, he might have no choice. (Richard Nixon resigned only after three Republican elders from the House and Senate told him he had to go because they could not guarantee enough Republican votes to keep him in office.) The trouble for Gore was that after 16 years in the House and Senate and eight years as vice president, he had very few friends on Capitol Hill. So, in one sense, he was back in his crouch: He had to weigh all his actions against how others might see them.

The first critical decision this influenced was whether to ask for a statewide manual recount of votes or just challenge the votes in four counties where the Democrats felt they had the best chance of gaining ground. This decision would be endlessly second-guessed, but aside from the physical difficulty of going to all 67 counties and asking for recounts, there was the impatience factor. "To be honest, there was public opinion saying, 'Get this thing over with,'" Baldick said. "The biggest thing we did wrong was right from the start when Al Gore didn't stand up and say, 'I won.' He should have said, 'We won the popular vote; we won Florida.' He should have stood up the next day and started building a transition team."

Gore might have been able to get away with that—after all, Bush was doing it—had he been a more likable public figure. But he was not. And he felt that if he pushed too hard, it would merely re-raise the issue that he was the candidate who would "say anything and do anything to win." This feeling so deeply affected Gore that it caused him to give away his most powerful bargaining chip: His popular vote victory.

In his first post-election address to the nation on November 15, Gore never claimed the final outcome of a recount would give him victory. Unlike Bush, he never expressed any optimism at all. "We should both call on all of our supporters to respect the outcome of this election, whatever it may be," Gore said. "Despite the fact that Joe Lieberman and I won the popular vote, under our Constitution it is the winner of the electoral college who will be the next president. . . . I don't know what the final results will show, but I do know this is about much more than what happens to me or my opponent; it is about our democracy."

Why didn't Gore claim that a fair recount would show him winning Florida, which was, after all, what he believed? Why didn't he give any indication that his claim to the office was no less legitimate than Bush's claim? "We always walked a fine line," Daley said. "We couldn't make it look like the campaign was continuing. People did not want that. He could not say he had won. We had to protect this guy in the likelihood that he became president. We didn't want him out there being some crazed lunatic saying all sorts of crazy things and then he becomes president in a number of weeks. He had to govern. And that was a concern. And for his own image for the long term we couldn't turn him into a slash-and-burn guy, which some people [in the campaign] wanted."

THE NEXT FIVE WEEKS WEREN'T PRETTY, BUT THEY sure were American: Two powerful men, vying for the most important job in the world, awaited the decision of ordinary citizens who had cast their ballots, hanging chads and all, in ways that had vote-counters squinting, lawyers wrangling, and the whole world waiting. Elsewhere in America, the people had spoken. In Florida, they mumbled. "The worm turns every couple of hours," Gore spokesman Chris Lehane said. "The worm is very dizzy." The worm was not the only one.

Unlike the Bush effort, where authority was delegated to a number of people, Gore ran the Gore effort. He sat behind the mahogany table in the dining room of the 30-room, white-brick Victorian vice president's mansion at the Naval Observatory typing out "don't-give-up-the-ship" memos. He took control of all scheduling and all photo ops. In his dining room/War Room he had two sets of phones and two laptop computers—one for vice presidential business and one for political business—and he continued to reach out to Democratic leaders, his political team, his legal team, Jesse Jackson, and supporters. "He has no speeches to give, no trips to plan, what do you expect him to do?" an aide said.

Now, November 17, as he typed away on his laptop for his second address to the nation, he was trying to put the best possible spin on a bad setback: Judge Terry P. Lewis of the Leon County Circuit Court had just ruled that Secretary of State Harris could certify the vote in Florida. Which would mean that Bush would be well on his way to the presidency. In Austin, Bush staffers threw their fists into the air and gave each other high-fives when the Lewis decision was announced. Certification of Florida and all that went with it were what they needed. Certainly the court battle would continue. But the public relations boost would be gigantic. The Bush campaign could call the major networks, newspapers, and newsmagazines and demand that their man now be referred to as "President-elect Bush." Bush could address the nation, visit members of Congress, demand briefings by Clinton's national security adviser, and even receive foreign heads of state in Austin to cement his image as the inevitable next president.

Without certification, none of this was possible. Harris was certainly willing. But that darn worm had at least one more turn left in it. Gore staffers noticed unusual activity around the Florida Supreme Court chambers in Tallahassee and quickly passed the word along to Washington: Don't let the VPOTUS (Washington shorthand for Vice President of the United States) go on the air quite yet. Reporters, standing in the autumn chill outside the vice presidential mansion, were waiting for Gore. Instead, they got platters of cookies and cups of coffee. Gore stayed inside watching TV and, along with the rest of America, heard the news that took him off the critical list: A clerk read a two-sentence statement from the Florida Supreme Court forbidding Harris to certify the election and ordering the manual count of ballots to continue. In Austin, enraged staffers threw pens at the TV screen. In Washington, there were whoops of glee. Gore turned to his laptop and typed a new statement. Typical of his steady-as-she-goes demeanor, however, it wasn't very different from his original: "The citizens of Florida surely want the candidate who received the most votes in Florida to be determined the winner of that state. That is why I am very pleased the hand counts are continuing." Then, in the only glimmer of the emotions that were raging within him, Gore allowed himself one partisan word. "They are proceeding," he said of the hand counts, "despite efforts to obstruct them. . . ."

The next evening in Austin, George and Laura Bush had dinner in the home of friends. Bush seemed "intrigued" by what was going on in Florida, one friend later told the *Washington Post,* but was not consumed by it. "It was not a detailed or prolonged conversation," the friend recalled. "We spent more time on the new Joe DiMaggio biography." Of course they did. Bush took baseball seriously. At the end of dinner, fortune cookies were distributed, but Bush refused to open his. A friend reached over and cracked it open. "You are entering a time of great promise and overdue rewards," it said.

THE GORE TEAM ALWAYS WANTED TO LASH OUT at the Republicans, but was instructed to go gently, except when it came to Harris. Katherine Harris was an obvious target from the beginning. Harris, who, depending on your point of view, was either the Joan of Arc or the Eva Peron of Florida, was one of those figures who suddenly find themselves thrust in the public eye and end up providing both high drama and low comedy. Instantly, her mascara became almost as talked about as Monica's beret. But the real scoop went to the *New York Daily News,* which reported that as a "wealthy citrus heiress" in the early 1990s, Harris "was second banana in a musical revue" where "she would exhort audience members to jump from their seats and dance like chickens." The first banana in the act, Robert Plunkett, said Harris "was really quite marvelous, walking around like a chicken in a gown that she [later] wore to the White House when George Bush was president." Asked how Harris was at counting votes, Plunkett replied, "I don't know if that's her strong point."

No wonder at least part of the world was laughing. Malaysian trade minister Rafidah Aziz, who was no friend of Gore's, said: "We are very puzzled how the great democracy can get into such a mess. Maybe we, all developing countries, should send an election watch every time they have a presidential election." And while few expected Malaysia to be able to teach America much about democracy, even some Americans were wondering how we had come to this point. "It's the most extraordinary case that we've dealt with as election lawyers ever," said Ken Gross, former head of enforcement for the Federal Election Commission and now a private election lawyer. "You have to skip a century to see anything like this. It's exciting." But how long before the excitement turns sour? "We're still within the zone of acceptability," Gross said. "The wheels haven't come off the train."

The media, long berated by academics and political scientists for over-concentrating on the "horse race" aspects of presidential campaigns rather than on issues, could now indulge without guilt in what had become a pure horse race story. As a result, the Florida recount received the "full O.J." from the media: blanket, repetitive, endless coverage of even the smallest details. Yet a poll by the *Wall Street Journal* and NBC News indicated that more than 80 percent of Americans were watching the recount closely, including 55 percent who were watching it "very closely." TV news viewership was up, and talk shows had callers jamming the phone lines. "Pound for pound, this is the biggest, most talked-about story in the past ten years," said Michael Harrison, editor of *Talkers* magazine, noting that the election "is being talked about not just on political shows but on sports talk and relationship talk. Everybody has an opinion." And for those who liked to look for silver linings, some 74 percent of people now said that the election "has increased the belief that every vote counts."

In Broward County, Judge Robert W. Lee, who presided over the election board, took in the show with a bemused smile. "It's like a flood," he said of the television cameras that burst in periodically throughout the day to watch the recount in action. "I'll be glad to return to my regular assignment, domestic violence," Lee said. "You need the same patience level."

THE NEXT CRISIS GORE FACED WAS THE COUNT of overseas absentee ballots, which was mandated by law. Gore's legal team wanted the ballots, which were mainly from military personnel and thought to be Bush votes, held to the strict standard of the law that stated that each ballot had to have a postmark to be counted. Many ballots mailed from military bases lacked postmarks, and Gore's lawyers objected to them.

As the count of overseas absentee ballots concluded with Bush 930 votes ahead, the manual recount of ballots in three counties showed Gore gaining ground. But Republicans, frustrated in the courts, threw up a barrage of arguments on TV. "We now have clear and compelling evidence from eyewitnesses that this manual recount process is fundamentally flawed, and it's no longer recounting but is distorting, reinventing, and miscounting the true intentions of the voters of Florida," said Bush communications director Karen Hughes. The Republicans also bitterly denounced the nullification of a thousand absentee ballots that lacked postmarks, while the

*Miami Herald* charged that more than 2,000 felons could have illegally voted in Florida.

Montana governor Marc Racicot, a Republican, was flown down to Florida and proved a compelling spokesman for Bush. "How can felons be allowed to vote while the men and women in our armed forces cannot?" he asked.

To combat Racicot, Lieberman was to go on the Sunday talk shows and defend the Gore position. Or, at least, that is what Gore thought. Instead, Lieberman went on "Meet the Press" and told Tim Russert, "If I was there, I would give the benefit of the doubt to ballots coming in from military personnel generally. Al Gore and I don't want to ever be part of anything that would put an extra burden on the military personnel abroad who want to vote."

Gore was shocked. Lieberman was way off the reservation on this one. And some would claim that if Lieberman had not given away the military absentee challenges, Gore would have finally gotten what he desperately wanted: a single day when he was ahead in the vote count. Later, however, cooler heads would defend Lieberman as having had no choice. Challenging military ballots was wildly unpopular with both the public and Congress. It was especially unpopular with congressmen, many of whom were Democrats such as Martin Frost of Texas, the chairman of the Democratic Caucus, who had large military bases in their districts and depended on military votes. A top aide made the case to Gore by saying, "How do you become commander-in-chief after trying to block military votes?"

Gore was not entirely mollified, and his relationship with Lieberman would never be the same. Later, Gore backers would wonder whether Gore had made the mistake of elevating Lieberman so high that Lieberman could challenge Gore for the nomination in 2004. Others said it did not matter: Hillary Clinton might challenge them both.

# DENIAL, ANGER, BARGAINING, DEPRESSION, ACCEPTANCE

"A FUNNY THING HAPPENED ON
THE WAY TO THE WHITE HOUSE."

—Bill Daley to author,
December 2000

MERICA HAD BEEN PLUNGED INTO AN unwanted civics lesson, one in which checks and balances had been replaced by chads and challenges. No branch of government—executive, legislative, or judicial—seemed to have the last word. "It was a roller coaster with a pause button," Nick Baldick said. "You'd have these amazing ups and downs but then we would have these three- or four-day periods where usually the Republicans would put us on pause through some court action. So you're sitting in a roller coaster at this angle going down a slope, and suddenly it's like, 'Stop!'"

While Gore could never seem to go ahead in the count, at least the Democrats were sticking with him. Senate Democratic leader Tom Daschle said that Democrats in Congress would not put pressure on Gore to concede, at least not yet. "I've talked with most of my colleagues over the last several days and there isn't any interest in conceding anything at this point," he said. "I think both sides have decided to take this election beyond the certification."

Both campaigns were feeling the same pressures. Democratic interest groups such as labor and minorities and Republican interest groups including the religious right didn't care if a concession would make their man look more statesmanlike; they would take an ignoble victory over a noble defeat. To African American voters, Florida was more than a case of confusing ballots. They had reported police cars blocking access to polling places, black voters being told they could not vote even though they were registered, and the most unreliable voting machines being placed in black precincts. To black people who a few decades before had faced police dogs, fire hoses, and mass arrests in order to vote, Florida was no political game. To them, it appeared an organized and nakedly racist attempt to disenfranchise them.

But to some in the Gore campaign, there had to be a balance point: Though it was once assumed that if Gore lost in 2000, he would be finished in terms of presidential politics, the nature of the loss and the fact that he received so many popular votes could make Gore a powerful candidate next time around. But Gore had to decide when, if ever, to pull the plug in 2000 to position himself for 2004. "He's been a great candidate," said Representative Bob Menendez of New Jersey. "And if we see a nullification of the votes here, he'll always be the presumptive candidate."

On November 17, the Florida Supreme Court prohibited Harris from certifying Bush as the winner in Florida, as she was planning on doing the following day.

Then four days later, Gore got the decision he had been waiting for: the Florida Supreme Court ordered Miami-Dade and the other counties where recounts were under way to finish by Sunday and to submit the results to Harris. Gore decided he must address the nation once again.

"I don't know that the public ever cared that much about the speeches," Eli Attie, Gore's chief speechwriter, said afterwards. "I mean, this whole thing was a story of a total disconnect between the public and elite opinion makers. I mean, the public didn't really care. It may well be that they just figured, 'We need a president in

January and not before,' as Warren Christopher said. It may be that they don't think the presidency is that important. It could be any number of things that I think made people feel like we can wait this out, it's not like a huge deal."

The elites in the echo chamber of Washington, which is where Gore lived, had a different view, however. "There really was a sense from the elites that, 'Oh my God, the Gore people are being so aggressive with all these legal challenges,'" Attie said. "And there even were people on our own team who thought we had to be careful and couldn't push it too hard, and we couldn't seem to have a scorched-earth strategy. The public—who knows if they paid attention?"

About 11 P.M., a beaming Gore takes to the airwaves but once again he refuses to predict what he believes: that a full, fair recount will grant him a victory in Florida. "The Florida Supreme Court has now spoken and we will move forward now with a full, fair, and accurate count of the ballots in question," Gore says. "I don't know what those ballots will show. I don't know whether Governor Bush or I will prevail, but we do know that our democracy is the winner tonight."

Gore then offers an olive branch: "I completely disavow any effort to persuade electors to switch their support from the candidate to whom they are pledged," Gore says, hoping to lure Bush into making the same statement. "I will not accept the support of any elector pledged to Governor Bush. Both Governor Bush and I should urge all our supporters to refrain from any comments, including comments on this evening's decision by the Florida Supreme Court, that could make it harder for us to come together as one nation when the process is completed."

DOWN IN AUSTIN, THEY HAVE HAD ENOUGH. UP to now, they felt they could fall on the ball until December 12 and win this thing. But the seven Florida Supreme Court justices, all of whom had been appointed by Democratic governors, were determined not to let this happen. And this is where James Baker proves his importance. As some have noted, Christopher is a lawyer who is also a politician. But Baker is a politician who is also a lawyer. And now Baker is ready to act like a politician. Maybe Al Gore was afraid of scorching the earth, but not Jim Baker. He would not only scorch it, he would roast it in the fires of righteous indignation. Jim Baker was going to war.

Almost vibrating with anger, Baker goes on TV near midnight and says of the 43-page opinion of the Florida Supreme Court: "All of this is unfair and unacceptable. It is not fair to change the election laws of Florida by judicial fiat after the election has been held." Having essentially called the ruling illegitimate, Baker then fires his next round. He notes that the Constitution gives the right to certify election results to the legislatures and he says, "One should not now be surprised if the Florida legislature seeks to affirm the original rules."

In other words, George Bush was taking his ball and moving to a different playing field. If the courts didn't give him the rulings he wanted, he would get that ruling from the Republican legislature.

This is, the Republicans knew, what the courts feared most. While the term "constitutional crisis" had been tossed around by the media since the beginning of the recount, in fact there had been no crisis. Everybody was playing by the rules: When the courts made a ruling, the participants obeyed it. A constitutional crisis would occur when one branch of government refused to obey another (if Richard Nixon, for instance, had continued to claim executive privilege and refused to turn over the Watergate tapes after the Supreme Court ordered him to). Now, Baker was threatening in no uncertain terms to create such a crisis: The Florida Supreme Court could make whatever ruling it wanted to, but the legislature could act on its own to make the ruling meaningless.

The next day, Bush said the court had "usurp[ed] the authority of Florida's election officials." The court "cloaked its ruling in legalistic language," he said. "But make no mistake, the court rewrote the law."

Anthony Lewis, writing in the *New York Times,* noted the danger of the course Bush and Baker were now charting. "Those menacing words—'usurpation,' 'judicial fiat'—recalled a dark episode in our recent history. They were exactly the words used by George C. Wallace and other Southern governors in defying court orders to end racial segregation. Why do the words matter? Because willingness to abide by decisions of the courts has been an essential element in holding this great, diverse, disputatious country together.

"When a court speaks, presidents accept. . . . So it is dangerous business when a man who would be president tries to delegitimize a court. And it is despicable when a lawyer as senior and powerful as Jim Baker denounces a judicial decision against him and says it will be muscled in the legislature."

The Florida legislature now knew that if it acted to name Bush the winner regardless of what the courts said, it would have the full support of the Bush campaign. And in Tallahassee, the lawmakers got busy.

A S IT TURNED OUT, THE REPUBLICANS WERE JUST warming up. The day after Baker declared war on the process, the confrontation in Florida moved to direct action. Republican telephone banks urged Republican voters to go to the Stephen G. Clark Government Center in Miami, where the Miami-Dade manual vote count was taking place, to protest. Miami's most influential

Spanish-language radio station, Radio Mambi, called on Cuban Americans to head downtown to do the same thing. According to the *New York Times*, a "lawyer for the Republican Party helped stir ethnic passions by contending that the recount was biased against Hispanic voters." Not all the demonstrators were from Miami, however. A large group was made up of congressional staffers, organized by Tom DeLay's office and paid for by the Bush campaign. DeLay, the House Republican whip, had said of the Florida Supreme Court ruling that "judicial aggression must not stand" and offered staffers free airfare, accommodations, and food if they would fly down to Miami. There were others who wanted to show their loyalty to the Republicans. "Almost every lobbyist, political organizer, consulting group with ties to the Republicans was represented," said one Republican official in Washington. "If you ever were or wanted to be a Republican, you were down there."

The melee that ensued was coordinated from a Winnebago parked outside the government center in Miami. The demonstrators descended on the building. Shouting and kicking doors, they attempted to storm the room where the counting was taking place. The chairman of the Miami-Dade Democratic Party had to be rescued by police after the crowd chased him down a hallway. People were reportedly kicked, punched, and trampled before sheriff's deputies restored order. "I was in the room and had people yelling and screaming at me," said John Hardin Young, the Gore campaign's lead recount counsel. "They were banging on doors, screaming. They had leaders that would tell the crowd what to say. They moved en masse like a school of fish. And they took their cues from just a couple of individuals. Clearly the crowd was pushing and shoving. They were there for the sole purpose of intimidating the board." The Bush campaign had always said that the manual recounts were "chaotic." Now, they were proving it.

*Wall Street Journal* columnist Paul Gigot was there, and wrote a column sympathetic to the demonstrators, calling what occurred a "bourgeois riot." He also reported that he was watching the count when: "Street-smart New York Rep. John Sweeney, a visiting GOP monitor, told an aide to 'Shut it down,' and semi-spontaneous combustion took over."

Representative Peter Deutsch, a Democrat from Fort Lauderdale, said later: "A group of out-of-state, paid political operatives came to south Florida in an attempt to stop county-wide recounts. They crossed state lines and intimidated the counting in a federal election, which is a violation of the Voting Rights Act."

In Miami-Dade, the "bourgeois" rioters were wildly successful. At the end of the demonstration, the commissioners decided to call off the recount for good. David Leahy, the nonpartisan member of the canvassing board, told the *Times:* "This was perceived as not being an open and fair process. That weighed heavily on our minds." Leahy later said, however, that he never felt intimidated. "These were people in ties and jackets," he said. "This was not a mob."

Leahy, 54, who had been supervisor of elections since 1981, said the reason the board started and quickly stopped its recount was that the members believed, based on the pace of the early hours of the Wednesday counting, that they would not be able to make the Sunday evening deadline set by the state Supreme Court. The Gore forces were furious. "The whiff of fascism is in the air," declared New York Democratic Representative Jerry Nadler. Fred P. Hochberg, deputy administrator of the U.S. Small Business Administration, added: "My family came here from Nazi Germany. My uncle was thrown down a flight of stairs . . . because of who he was. To have it happen in America is just shocking."

Those who dismissed the melee as just a bunch of yuppies acting out underestimated the racial component: If you lived in Miami, you did not want to be branded as anti-Cuban. Cuban Americans, who voted heavily for Bush, felt their victory was being stolen. "We were trying to stop the recount; Bush had already won," said Evilio Cepero, a reporter from Radio Mambi. "We were urging people to come downtown and support and protest this injustice." Cepero roamed around the building with a megaphone and regularly cut into Radio Mambi broadcasts urging people to come downtown to protest. In Palm Beach, another county where Gore had demanded a recount, the *New Republic* reported that Donato Dalrymple, the house cleaner (often called a fisherman) who had rescued Elián González from the Atlantic Ocean, was part of an anti-Gore demonstration and shouted: "No more Gore! Al Gore is a communist! He supports Castro!"

When word reached Michael Whouley about what was happening in Miami-Dade, he was enraged. The Republicans thought they could muscle him? They thought they could send some Hill weenies up against him? Didn't they know he could pick up a phone and have a hundred Teamsters on their asses in two minutes? If they wanted a piece of him, it would be like Mike Tyson vs. Cicely Tyson!

But Whouley was told to cool it. There would be no confrontation with the protesters. Further trouble would just support the Republican position that the recount was "chaotic." It was an especially bitter pill for those in the Gore campaign who knew how hard Gore had worked to prevent riots from breaking out when black voters learned how their votes were being thrown out. "Following Election Day, there were riots that were brewing in Miami and in Palm Beach," Gore's traveling chief of staff, Michael Feldman, told me. "There were people that were ready to take to the streets. Gore personally turned the volume down on that stuff. He calmed people down. He told them not to do that. He elevated the process.

He instructed his team: 'I want to make sure this doesn't get out of control.'"

But no good deed goes unpunished, and now it was decided that Gore could not even go on the air to denounce what happened in Miami-Dade. It would look too partisan. So a somber Joe Lieberman went on television to condemn the demonstrations as "designed to intimidate" and as "a disservice to our democracy." Lieberman said, "This is a time to honor the rule of law, not surrender to the rule of the mob."

The Bush campaign dismissed Lieberman and the Democratic complaint with a shrug. "I don't recall Senator Lieberman opposing Jesse Jackson's organized protests orchestrated with the AFL-CIO in Palm Beach County," said Ari Fleischer.

In Washington, in his dining room bunker, Gore was distraught over the halt to the counting in Miami-Dade and also the strange silence of Miami-Dade County Mayor Alexander Penelas. The mayor, 28, handsome, dynamic, and eloquently bilingual, was a rare Democrat in the Cuban American community. He was also a client of Tad Devine, one of Gore's top political strategists. Some in the campaign thought that Gore went public for keeping Elián González in the United States as part of a deal with Penelas for his support. But after Elián was snatched by armed federal agents and many Cuban Americans blamed Gore along with Clinton, Penelas's enthusiasm for Gore seemed to cool. After securing his own reelection in the September primaries, Penelas took a trip to Spain and made no campaign appearances in Florida for Gore. "I had to take care of myself," Penelas said. And when it came time for some prominent official to come forward, denounce the demonstrations, and publicly ask the board to continue counting in Miami-Dade, Penelas was AWOL. In 1996, Clinton carried Miami-Dade by 117,000 votes. Gore carried it by 39,000 votes. Had Gore managed to get the

Cuban American support that Clinton got—in other words, if the Elián case had never happened or if Elián had not been sent back— Gore would have easily carried Florida.

THE DEMONSTRATIONS, AS IT TURNED OUT, DID have one plus for Gore. "It solidified Democrats not to break from us," Daley said. "Baker's comments, Bush's tough speech—no conciliation, no outreach—and then the mayhem in Miami and, bingo, Democrats were locked in."

The next night, Thanksgiving, the Bush-Cheney Recount Fund threw a party for the protesters and other volunteers at the Hyatt hotel on Pier 66 in Fort Lauderdale. The food and booze were free, and Wayne Newton sang "Danke Schoen." The highlight, though, was a conference call from Bush and Cheney thanking everyone. Both joked about the battle of Miami.

The Democrats sponsored no Thanksgiving celebration for their workers. Instead, everybody kept working. "When this is over and done with, we want to be able to say that we did everything possible to make sure every vote counted," said Luis Rosero, a Democratic Party spokesman. "Then we can rest and have drinks and have some singer brought in to us."

ON NOVEMBER 26, AT 5 P.M., HARRIS CERTIFIED the final vote, giving Bush a 537-vote victory over Gore. The official ceremony in Tallahassee was conducted in near silence. The certification document was then taken to Jeb Bush, who, fearful that Gore would try to block him with an injunction, quickly signed it at his dining room table.

As expected, Gore vowed to contest the election in state court and then conducted a series of television interviews to make sure everybody knew the election was not a done deal. In Austin, Bush stood in front of a bouquet of yellow roses at the Texas capitol and claimed victory, saying that "Secretary Cheney and I are honored and humbled to have won the state of Florida, which gives us the needed electoral votes to win the election. We will therefore undertake the responsibility of preparing to serve as America's next president and vice president."

There was almost no celebration. No bands, no balloons. The audience was made up mostly of reporters and TV producers. Everybody knew the roller coaster had just paused, not stopped. With the exception of Frank Bruni writing in the *New York Times*, hardly anybody in the media referred to Bush as the "president-elect." Both the White House and the General Services Administration, which controlled transition funds, said they would not treat Bush as if he were the president-elect until the situation was resolved in the courts.

The next morning, Bush left the capitol on his way to the nearby University of Texas campus to exercise. As he passed a small group of reporters, one asked him what he now wanted to be called.

"Sir, at least in your case," Bush responded.

The legal case now proceeded down twin tracks: Both sides filed briefs with the U.S. Supreme Court, and Leon County Circuit Judge N. Sanders Saul began hearing Gore's suit on the contested ballots.

As November waned, a Florida legislative committee recommended that a special session be held to give Bush the state's 25 electors no matter what the courts decided. Ever since Baker's attack on the Florida Supreme Court, the legislature had been plotting to take the matter into its own hands, consulting both with the Bush campaign and Jeb as it did so. Now, Jeb, who had earlier declined to get involved, said he would sign such a bill into law.

On December 4, Judge Saul rejected all of Gore's arguments and seemingly drove a stake through his efforts. But four days later, the Florida Supreme Court resurrected Gore by repudiating Saul and ordering manual recounts of the undervotes in every county in Florida, which was more than Gore had asked for. The court also restored votes that had previously been excluded from Gore's count, and Bush's victory margin now dropped to a little more than 100 votes.

In Austin, the Bushes were in the living room of the governor's mansion with two photographers waiting to record what Bush had assumed would be his final victory moment. Instead, Bush heard the Supreme Court's order.

"I'll be damned," he said.

The Republicans in the Florida legislature were incensed. They met in a special session and decided to reconvene on December 12, the electoral college deadline, to seat Bush's 25 electors.

The Bush campaign appealed to the U.S. Supreme Court, and the next day, Saturday, at 2:40 P.M. five justices, a bare majority, ordered the count to be halted in Florida pending a hearing on Monday.

Gore was genuinely shocked. He had always believed—along with a number of legal commentators—that the U.S. Supreme Court would stay out of the case. He believed strongly that the court would never substitute its judgment for the will of the people. To do so would be nakedly political.

Bill Daley called Gore to provide a political analysis. "Forget it," Daley told him, pointing out that five of the nine justices were conservatives appointed by Republican presidents. "Five Republicans. We're going right in the tank." Maybe it's because Daley grew up in Chicago at his father's knee, but he understands what Gore does not: There is no place in America—no institution—free from politics. Life is politics. And the justices live in the real world. Michael Isikoff of *Newsweek* reported that at an election night party in Washington attended by Justice Sandra Day O'Connor, she became visibly upset when the networks (incorrectly) called Florida for Gore, and she was overheard to say, "This is terrible. This is terrible." As more states were called for Gore, she walked out of the room in apparent disgust. Her husband later explained to the other guests that O'Connor had been hoping to retire in the next four years and didn't want a Democrat to name her successor. Besides, if the Supreme Court did not intervene, a huge battle might spring up between the Florida Supreme Court and the Florida legislature. The next president might have to be selected by the U.S. Congress, which is provided for in the Constitution. But nobody wants to even think about that.

Gore does not buy Daley's assessment. Gore is optimistic. They will win in the Supreme Court 5 to 4, with O'Connor providing the swing vote, and the matter will be sent back to Florida for the counting to continue. Daley would see. No U.S. Supreme Court would ever decide that it did not want to hear the will of the people.

GORE IS SO CONFIDENT OF VICTORY THAT ON the day after his lead attorney, David Boies, argues before the Supreme Court—the same day that the Florida House of Representatives votes to certify a slate of electors for Bush—Gore calls Eli Attie and says, "I'd like to sort of work on an op-ed piece to run somewhere that would sort of say, look, there's a reason why all these branches of government can't decide this, because the courts determine what the law is, but a court can't really determine the will of the people."

Gore decides the piece can run either before the Supreme Court rules—he expects it might take the court days and days—or even after the court rules, because he is sure the court will let the vote count proceed.

Attie asks some questions, and he and Gore start faxing drafts back and forth. Then Gore calls back and says, "Why don't you come over to the house and we'll do some more work on this?"

It is a cold day, and while Attie normally enters the Naval Observatory through a back gate down by the British Embassy to avoid the media at the front gate, he doesn't want to walk around in the cold and so he tells the cab to take him to the front gate. "And all of a sudden, like John Yang [of ABC News] just kind of appeared as if out of the bushes and started like running toward me, like kind of calling my name," Attie says. "And it occurred to me in a flash that, oh my God, they think I am here to write a concession speech." Attie runs away from Yang and gets in the front gate, but by the time he gets into the vice president's mansion, there is a call for him from Gore aide Monica Dixon saying she has already gotten a dozen phone calls from reporters asking if Attie has come to the mansion to write a concession speech.

Even Gore has heard about it, and when he sees Attie he just shakes his head and says, "Should have used the back gate."

They keep working on the piece. Rob Reiner shows up for dinner with the Gores, and naturally, everybody keeps one eye on the television. When not working with Attie, Gore is on the phone with lawyers, getting his feelings confirmed that nothing bad will happen.

At 10 P.M., word comes down that a ruling is imminent. Gore and everybody else head for the dining room.

The ruling is 65 pages long, and the TV reporters struggle to read it while simultaneously trying to tell their viewers about it. It is a hopeless muddle. The ruling is so densely worded that at first nobody can tell who won and who lost.

Even though it is only 9 P.M. in Austin, Bush is already in bed but is watching the TV and immediately gets on the phone to try to find out what the court has actually said. He reaches Karl Rove, who is also in bed watching TV.

"I'm watching NBC, and it's good news," Rove says.

"I'm watching CNN, and it's bad news," Bush says.

"Well," Rove replies, "then watch NBC."

"I'll tell you what," Bush says. "I'm calling a lawyer."

Eventually, the TV reporters realize it may be easier to figure out what the Supreme Court has said by reading the dissents.

"Although we may never know with complete certainty the identity of the winner of this year's presidential election," wrote Justice John Paul Stevens, "the identity of the loser is perfectly clear. It is the nation's confidence in the judge as impartial guardian of the rule of law."

Five justices—Chief Justice William Rehnquist, Sandra Day O'Connor, Antonin Scalia, Clarence Thomas, and Anthony Kennedy, all appointed by Republican presidents—formed a majority in an unsigned opinion that said there were constitutional problems with the Florida Supreme Court decision and there was no way to remedy them in time. They said that the differing methods of determining what was a legitimate vote in Florida—hanging chad? dimpled chad?—violated the equal protection clause of the Constitution, a unique line of reasoning the court had never made before. And while the court seemed to be saying that every county in the United States now had to agree upon one standard for counting ballots, the court quickly added that its ruling in Florida had no relevance for the rest of the nation.

The dissenting justices wrote with a cold anger.

"To recount . . . manually would be a tall order," David Souter wrote, "but before this court stayed the effort to do that, the courts of Florida were ready to do their best to get that job done. There is no justification for denying the state the opportunity to try to count all disputed ballots."

Stephen G. Breyer wrote: "In this highly politicized manner, the appearance of a split decision runs the risk of undermining the public's confidence in the court itself. That confidence is a public treasure." He also wrote that the majority decision was "a self-inflicted wound" for the court.

Gore, who has been faxed the decision page by page, makes no decision on what to do. Technically, the Supreme Court has returned the matter to the Florida Supreme Court and, technically, Gore could try to fight on there. Gore tells everybody to sleep on it; they will decide in the morning what to do.

Down in Florida, the Gore team members want to fight on. They are way beyond angry. If the court had not stopped the recount on Saturday, the recount would be completed by now; Gore would have gotten the most votes and he would be the next president. They are sure of that.

Why did the court stop the count before it ruled? Why didn't it let the count go on and then rule? It was proof, they felt, that the conservative majority on the court simply wanted Bush for president and would find a way to make that happen.

Whouley remembers the personal calls Gore had made during the 36 days to the team in Florida to try and boost their spirits with jokes. "When this is all over," Gore told them one day, "just let me know what countries you guys want." Nobody is talking about ambassadorships anymore. Whouley gets on the phone with Gore and tells him the team in Florida is willing to stay down there, to go back to the Florida Supreme Court, the lawyers are ready to go back in, all he has to do is give the word. Gore makes no commitment.

At 10 the next morning, there is a conference call, and the

Florida team gets the word that Gore is pulling the plug. It's over. Bush has won. Maybe not at the ballot box, but Bush has won.

Whouley calls his staff together. He tells them that sometimes you learn more from your defeats than you do from your victories, and that they were great people and they should stay involved in politics. "The scoreboard broke," Whouley tells them. "That's all. Sometimes those things happen."

Then he begins packing up the office. That night, he does something he has not done in 36 days in Florida. He locates the Atlantic Ocean and goes for a swim.

THE NEXT MORNING, ATTIE GETS A CALL FROM Gore.

"Why don't you come over and bring a laptop?" Gore asks him.

Attie goes over—he uses the back gate this time—and Gore is in blue jeans and a long-sleeve T-shirt. They spend the whole day working on the concession speech, Gore dictating parts, Attie working them over, printing them out, draft after draft.

"His mood was pretty good," Attie says later. "He was really stoic. He really wanted to make sure he had a good speech. He had a big Christmas party scheduled for that night and so we sort of worked all day on it."

Some Gore supporters don't want him to use the word "concede" in his speech because that would be an admission he has lost. Gore rejects the argument. He tells them the speech will be read with a fine-tooth comb and he wants to be gracious toward Bush and not grudging. He also insists on referring to Bush as the "president-elect."

The hour grows late and Gore's guests start arriving for the party. He greets them and then searches out Attie and suggests more changes for the speech. Finally, the traveling group gets in the motorcade—it is smaller than the one they had in Nashville—and pretty soon they are at the Old Executive Office Building next to the White House where the vice president has a suite of offices.

Gore goes to the office of Jim Kennedy, his spokesman, and gets his TV makeup applied. He and Attie discuss some last points, and Attie loads the speech into the TelePrompTer. Gore calls Bush in Austin and congratulates him on becoming the 43rd president. He also tells him he won't be calling back to change his mind this time. Then Gore walks into the Ceremonial Office and addresses the nation.

"Let there be no doubt, while I strongly disagree with the court's decision, I accept it," he says. "I accept the finality of this outcome, which will be ratified next Monday in the electoral college. And tonight, for the sake of our unity of the people and the strength of our democracy, I offer my concession.

"Now the political struggle is over and we turn again to the unending struggle for the common good of all Americans and for those multitudes around the world who look to us for leadership in the cause of freedom."

Gore has decided to end on a joke. In 1992, running for vice president, he said of the Bush/Quayle administration, "It is time for them to go."

Now, in his last speech as vice president, Gore says: "And now, my friends, in a phrase I once addressed to others, it's time for me to go."

THEN HE GOES BACK TO HIS HOME, WHERE THE Christmas party is in full swing, and he dances as if nobody is watching. Sometimes smiling, sometimes biting his lip, his arms moving, his hips swiveling, his eyes usually gazing deeply into Tipper's, he dances with the same concentration that he brings to just about everything else he does in life. He dances until 2:30 in the morning and the bar has been drunk dry. He and his campaign have gone through the five stages of impending death as identified by Elisabeth Kübler-Ross: denial, anger, bargaining, depression, and acceptance. Acceptance is now upon them all, and even though some of the guests had cried watching Gore concede on TV, there are few tears at the party.

And all night long people come up to him and say exactly the same thing: "You won! You won!"

DOWN IN FLORIDA, MICHAEL WHOULEY IS watching TV, waiting for Gore to concede, when he gets a call. It is Michael Feldman. Thirty-six days ago, Whouley had paged Feldman in Nashville and told him to stop the concession because Gore had not really lost. "Dude," Feldman now says. "I'm still waiting for your page!"

GORE DOES NOT WATCH BUSH GO ON TV AND give his acceptance speech.

Speaking in Austin from the House chamber in the 112-year-old pink granite state capitol, the space dominated by a 30-foot Christmas tree, Bush says: "Our nation must rise above a house divided. Americans share hopes and goals and values far more important than any political disagreements. Republicans want the best for our nation. So do Democrats. Our votes may differ, but not our hopes."

． ． ．

ABOUT 3 IN THE MORNING, PRESIDENT CLINTON IS returning from Ireland aboard Air Force One. He has already called Bush and Gore. He is in an upbeat, nostalgic mood, and he tells a joke he has heard.

"Gore got the best of all worlds," Clinton says. "He won the popular vote and doesn't have to do the job!"

GEORGE BUSH IS ELECTED TO THE PRESIDENCY with just 47.9 percent of the total vote, which is 24.5 percent of the electorate. He is the first president elected since 1888 to have lost the popular vote.

Al Gore loses the presidency, but wins more popular votes than any presidential candidate in U.S. history except for Ronald Reagan.

So did the people like him? Did they really, finally, like him?

"To tell you the truth," Bill Daley says, "I think they never really liked either one of them."

W hy was the presidential election of 2000 as close as it was? Because candidates with similar goals and similar strategies marketed themselves to the American people in similar ways. Close elections often signify a great chasm over a key issue or crisis. Not this one. "If anything, this is a testament to the social stability of the United States as it enters the twenty-first century; I don't see a great social divide ripping this country apart," said presidential historian Gil Troy. "It also signifies the growing irrelevance of politics to the lives of many people."

The Democratic and Republican parties, using nearly identical methods of polling, people-metering, focus-grouping, ad-making, and fundraising, reached parity. And the close popular vote may indicate that people weren't divided so much as they were ambivalent. According to exits polls, 55 percent of voters said they had reservations about the vote they had just cast.

Bill Clinton cast a long shadow over both candidates. They studied both his centrist politics and his seductive use of stagecraft. Thus, we got two candidates in the general election who avoided hot-button issues and the extremists of their parties. We got two candidates who sought to be not just president, but First Friend to the nation. Clinton's legacy was complicated. Americans can be forgiven if they appeared to apportion their votes by a coin flip. When you can turn on your TV set and see the two candidates being warm, fuzzy, and winsome with Oprah or Letterman or Leno, it's hard to see much difference between them or draw any political lessons from their performances. It's not that George W. Bush and Al Gore are identical or without ideologies or have exactly the same view of the role of government. But as they ran for president, they relentlessly played down their ideologies in a dash to the center of the American political spectrum, and this inevitably blurred the differences between them.

In eight years, Clinton also made the presidency seem less imposing, less grandiose. "It is a *job*," he told Joe Klein in *The New Yorker*. "There's a lot to be said for showing up every day and trying to push the rock up the hill." Both Gore and Bush looked capable of pushing a rock up a hill. As Michiko Kakutani wrote in the *New York Times:* "Citizen Clinton's tenure in the Oval Office helped shape the tone of the 2000 presidential campaign—a campaign uncommonly focused on personalities and character flaws, on sighs and smirks and spousal kisses. . . ."

According to exit polls, Gore won voters who decided late, and 15 percent of those who voted made up their minds in the last week before the election. This was a time when Gore was at his best, campaigning vigorously and turning what had been a negative ("slash and burn") into a positive ("I'm fighting for you!"). Bush maintained a much more leisurely pace and was thrown off track when five days before the election it was revealed that he had been arrested for drunken driving in 1976. Bush was supposed to be the candidate of honesty and values, and the focus of the stories was not so much on his misdemeanor offense as on his 24 years of covering up the event. (The Bush campaign believed the story cost Bush the state of Iowa.)

Both men ran relatively innocuous campaigns in the general election. But in the primaries, where passions run higher, this was not always possible. In the primaries, a candidate of true excitement can come along and sweep voters off their feet. Bush faced this problem with John McCain and avoided defeat only by veering away from the center and dashing over to Bob Jones University to embrace the right wing of his party. That he was able to make most voters forget this in the general election is a testament to his campaign's abilities. Some voters did not forget, however.

One spectacular failure of the Bush campaign was its inability to attract black votes. Bush made an enormous effort and spent time and money trying to woo black voters, but got a lower percentage of the black vote than any candidate since Barry Goldwater, who had voted against the Civil Rights Act of 1964. Black voters did not forget Bush's visit to Bob Jones, his refusal to oppose the flying of the Confederate battle flag in South Carolina, or Dick Cheney's vote against freeing Nelson Mandela from prison. And many were offended rather than impressed by the parade of black faces at the Republican convention. While nationally Bush got 8 percent of the black vote, in Texas he got only 5 percent. (When he ran for reelection in Texas in 1998, he had received 27 percent of the black vote.)

"This is a blot on the party of Abraham Lincoln," said Governor Frank Keating of Oklahoma, a Republican. "The first order of business for Republicans in Congress, governors, and a Republican administration must be to determine what went wrong and why." The ability of Democrats to dramatically increase African American turnout in targeted states and black fury over what was perceived as being disenfranchised in Florida create a problem the Republican Party must address.

One of the great ironies of the post-election period is that while Democrats sharply turned on one another for losing the White House, conservative analysts noted disturbing trends in the vote that bode ill for Republicans: If you combine the totals of Al Gore and Ralph Nader, 51.1 percent of voters went for a left or left-center candidate. There were 2 percent more voters identifying themselves as liberals than in 1996 and 3 percent fewer calling themselves conservatives. There were also 5 percent fewer voters calling themselves Republicans and 2 percent more calling themselves Democrats. "The election revealed more negative than positive trends for Republicans," Fred Barnes wrote in the *Weekly Standard*, pointing out how "Latinos are still basically a Democratic constituency" and "more than ever, blacks are a monolithic voting bloc." David Brooks, writing in the same magazine, noted that the "geographic picture, on the whole, is ominous for Republicans" because, among other things, "information age elites are trending Democratic." He also quoted analysts saying "the Democrats have a huge issue advantage" and "the only reason Bush was able to tie the election is that he blurred policy differences and thus could highlight Gore's personal weaknesses." A conservative Republican congressional staff member told me after the election: "Given the ability of the Democrats to turn out their base, the conventional wisdom, which is probably accurate, is that we won't be in a majority two years from now in either house."

People who lived in big and medium-size cities tended to vote for Gore, and those in small towns and rural America tended to vote for Bush. In the suburbs, which used to be safely Republican, Bush edged Gore by just 2 percentage points. The bad news for Republicans, according to veteran political analyst Charlie Cook, is that "rural and small-town America is becoming more Republican, but its proportion of the electorate is shrinking. With Democrats now winning large- and medium-size cities by bigger margins and with Democrats now running competitively in the suburbs, Republican hegemony in presidential elections is, for now, over."

Bill Kristol, publisher of the *Weekly Standard*, said: "Conservatives have always assumed that the people are with us. It looks as if it's a moderately liberal country as much as a moderately conservative one."

So why didn't Gore do better than 48.4 percent of the vote? "I think people felt that George Bush was a moderate, acceptable, engaging, and charming guy," said Michael Whouley, "and we couldn't portray him as an unnecessary risk." According to Gore pollster Stan Greenberg, voters agreed with Gore on the issues, but agreed with Bush on values. "In the end, almost half the electorate threw up its hands, unable to differentiate the proposals of the two candidates. The overall impact of Bush's neutralization campaign was to allow those voters who supported Democrats on the issues to prioritize and vote their cultural concerns."

Greenberg found 48 percent of the voters believed that "with the nation at peace and the economy as it is, we should continue with the Democrats in the White House." But 48 percent also felt "after eight years of the Clinton-Gore administration, it's time for a change." Talk about a divide.

An even larger divide developed after the election among Democratic activists, who split between those who thought Gore blew the election by going too far to the left and not embracing Bill Clinton and those who believed Clinton and his scandals sank Gore's chances. "Clinton fatigue was the ice on our wings," a senior Gore staffer who also had worked for Clinton told me. "Without the Clinton scandals, Gore wins by 10 percentage points."

Political analyst Mike Berman, writing in *Washington Political Watch,* pointed out that while Clinton enjoyed positive ratings overall, the story was vastly different among likely voters. "In October, the President's positive/negative score was 48/44 percent and by early November, just before the election, those likely voters had gone negative in their feelings, reflected in a 42 percent positive, 46 percent negative rating" for Clinton, he wrote.

And even though voters believed the country was better off than it had been eight years before, 55 percent of Americans said that they were not going to miss Clinton. "This does not suggest that the Gore campaign choice on whether to use Clinton was the right decision," Berman wrote, "but it does suggest that it was not as obvious a call as many thought."

The use or misuse of Clinton was the question that kept Democrats talking long after Gore conceded and, in fact, was the subject of an "air-clearing" meeting between the two a few weeks after the election. John Harris of the *Washington Post* reported that "for more than an hour, in what sources close to both men described as uncommonly blunt language, Gore forcefully told Clinton that his sex scandal and low personal approval ratings were a major impediment to his presidential campaign. Clinton, according to people close to him, was initially taken aback but responded with equal force that it was Gore's failure to run on the administration's record that hobbled his ambitions."

It was the scab that Democrats could not refrain from picking. On the night of Gore's concession speech, Governor Gray Davis of California told Bill Daley that he had misused Clinton.

Daley was tired of hearing it. "Tell me what states, had we used Bill Clinton better, we would have won that we lost. Michigan? Pennsylvania? California? Washington? Oregon? Wisconsin? Minnesota? Illinois? New York? Where?" Daley said. Gore had won all of those states.

"Arkansas," Davis said.

"Okay, Arkansas is a unique state," Daley replied. "But don't you think it would have been a little awkward if we asked the president of the United States to basically camp out in Arkansas for a month? Don't you think that would have been demeaning? We had him go the last weekend, and he was helpful, and we won the congressional district he campaigned in."

"Tennessee," Davis said.

"Well, Clinton had nothing to do with Tennessee," Daley said. "Forget it."

Though Gore could not have known in advance that losing Tennessee (or West Virginia or Arkansas) would cost him the presidency, he did realize it would be a great embarrassment for a presidential candidate to lose his home state. Yet his campaign handled Tennessee poorly. Gore did not pay enough attention to it and was late in making personal appearances and putting up TV ads. In Tennessee, voters could start voting as early as October 18, and 36 percent of the electorate cast their ballots before Election Day, many of them having missed Gore's attempt to win the state. But what really sank Gore in Tennessee (as in West Virginia and Arkansas) was a very effective campaign by the National Rifle Association, which bought $600,000 in ads in Tennessee, and flew Charlton Heston, NRA president, in for big rallies.

Clinton had succeeded in making gun control a mainstream political issue and was able to convince hunters that banning assault rifles and cop-killer bullets would in no way harm their sport. Gore was not able to pull this off. Gore was not able to counter NRA attacks and was not able to reach across the cultural divide to hunters, many of whom were among the lower-income white males that he, in general, did poorly with. Guns worked for Bush. About half the voters in 2000 said they had a gun at home. Of the gun owners, 61 percent voted for Bush. Of the non-gun owners, 58 percent went for Gore. But union households, which overall gave Gore 59 percent of their votes, split 50-50 when there was a gun in the house.

Gray Davis was not convinced by Daley's explanation. He believed Gore should have embraced Clinton, his economy, and his popularity.

"Why don't you do this?" Daley snapped at Davis. "When you run for president, you have him campaign for *you!*" Later, Daley told me: "You know, I got so pissed off at him. We did *win* by 539,000 votes. So, yes, we lost the presidency. But it wasn't because of how we used Bill Clinton. It was Ralph Nader. Ralph Nader cost us Florida—he got 96,000 votes in Florida. I got to believe we would have picked up 500 of those if he wasn't on the ballot."

NADER, NOMINEE OF THE LIBERAL GREEN PARTY, has a slightly different view of things. "Gore lost Florida because of the Democrats," he told me after the election. "He was done in by Democratic counties: Miami-Dade didn't even recount, and Palm Beach took off [its manual vote recount] for Thanksgiving. The mayor of Miami, I think, was the key. Where was he? With friends like these, who needs Republicans?"

But did Nader feel bad that having siphoned votes from Gore, he might have been responsible for putting a Republican in the White House?

"Between a party that says the right thing and does nothing and a party that says the wrong thing and does nothing, what's the difference?" he said. "It's what I call 'protective imitation.' Bush tried to steal Clinton's issues. So Bush and Gore agreed 32 times in the second debate. It was Pepsi vs. Coke, GM vs. Ford, aspirin vs. Tylenol. The whole campaign was an intricate kabuki dance.

"The president is increasingly insignificant in making key decisions anyway. There is a permanent corporate government in power in Washington whose biggest influence is corporate lobbyists and corporate political action committees."

Nader got only 2.7 percent of the vote in 2000—a poor showing he largely blames on being excluded from the presidential debates—but the cause of reducing the influence of big money in Washington had other, more powerful, advocates.

.  .  .

SHORTLY AFTER BUSH BECAME THE PRESIDENT-elect, John McCain served notice that he would bring the McCain-Feingold campaign finance reform bill to an early vote in the Senate. McCain knew that Bush would not be pleased by this—Bush opposed the bill throughout his campaign—but McCain also saw its passage as his legacy to the nation.

After Bush's inauguration, the usual honeymoon period commenced, and Bush began a charm offensive among powerful leaders of Congress. Relations between the Bush White House and McCain remained extremely poor, however. "I'll tell you how bad it is," a McCain staff member told me. "Since McCain's surgery [for skin cancer in August 2000], about once every two weeks we get two or three or four calls from reputable journalists who have been told by Karl Rove that McCain is terminal. And for the life of me, we can't figure out what the point of that is. You know, why? Why? McCain doesn't know about it. I mean, we never even bother telling him about it. But that kind of stuff goes on."

For their part, McCain's Senate and old campaign staffs took some guilty pleasure at Bush's narrow victory. They believed that had McCain been nominated he would have beaten Gore easily in both the popular and electoral college vote. Some on McCain's staff also believe Bush supporters are missing the point of the closeness of the election. One told the story of how, after Election Day, a group of Republican legislative directors who work for the deputy whips in the House met in private to figure out how to reduce black turnout and union turnout in the future. Ideas included making sure that in contract negotiations management did not grant workers Election Day off to vote. "The whole point was, how can we stop, how can we suppress their people from voting?" the staffer told me. "Besides its offensive ideological quality, it's just so stupid. Why don't we try to start winning some labor votes and some black votes? Why don't we give that a shot?" The staffer made a disgusted noise. "We could poll-tax them," he said sarcastically. "And giving them shitty voting machines seems to be the latest tactic."

McCain was somewhat—but only somewhat—more sanguine when I interviewed him in his Senate office. "Running for president was just a great ride and an exhilaration that I've never experienced in my life," he said, "except perhaps maybe the day I came home from prison."

I asked him if passage of the McCain-Feingold bill banning soft money would change the face of American politics and government for generations.

"No," McCain said. "Actually, it'll change it until smart guys find another way to corrupt it. Twenty to 30 years from now there'll be another McCain and Feingold who'll say, 'Look, we got to clean up the system.' It could be a good bipartisan victory to start out with. Now, will that happen? I don't know. I think the odds are against it."

(Professional fundraiser David Jones agreed. "McCain-Feingold would make professional fundraisers 10 times more valuable than they already are; it would be a boom for the industry," he said. "It would make hard money more valuable, which means instead of a few people writing large [soft money] checks, you would need many more people writing smaller [hard money] checks, and you need fundraisers to find those people.")

McCain said he had no commitment from Bush to sign the bill should it pass Congress. "But I think if it passed it would be hard for him as his first act to veto a major reform," McCain said.

As to the election results, McCain was as gloomy as other Republicans. "We lost California, the fastest-growing state numbers-wise. We lost all of the West Coast, where you've got economic and population growth. We lost all of the Northeast. We lost several of the—quote—battleground states," he said. "Perhaps more important than that, African Americans voted in larger percentages for Gore than they had for Clinton. I mean, it's remarkable. And the Hispanic vote in California is becoming more and more polarized, and that is a problem for all of us because Hispanics are now living everywhere, and they're the fastest-growing part of our population. And states like California, Texas, Arizona, New Mexico are going to become more and more heavily Hispanic. And if we don't reverse that trend, there is no doubt about our status. So President Bush has a huge challenge. He not only has to reach out to Democrats, but he's going to have to reach out to those demographics as well."

McCain was also upset about what America had learned about voting methods in the last election. "Is it fair for the poor parts of America to not give people the same assurance that their vote will count as the wealthier areas?" he said. "What's wrong with that picture? California, in the wealthier areas, had touch-screen voting. In some of the poorer parts of America, we had this antiquated system. That has to be fixed."

If this sounds like a future presidential candidate talking, McCain says that is unlikely. "I think that President Bush will clearly run for reelection," he said. "I can't imagine a scenario where I would run against him in a primary. [Which does leave the door open for McCain to run as an independent.] I just don't imagine it. I think he'll be a good steward. I think he's surrounding himself with good people. And I think he may have a tough time—there's no doubt about that. But to think that he would be a failure is just not something I would imagine."

But are there still some people who would vote for you in 2004? I asked.

"Oh, yeah," McCain said with a grin. "You know, the McCainiacs are still out there. They really are."

ELEVEN DAYS AFTER BEING INAUGURATED, George W. Bush once again forgot that it is best to treat all microphones as if they were live. Meeting with a group of Roman Catholic leaders in the White House and not knowing his remarks were being piped into the press room, Bush said: "I'm about to name my brother the ambassador to Chad."

AT THE END OF JANUARY, STEVE ROSENTHAL, political director of the AFL-CIO, gave a clear signal that likability was going to continue as an issue in American politics. "The key question we should ask the prospective Democratic candidates for president in 2004 is, 'Can you hang?'" Rosenthal said. "Let's see how you can hang on a corner in South Philadelphia. Bush can hang, you know. Clinton can hang. Al Gore, I've seen him, he can hang, but he didn't show it in this election."

JOAN BISKUPIC OF *USA TODAY* WROTE IN LATE January that the U.S. Supreme Court had been "bombarded with thousands of letters from angry Americans, some of whom have sent in their voter registration cards suggesting that going to the polls in November was a waste of time. . . . Sandra Day O'Connor has told people close to her that in her two decades on the court, she has never seen such anger over a case."

·　·　·

KATHERINE HARRIS SAID ONE OF HER PRIORITIES as Florida's secretary of state was to improve the voting system. "Let's just pray in 2004 for a landslide," she said.

THE SPEAKER OF THE FLORIDA HOUSE, TOM Feeney, said state legislators were likely to take a look at how the Florida Supreme Court operates, and might consider imposing term limits.

ON A TRIP TO CHICAGO, BILL CLINTON PRAISED Bill Daley, saying, "I think he did a great job of leading Vice President Al Gore to victory. Our candidate won the popular vote and the only way [the Republicans] could win was to stop the counting of votes in Florida."

BEFORE LEAVING AUSTIN FOR THE WHITE HOUSE, George Bush personally supervised the packing of his belongings. Standing on the ground floor of the Governor's Mansion, he shouted up the stairs to the movers, "Don't forget my pillow!"

Earlier, he had packed his autographed baseballs himself.

ON HIS LAST FULL DAY AS PRESIDENT, CLINTON signed an agreement admitting that he made false statements under oath about his affair with Monica Lewinsky. He agreed to lose his law license for five years and pay a fine. In return, a federal prosecutor agreed not to indict him when he left office.

Bush said: "It's finally over with. It's now time to move on. I think the country is pleased that it's time to move on and that's exactly what we're going to do."

But the country did not move on. It could not. Not yet.

On January 20, just hours before Bush took his oath of office, Clinton issued more than 100 pardons for a variety of unsavory but well-connected characters such as billionaire Marc Rich, one of the FBI's 10 most wanted fugitives, whose ex-wife had donated $450,000 to Clinton's library and more than $1 million to the Democratic Party and Hillary's Senate campaign. Other people seeking a pardon had used Clinton's half-brother, Roger, to approach the president. Hillary's brother, Hugh Rodham, took a fee of $400,000, which he was forced to return, to gain pardons for two men.

As both Congress and a federal prosecutor in New York began investigations, even Clinton's closest associates found themselves unable to defend him. "It's terrible, devastating, and it's rather appalling," Bill Daley said. "Bush ran on bringing dignity back, and I think the actions by Clinton of the last couple of weeks are giving him a pretty good platform."

The Clintons returned gifts and furniture valued at $28,500 that they had improperly removed from the White House in 2000 and moved to their home in New York. Clinton also abandoned plans to rent office space in Midtown Manhattan that would have cost taxpayers $738,700 a year in rent. After a flurry of negative publicity, Clinton found cheaper quarters in Harlem.

While Bush had an impressive, sure-handed first month in office, the public seemed to pay little attention. His 53 percent job approval rating was the same as Bill Clinton's and Ronald Reagan's had been during each man's first month in office.

Bush found himself where Gore had found himself for eight years: In the shadow of a man who seemed unwilling or unable to step out of the spotlight. On February 22, the day of Bush's first news conference, ABC, CBS, and NBC spent a combined 5 minutes of their nightly newscasts reporting on Bush and a combined 21 minutes reporting on Clinton.

Terry McAuliffe, a fundraiser and Clinton loyalist whom Clinton, in his last weeks, had picked to head the Democratic National Committee to ensure that Clinton and not Gore would be the senior spokesman for the party, did not see any problems with the unending Clinton publicity.

"I think it's a problem for President *Bush*," McAuliffe said. "Because Bill Clinton is in the newspapers every day. And it's not a problem for us."

Giving a speech on February 27 at a media business conference for which he was paid $100,000, Clinton said he wanted to "get out of the news" and "have a life."

He did not say when.

# ACKNOWLEDGMENTS

George W. Bush and Al Gore were very generous in granting me private interviews throughout the campaign, as were John McCain, Bill Bradley, and Ralph Nader. I am very grateful to all the candidates and their staffs for their time. The research for this book took place during 18 months of traveling with the campaigns and 16 months of covering the Clinton White House before that. I tape-recorded virtually all my interviews, and to Ron Wilson of *U.S. News & World Report*, who transcribed the tapes, a special thanks and I promise never to interview anybody at lunch or dinner again. He tells me the clatter of silverware nearly drove him crazy.

This book would not have been possible without the generous, extensive, and continuing support of *U.S. News & World Report*, its editor in chief, Mort Zuckerman; its editor, Steve Smith; its executive editor, Brian Duffy; and especially its U.S. news editor, now managing editor, Brian Kelly; and the extraordinary staffs of its library, copy desk, and fact checkers, none of whom are to blame for any errors of thought, word, deed, or grammar contained herein.

Of the many people on the campaign staffs and at the White House who helped me, my thanks especially to Bill Daley, Chris Lehane, Michael Feldman, Eli Attie, David Morehouse, Michael Whouley, Nick Baldick, Jim Loftus, Brandon Thomas, Ron Klain, Carter Eskew, Tony Coelho, Mark Fabiani, Nathan Naylor, Bridger McGaw, Karl Rove, Joe Allbaugh, Don Evans, Karen Hughes, Josh Bolten, Mike Gerson, Ari Fleischer, Eric Hauser, Anita Dunn, Jon Lenzner, David Beckwith, Mark Salter, Nancy Ives, Dan Schnur,

Mike Murphy, Rick Davis, Howard Opinsky, John Weaver, Todd Harris, Greg Mueller, Juleanna Glover Weiss, Doug Sosnik, Rahm Emanuel, John Podesta, Mike McCurry, Joe Lockhart, and Pat Ewing.

Friends, colleagues, and the best road warriors anyone could find include Dan Balz, Jodi Enda, Terence Samuel, Dan Solomon, Laura Dove, Gloria Borger, G. Robert Hillman, Nancy Balz, Mary Ann Akers, David Jones, Susan Feeney, Jack Torry, Michael Tackett, Frank Foer, Adam Rogers, Olivier Knox, Muriel Massenburg, Flynn McRoberts, Monica Davey, Jim Angle, Mark Z. Barabak, Naftali Bendavid, Rick Pearson, Bob Kemper, Rick Kogan, Paul Galloway, Alan Sipress, Ellen Nakashima, Rick Berke, Mark Halperin, Angie Cannon, Ellen Gamerman, Michael Barone, Paul Bedard, Jeff Glasser, Chitra Ragavan, Marianne Lavelle, Kevin Whitelaw, Kit R. Roane, Michael Schaffer, Gary Cohen, Joan Gartlan, Leslie Goodman, Richard Folkers, Ty Trippet, Ilyssa Panitz, Shannon Thompson, Lisa Stein, Lynn Sweet, Elizabeth LaGrua, Jenn Poggi, Stanley Kayne, Alison McIntyre, Jim Lo Scalzo, Chick Harrity, Charlie Archambault, Scott Goldsmith, Kenneth Jarecke, David Butow, Jeff McMillan, Alex Quesada, and Jamie Carpenter.

At Creators Syndicate, special thanks to Rick Newcombe and Anthony Zurcher.

As with any endeavor, a few people proved indispensable: my agent, Bob Barnett; my editor, Emily Loose; and my wife, copy editor, and best friend, Marcia Kramer.

# INDEX

# ABOUT THE AUTHOR

R OGER SIMON is a bestselling author, nationally syndicated columnist, and chief political correspondent for *U.S. News & World Report*. He has covered every presidential election since 1976 and is the winner of more than three dozen journalism awards. He is a former White House correspondent for the *Chicago Tribune* and a former columnist for the *Baltimore Sun* and *Chicago Sun-Times*. He is the only person to win twice the American Society of Newspaper Editors Distinguished Writing Award for Commentary. He lives with his wife, Marcia Kramer of the *Washington Post*, just outside Washington's Beltway.